# Looking Forward

## Challenges to Canadian Music Education

Betty Hanley & Brian A. Roberts, Editors

©2000

40 Years of Leadership in
Canadian Music Education

Cover design by Mo Alton.
Book design by Betty Hanley.
Printed and bound in Canada by Friesens.

Canadian Cataloguing in Publication Data

Main entry under title:

Looking Forward

Challenges to Canadian Music Education
Includes bibliographical references.
ISBN 1–55056–766–7

1. Music — Teaching and learning — Schools — Canada. 2.
Education — Canada — Curriculum
I. Hanley, Betty, 1942– II. Roberts, Brian A. 1947– III. Canadian
Music Educators Association.

# Contents

# The Authors

**Dr. Rodger J. Beatty** is Associate Professor in the Preservice Department, Faculty of Education, Brock University, St. Catharines, Ontario, where he teaches music education curriculum methods and supervises and counsels teacher candidates. Prior to his appointment at Brock University in 1994, Rodger taught 17 years in Ontario elementary schools. Professor Beatty recently completed his Ed.D. in Curriculum at the Ontario Institute for Studies in Education of the University of Toronto. He holds an honours B.Mus. degree (University of Western Ontario), B.Ed. (University of Toronto), M.Ed. (Queen's University) and an A.Mus. diploma — Vocal Performance (Western Ontario Conservatory of Music). He is past president of both the Canadian and Ontario Music Educators Associations. As a specialist in choral music at the elementary school level, Dr. Beatty is a frequent guest speaker, choral conductor, clinician, adjudicator, and workshop leader for various teachers' federations, numerous school boards, and music festivals across Canada and the United States. His research interests include assessment and evaluation in music education, orientations of preservice teacher candidates, curriculum design in music/arts education, and selection of curriculum materials.

**Dr. Carol Beynon** is a faculty member at the University of Western Ontario where she teaches elementary and secondary choral music pedagogy. She is a specialist in vocal and choral pedagogy, especially in the development of boys' and young men's voices. She is founding co-director of the award-winning *Amabile* Boys' Choirs and a choral clinician and adjudicator for music conferences and festivals across North America. Dr. Beynon's research focus is in teacher development and she is a published author in such journals as the *Canadian Music Educator*, the *Alberta Journal of Educational Research*, the *Journal of Professional Studies*, and *Teaching Education*. In the fall of 2000, Prentice Hall Canada will publish *Learning to Teach: Cases and Concepts for Novice teachers and Teacher Educators*, co-authored by Dr. Beynon and colleagues, A. N. Geddis and B. A. Onslow. She is the recipient of the President's Prize of Phi Delta Kappa for leadership and the Kappan Award for service in teacher education, and in 1998 and 1999, she received an award for excellence in teaching from the University of Western Ontario's Students' Council.

**Eric Favaro** is the Arts Education Coordinator for the Cape Breton-Victoria Regional School Board in Nova Scotia. Trained as a music educator, Eric has taught elementary classroom music and instrumental music in Calgary and Sydney and has taught summer courses in Music Education at universities in Alberta and Nova Scotia. In his current role, he has been instrumental in the development and implementation of new arts curriculum documents at the Nova Scotia Department of Education and Culture and has developed courses unique to Cape Breton, including Traditions of East Coast Music and Community Gaelic Arts and Entrepreneurship in the Cultural Industries. Eric serves on the Board of Directors for the International Society for Music Education and is past president of the Canadian Music Educators Association. As president of that organization, he initiated and chaired the first National Symposium on Arts Education in Cape Breton and co-chaired the second in Victoria. He currently serves on the National Advisory Board of this organization.

**Dr. Harold Fiske** has been a member of the Music Education Department of the Faculty of Music at the University of Western Ontario since 1974, where he instructs courses in psychology of music and research methodology and also serves as a graduate thesis advisor. He holds B.Mus. and M.Mus. degrees from Boston University and a Ph.D. from the University of Connecticut. He has presented papers at many music education research conferences in Canada and elsewhere, most of which have been published. He is also the author of three books, *Music and Mind, Music Cognition and Aesthetic Attitudes,* and *Selected Theories of Music Perception,* as well as a contributor to several multi-authored texts including the first edition of the 1992 *Handbook of Research on Music Teaching and Learning.* He has served as chair of the Research Commission of the International Society of Music Education, the chair of the Canadian Music Education Research Council, and is chair-elect to the Research Alliance of Institutes for Music Education. Currently he is a member of the editorial boards of the *Psychomusicology* journal and the *Bulletin of the Council for Research in Music Education.* He is a former chair of the Music Education Department at Western. Prior to his university assignment, Harold Fiske taught instrumental music at the elementary, intermediate, and high school levels.

**Dr. Barbara Graham,** vice-president of the Canadian Music Educators Association, has been a music teacher, performer, and arts consultant. At the present time she is on a leave of absence from her position as teacher Team Leader with the Seven Oaks School District Division #10 in Winnipeg, Manitoba, and is teaching in the Department of Secondary, Higher, and Foundations of Education at Ball State University. She completed her undergraduate work in piano, viola, and voice in Winnipeg, holds a M.Mus., Piano Performance from Ithica College, and a Ph.D. in Education from Simon Fraser University. She was a member of the viola section of the Winnipeg Symphony Orchestra and the Nurnberg Symphoniker, continues to teach a small number of piano students, and enjoys playing chamber music. She is a member of Music for Children, Carl Orff Canada, the Manitoba Choral Association, Manitoba Registered Music Teachers Association, was president of the Manitoba Music Educators Association, and served as member-at-large and secretary-treasurer of the CMEA.

**Dr. Peter Gouzouasis** is Coordinator for Music Education in the Department of Curriculum Studies at UBC. His neo-organicist perspectives on music acquisition and music learning have led him to explore research in traditional and New Media contexts. He is the former music director of WRTI, JAZZ 90 in Philadelphia, which was the most-listened-to 24-hour jazz radio station in North America during the 1980s, and is also recognized for his work in writing television and radio commercials broadcast across North America. Peter is a lifelong learner of music and still pursues serious studies of guitar and other fretted instruments and performance in jazz, North American folk, Celtic, and Greek music contexts. His cutting edge work at UBC led him to the creation of the state-of-the-art MUSES Computer Laboratory for Research in Acoustic Media, Visual Media, and Multimedia in 1990.

**Dr. Betty Hanley** teaches music education in the Faculty of Education at the University of Victoria. She earned a B.A. in Music (University of Western Ontario), M.Mus. (Wayne State University) and a Ph.D. (University of Minnesota). Dr. Hanley co-organized the 1989 symposium *Re-Thinking Music Education in British Columbia*, chaired the second National Symposium on Arts Education (NSAE), Victoria 1998; and has published articles in the *Canadian Music Educator*, the *Canadian Journal of Education*, the *Journal of Music Teacher Education*, and the *British Journal of Music Education*. She is a co-author of *Making Music Meaningful: A Source Book for Beginning Teachers* (1991) and *The State of the Art: Arts Literacy in Canada (1993)*, author of *Foundations for Music Education* (1995), and editor of *Leadership, Advocacy, Communication* (1999). She is a member-at-large on the CMEA Board and a member of the steering committee for the National Symposium on Arts Education. Prior to her assignment at the University of Victoria, she taught instrumental music at the high school level and general music at the elementary school level.

**Mary Kennedy** received her B.Mus. and M.Ed. from the University of Victoria, British Columbia, Canada. At present, she is enrolled in the Ph.D. program in the School of Music at the University of Washington in Seattle. Ms. Kennedy has taught music at all levels from kindergarten to grade 12 and has been a lecturer at the Universities of McGill, Victoria, British Columbia, and Washington. Ms. Kennedy has been a presenter at the British Columbia Music Educators' Conference, Desert Skies Symposium on Music Education, Music Educators National Conference, and the National Symposium on Arts Education. She will be presenting at the International Symposium on Music Education in Edmonton, July 2000. Publications include articles in the *British Journal of Music Education*, the *Canadian Music Educator*, and the *Choral Journal*.

**Dr. Anne S. Lowe** a exercé un rôle comme éducatrice dans le secteur musical privé et publique comme enseignante de piano, musique générale, chant chorale et musique instrumentale de 1966 à 1990. En 1990, elle a été embauchée par l'Université de Moncton à la Faculté des sciences de l'éducation en tant que professeure de cours de didactique de la musique au primaire, un poste qu'elle a occupé jusqu'en décembre 1999. À l'heure actuelle, en plus de son travail en musicale, elle occupe le poste de vice-doyenne à la Faculté des sciences de l'éducation, responsable de la vie académique au premier cycle et de la coordination des programmes du 2e et du 3e cycle en éducation. Elle détient les diplômes suivants: Baccalauréat en éducation musicale de l'Université de Moncton (1975), Maîtrise en musique de la University of Western Ontario (1985), Doctorat en éducation de la University of Illinois (1995). Elle est l'auteure de plusieurs publications qui paraissent dans les journaux d'éducation et d'éducation musicale et elle donne des conférences au Canada et aux Etats-Unis, traitant de l'intégration de l'éducation musicale dans les classes de français langue seconde et langue maternelle.

**Dr. Charlene Morton** is Assistant Professor of Music at the University of Prince Edward Island where she teaches elementary school music methods, philosophy of music education, ear training, and introductory music theory. She is currently doing research to develop strategies for teacher renewal including how to address (mis)representation in music programs, heritage projects, and musicals. Her work is published in academic journals and anthologies such as the *Philosophy of Music Education Review*, the *Philosophy of Education Society Yearbook*, and *Feminism and Education: A Canadian Perspective*, and she continues to present papers at conferences in Canada and abroad. Before obtaining her M.Ed. (UWO) and Ed.D. (OISE/UT), she taught elementary school music in Manitoba, Nova Scotia, and Ontario, and completed four levels of Kodály summer programs and a year of music studies in Hungary.

**Dr. Amanda Montgomery** is currently a professor in the Faculty of Education at the University of Alberta where she teaches undergraduate and graduate courses in music education. Dr. Montgomery also teaches music to the kindergarten–grade three children enrolled in the Department of Elementary Education's Child Study Centre. As president of the Canadian Music Educators Association and past-president of the Kodály Society of Canada, Dr. Montgomery provides leadership to many music educators across Canada. Formerly a professor at the University of Western Ontario and the University of Prince Edward Island, Dr. Montgomery received her graduate degrees with distinction from Indiana University. Her research includes studies in early childhood music, musical preference, and teacher education. Articles by Dr. Montgomery may be read in several national and international journals.

**Dr. Brian A. Roberts** received his B.Mus. and M.Mus. degrees from the University of Western Ontario and his Associate Performance Diplomas in trumpet and singing from the Western Conservatory of Music. Further studies in England and Germany led to the completion of the Künsterliche Reifeprüfung in Singing at the NWD Musikakademie in Detmold, Germany. His doctorate in sociology is from the University of Stirling in Scotland. Dr. Roberts has a world-wide reputation as a leading scholar in the field of music education with more than 150 books, monographs, and articles in the field. Currently, he is the editor of the national journal, the *Canadian Music Educator* and has recently served as guest editor for the *International Journal of Music Education*. Dr. Roberts has performed extensively. Invitations to perform major operatic roles have come from Europe as well as both North and South America. Included among these are the title role of the Canadian opera, *The Fool*, by Harry Somers and Strauss' *Ariadne auf Naxos* at the Stratford Festival in England. Since returning to Canada in 1981 to take up a position in music education at Memorial University of Newfoundland, Dr. Roberts has continued to perform throughout Canada and Europe.

**Dr. Joan Russell** is a full-time professor in the Faculty of Education, Department of Culture & Values, McGill University. Recently she has developed four new professional seminar courses for music specialist teachers, a Dalcroze-based course for teachers, and a graduate course that explores issues of cultural literacy and education in the arts. At present she is a member of a committee that is designing a new doctoral program in Education. Her research interests include ethnographic studies of the musical practices of diverse cultural groups, descriptive-interpretive case studies of expert music teachers with an emphasis on the sociocultural and disciplinary contexts of teaching, and the mediating role of verbal language in the construction of musical knowledge. She is a reviewer for the *International Journal of Arts Education, McGill Journal of Education,* and *Arts & Learning Research.*

**Dr. Katharine Smithrim** (Ph.D. Eastman) is a professor in the Faculty of Education at Queen's University, where she teaches curriculum courses in elementary music and graduate courses in arts education. Her research interests include teacher transformation through the arts, the role of singing in women's lives, and the relationship between rhythm and cognition. Katharine sits on the six-member Music in Early Childhood Commission of the International Society of Music Education which vets international research for presentation and publication. In order to keep in touch with teaching and learning in the schools while she is involved in teacher education at the university, she continues to teach music in elementary schools on a volunteer basis, a different grade each year.

**Dr. Betty Anne Younker** is an assistant professor at the University of Western Ontario where she teaches "Introduction to Music Education and "Commu-nications in Music Education" at the undergraduate level, and "Philosophy of Music Education" and "Qualitative Research" at the graduate level. Dr. Younker's research areas include musical thinking and composing in the music classroom. Her teaching experiences include 10 years in the public school system, 9 years at the university level, and 20 years as a private flute instructor. Dr. Younker continues to perform in choral and instrumental settings.

# Introduction

Canadian music educators and their students continue to make an abundance of beautiful music and have experienced both the invigoration of success and the frustration of adversity since the Canadian Music Educators Association/l'Association Canadienne des Éducateurs de Musique (CMEA/ACEM) was founded at the 1959 convention of the Ontario Music Educators Association (OMEA). Since 1959, the CMEA/ACEM has overcome geography, insufficient funding, and a small population from which to draw membership to remain the national voice for Canadian music education and its official representative to the International Society for Music Education (ISME). Its survival and success are a testimonial to the efforts of the many individuals who have worked to achieve a strong national vision and vibrant demonstration of Canadian music education.

As the 20th century came to a close, the CMEA/ACEM was active in initiating and sponsoring the National Symposium on Arts Education and its two publications. These events were important advocacy initiatives seeking to raise the profile of arts education in Canada. Now, as the 21st century begins, the CMEA/ACEM continues its historical roles but is also undertaking new initiatives. One such venture is *Music of the Spheres* (ISME summer 2001, hosted and organized in Edmonton), an international symposium that will provide a gathering place for music educators and musicians from around the world. The CMEA/ACEM is also working with the Coalition for Music Education in Canada to develop a national document that will serve as a policy framework for music curriculum. A third undertaking is the desire to initiate a national dialogue about the future of Canadian music education in the form of this book.

The authors of *Looking Forward: Challenges to Canadian Music Education* have provided a diverse and rich description of the many issues which Canadian music educators will encounter in the coming years, issues which will require difficult decisions. Hanley selected five ideas — egalitarianism, instrumentalism, postmodernism, constructivism, and collaboration — and examines their impact on Canadian music education in the coming decades. Adopting a broad perspective, Favaro considers the political landscape of arts education and identifies some opportunities as well as pitfalls that music educators will be encountering. Lowe describes recent directions in music curriculum development in New Brunswick, our only officially bilingual province, and the challenges of implementing a learner-centred program. Russell discusses the cultural, religious, and social forces which led to the development of current teacher education programs for the English-speaking sector in the province of Québec. Picking up on the teacher education theme and interested in who will be the music teachers of the future, Beynon reports on research about the important role of the practicum in preservice music teacher education, the necessary links with sponsor teachers, and the conflicting expectations of students, sponsor teachers, and the universities.

Hopeful for the future, Montgomery focusses on the elementary music curriculum and discusses the need for cooperation among teacher educators, music specialists, and classroom teachers. Kennedy raises issues for secondary music programs when she examines low student enrolment in secondary music classes and proposes that composition would provide a viable alternative to performance classes for many students.

The next two writers look at special components of music programs. Starting from the impact of the sounds which surround us, Graham examines the role of active listening in expanding sonic horizons. She discusses how students can grow into a musical life with deeper musical understanding and knowledge. Using Dewey's work as a foundation, Younker reviews how critical thinking is described and supported in three Canadian elementary music curriculums and concludes with suggestions for implementation.

Assessment is of great concern to music educators. Beatty reviews the merits of and options for authentic assessment, focussing on how the latter contributes to student success. Smithrim examines the role of arts assessment in a postmodern age. She notes the extremely high standards expected of artists; yet, in the schools, the kinds of excellence promoted by the arts is not highly valued. She further questions whether assessment can illuminate the aesthetic process.

Drawing on historical narrative as his vehicle, Gouzouasis asks music educators to stop pretending that nothing has changed in music and music education since the advent of technology and to take a proactive stance toward the changes, including the possible displacement of musicians. Morton reviews a different kind of change: the change brought on by increasing multiculturalism in Canada. She examines multicultural policies, the literature, the need for inclusiveness, and the dangers of racism, and argues for the need to develop a vision of multicultural music education that acknowledges the significance of recognition. Fiske brings the book to a close as he looks at past prophecies for music education and bravely undertakes a few predictions of his own based on a comprehensive survey of important areas of research in music education.

While some of the authors share similar perspectives, others do not. What to do with music notation is one area of contention. A definition if music literacy is another. Yet another is what the music classrooms in the new millennium will look and feel like. The different views presented in this book are very useful because they can help us clarify our thinking. Vive la différence! There are also some recurring themes. One is the need to consider the role of music education in the larger educational context. Another is the need for knowledgeable and musical teachers.

Who could benefit from reading this book? The list is long, ranging from students, to administrators, to parents. Certainly the book is for music educators. The challenges described in the book are not limited, however, to Canadian music education. So musicians and music educators from many other countries might feel right at home in these pages.

*Looking Forward* did not just happen. It is the result of the efforts of many individuals. We are grateful to the CMEA for initiating the project and supporting it financially; to Duane Bates (Queen's University), Bob de Frece (University of Alberta), and Mary Hookey (Nipissing University College) for generously reviewing the proposals at a busy time of the academic year for their helpful suggestions; to Mo Alton from Royal Roads University in Victoria for his stunning cover design; and, of course, to the authors, without whom there would be no book.

We suspect that you will encounter ample opportunities to flex your thinking muscles as you peruse these pages and that you will find the content provocative, sometimes disturbing, and yet reaffirming. Above all, we hope you become part of a dialogue which ensures a strong and vibrant music education in all Canadian schools and communities.

Betty Hanley
February 29, 2000

# Editorial
## A Framework for the Future

*Brian A. Roberts*

My son's great-grandmother was 12 when the last century opened in 1900, and my wife and I were very happy that he was able to get to know her. She lived until just before her 100th birthday in 1988. We talked often with our son about the huge changes she witnessed through her very long life — the beginnings of the trend to have two automobiles in every garage, the growth of electrical appliances for every home such as refrigerators and stoves, the telephone in every home, the television, airplanes, and a man or two on the moon! When great-grandma moved from England to Canada she took a very slow boat. Today she could hop on a Concord, check her digital wristwatch, and arrive across the other side of the Atlantic earlier than she left England.

We are told that the rate of change increases every year, as is evident every time you open a newspaper or turn on the TV. What just a few years ago would be considered impossible is now commonplace. Not only can you drive in some considerable comfort to work these days, but from your car, while stuck in a monster traffic jam, you can call on a cell phone (or digital phone if you are really up to date), fax your office, work on your laptop and e-mail your work to your colleagues, who think you are in the next room. You can carry around more information on a single five-inch silver disk than a Britannica salesman could actually lift just twenty years ago, and the encyclopedia that you now own not only has pictures of composers and stories about them, it will play their music to you as well.

Now that I am connected through a cable modem to the internet, my computer is "on-line" the entire time it is running. I can e-mail my word processing documents directly with the click of a single button and interact with the whole of the web at any time and with amazing speed. I have a commercial web site which is mounted in California with which I can negotiate as if it were in the next room. On the web I can talk with people using the built-in microphone on the front of my computer and I can even take a live-time piano lesson with a teacher who can be anywhere in the world and who can hear what I am playing at the same time as I play it. We can even play duets together if we want, me here in Newfoundland and my teacher in South Africa, Germany, or wherever.

Telephone long-distance rates have fallen so far and so fast that it is now cheaper to pick up the phone and call England than to stamp a letter. I sit and marvel that I can put a piece of paper in my fax machine and an exact copy comes out in Australia at the same time as my machine is spitting the paper out the other side.

My regular daily list of personal contacts includes people from all over the world. I do business with people whom I have never met and will likely never meet AND who live in places I have never visited and will not ever likely visit. At the university, our chief method of contact has become e-mail. While one could phone, the chance of the other person being there is always remote and with e-mail, you get to have some sort of permanent record of the request and answer. But this technological advance has been so pervasive that I can be almost anywhere in the world and operate my computer, check my e-mail, send messages, ask questions, and function no differently than if I were actually in my office in a way that would defy anyone knowing where I might be physically at any given time. With the availability of call forwarding and e-mail that announces the arrival of every new message, I can operate from a hotel room, my home office, or from anywhere else for that matter, completely seamlessly with the appearance of actually being physically located where I might be expected to be.

This technology has been so pervasive that the university wishes me to teach students over the web because the institution believes that a greater number of fee-paying units will enrol. So I don't even have to appear in my physical office at the university for classes either. I could, in fact, hold a fully functioning position at the University of Toronto or North Texas or Sydney Australia that could give everyone with whom I needed to be in contact the impression that I was physically in an office on their campus.

What has this discussion to do with the future of music education? Well actually — nothing and everything. It depends on what your idea of a musical education really is and how your ideas support a person's interaction with things musical.

We can certainly predict with some safety that the role of computers in learning and performing music will become ever greater. The delivery of recorded music will become ever pervasively tied to our ability to download what we want, whenever we want. Digital music files are, after all, only digital files. With the current ease with which we can capture these and burn them on our own CDs, the future for moving all sorts of musical recording around is dazzling.

We also have seen gigantic gains in the technological ability to devise instructional materials for use in a digital medium. Yes, we can take a piano lesson with a live teacher on the web who can hear us play at the same time we play and can talk with us about our performance in a way that is not dissimilar to what a piano teacher might do with your son or daughter who lives only a couple of blocks away. This technology will have a major impact on the way rural society can learn and spend its time. No longer will access to a neighbourhood teacher be the determining factor in whether a child can actually study piano.

In fact, the ability of the computer to take on the entire instructional job is not far removed. Witness the phenomenal development that Adventus has made with its *Piano Suite* product. The error detection algorithms are very impressive and allow a student to be corrected in a variety of fashions that suits the need of the student at any given time. *Piano Suite* is not the only product making gains in this direction.

The theoretical aspects of music are as easily taught using computer-assisted instruction as any part of music. Really exciting CDs are now available to introduce serious music students to our entire Western music tradition. One need look only at the collection of CDs that is published by Zane to see fabulous CDs connecting art and music together, the history of Jazz, and the history of music. These multimedia teaching aids stand alone and offer interested students complete and thorough introductions to their contents. They contain text and music samples. They are informative and easy to use. They approach the TV and video games for ease of use and entertainment appeal.

The recent advances in piano-keyboard links to the computer have made their use so easy that the piano keyboard has become the second most purchased periphery for computers after a mouse. What used to be a nightmare of confusion with MIDI patches and odd collections of cables is now usually a simple serial-connection plug away. New software such as *Sibelius* has transformed the whole notion of being a composer or arranger. My own experience with *Sibelius*, after several years of frustration with a leading competitor, was that both my son and I had playable arrangements out of the printer within the first weekend after the Friday installation. The program thinks like a musician. It is intuitive and moves logically through the composing and arranging process. As a result, what used to be so thoroughly labour intensive as to make the process unthinkable now requires little more than a spark of creation and a few minutes to put it on the page. I am not trying to make light of the hard work of composing or arranging. The hard work remains like before, except that 90% of the time can now be spent on the musical work rather than on the drudgery of writing out the parts. Ideas can be tried right in front of you on the screen. Notate the idea and play it back.

Most subjects have developed instructional use of computers, and certain advantages become obvious. In science, dangerous or expensive experimentation can be done without the dangers of actually handling the chemicals. Interactive computing can lend a hand in a variety of ways never before possible and hardly imaginable only a few years ago. Furthermore, science and other subjects with expensive and limited access, particularly in rural or other low-density schooling areas, can gain access to instruction otherwise not reasonable or possible.

I am, on the other hand, troubled by the isolation that can be created in this technological world. Music is for me and many, if not most, students principally a social activity. My son is typical; he is disturbed by not attending band practice as much because he cannot see his friends as he is about missing the music itself. While much musical instruction can take place in schools or at home or in the isolation booth of the computer lab, the essential human element must take place together with others. This point may be self evident, but it is the critical and *sine qua non* of school music that choirs and bands of all sorts must remain the central focus of our attention. As more and more is given over to the computer, people will need bands and choirs to remain "human." Somewhere our children will need places where they can make friends and grow up as kids ought to. Schools will be transformed, and the role of music will become ever more necessary to the development of a person who can interact with people as well as with a machine.

The future of schooling also will demand of our society an effort to define what schools ought to be rather than what they become because other social agencies drop responsibilities on the backs of teachers. Society will also have to have a look at itself to see what it will define as the core identity of being Canadian. As long as minority groups exercise their "rights" by displacing the majority, schools will never function effectively as a healthy socializing agent. We cannot ask 30 children to refrain from singing in school because one or two or twenty find singing against their social order or religion. Our schools are becoming fragmented over special interests. Some believe that arts schools are just one example of this specialization. Arts schools do not, however, trample the rights of others except to the extent that those students who excel in the arts are removed as leaders from their otherwise assigned schools. Here our schooling authorities must ask the questions that direct where the educational dollars are best spent. The question to be answered in this case is whether the disadvantages to the remaining students who are deprived of their cohort leaders outweigh the advantages to the arts students in special schools designed to foster the great potential otherwise lost to our society.

Our schooling systems as a whole do a poor job with advanced students in most areas. In fact, music is typically the only subject where private out-of-school tuition is encouraged for the best students. While the math teacher seeks help for students doing poorly, the music teacher identifies and fosters the achiever. Do we as a society not miss an opportunity by ignoring the potential that rests in those students who otherwise could maximize their potential in mathematics. Will the pressure from special interests eventually put this kind of support into our schools? Will music benefit from the kind of special tuition available currently only from the private sector. In fact, will schools or parts of schools become contracted out to special interest groups. Will parents be able to buy courses for their children with an educational tax credit system? What might remain of a public school system in this form?

We must never lose sight of the fact that music is an enjoyable experience for students. It is a social enterprise where learning styles and commitment can be displayed. It is a place where excellence can abound, where excellence is expected, where excellence can be respected.

What will our children's children see at the end of this new century? Great grandma could never have predicted the changes in her lifetime. It is impossible to guess the unimagined. What will remain is the need for people to interact with one another, face-to-face, where they can shake hands, hug or even kiss. Music is a symbolized act of love, and we can all use a lot of love. School music will be needed more than ever before in the schools in our future, in no matter what form.

Chapter One

# What's Ahead?
## Challenges for Music Education in Canadian Schools[1]

*Betty Hanley*

*Perhaps we need to locate our radical thinking within the perspective of the wider debate about the changing nature of teachers' work and culture in the post-modern age, in which Hargreaves (1994) observes the disjunction which comes about when society changes, but the basic structures of teaching and schooling do not. Music teachers may soon be required to devise a radical solution to this dilemma.*
(Cox, *Secondary School Music Teachers Talking*, 1999, p. 44)

Since its early appearance in the late-19th century, music education in Canadian schools has experienced considerable success. The successes include many bright lights, from successful instrumental and choral programs which produce high-level performing groups across the country, to articulate and sometimes vociferous parental support and advocacy for instrumental music programs, which has on many occasions saved programs targeted for extinction.[2] We have basked vicariously in the publicity generated by the films, *Mr. Holland's Opus* and *Music of the Heart,* and by American musicians and celebrities speaking out in defence of music in the schools. Our own David Foster sang the praises of music education on national television at the 1998 Juno Awards and honoured his high school music teacher in Victoria, Mr. Dave Dunnet. In addition, the theory of multiple intelligences (Gardner, 1993) which hypothesizes a musical intelligence, Goleman's theory of emotional intelligence (1996), writers who support the importance of imagination and intuition (Eisner, 1997; Pitman, 1998), writers who acknowledge the limitations of the Western preoccupation with rational intelligence

(Saul, 1993), and research demonstrating the non-musical benefits of music education (Cutietta, Hamann, & Walker, 1991) have contributed to the greater academic legitimacy of music programs. There is much to celebrate.

Indeed, Canadian music education has been remarkably resilient in the face of daunting obstacles (or challenges, depending on your point of view). But the challenges are many. In the recent past, these challenges have included severe cutbacks, a conception of teachers as generalists (able to teach all subjects), the arts as a generic field, and the traditional skills-based view of music teaching which is disputed by contemporary educational trends and research. Malcolm Ross, a British drama educator, arts education researcher, and author of iconoclastic articles on music education, writes a little too convincingly that music teachers do not acknowledge that the purpose of music education is to help students "find their authentic, expressive voice, (1995, p. 185) and focus instead on teaching "a collection of facts and techniques which need to be learnt, mastered and remembered" (p. 195). Ross (1998) provides an uncomplimentary description of a music teacher as a "martinet" and claims that music education has failed to "modernise, that is, it has somehow been impervious to the creative developments in classical and popular music" (p. 255). According to research by Ross (1995) which spans decades, British students are bored with music classes and opt out of music (unlike art and drama) in spite of their love of music outside the school context and their view of music as a "badge of identity" (see North & Hargreaves, 1999). Does Ross' criticism apply to the Canadian context or can it safely be disregarded?

Where are we now? There are many ways to view the challenges facing Canadian music teachers. I have chosen to contextualize these challenges using as a framework a five key ideas which I have come to view as significant in terms of their potential to necessitate fundamental changes to Canadian music education as the 21st century begins: egalitarianism, instrumentalism, postmodernism, constructivism, and collaboration (or who owns the curriculum).

These five ideas are interconnected, if sometimes conflicting (their strength lying in their particular convergence at this time), but I will discuss each separately for convenience, exploring the interrelationships and teasing out their implications for music education in Canada. Finally I will identify what I consider to be some of the major challenges facing Canadian music educators in the next few decades.

## Egalitarianism[3]

Aspects of egalitarianism, "the belief in equality among people" (Hoffer, 1986, p. 24) are evident in:

1. the denigration of specialists (Koroscik, 1997) and the accompanying belief that "almost everyone is equally capable of informing and advancing knowledge on any subject" (Koroscik, p. 5) and the consequence that it doesn't seem to matter what or if the students are learning and

2. the emancipation from the "drudgery" of skill development with the attendant freedom to be creative facilitated by technology.

In this egalitarian world the conventional meaning of words becomes blurred: thus, everyone can be creative, intelligent, and above normal; emphasis on the effort and work necessary for success gets minimized, and unearned rights are taken for granted.

I should clarify that I do not refer here to an egalitarian vision which allows for individual differences and personal excellence while preserving equality before the law, but rather one which tends to reduce everyone to dreary mediocrity and the lowest common denominator under the guise of democratic ideals.[4] Within egalitarianism there has existed a cross-purpose which continues to erode the ideal as it is lived in our schools. On the one hand it seems that excellence is a desirable goal (especially in international science and math competitions or music festivals), but, at the same time, the search for excellence is suspect because one outcome is that some students will achieve at higher levels than others. Indeed, there is a deep-seated anti-intellectualism in our country, one which fundamentally devalues education and intellectual and artistic accomplishments while at the same time seeking to maintain a competitive edge in the global economy. We want people to be smart and accomplished in their fields, yet we are suspicious of experts (Koroscik, 1997). How is egalitarianism impacting on music education? I will focus on two aspects of the issue: the role of the music specialist and the use of technology in music programs.

Should there be specialist music teachers? Grumet (1995) has some provocative words to say about arts specialists as a group:

Advocacy groups of arts teachers have been isolated within their specializations, lodged in their music rooms and studios (when they have
them), often isolated from the rest of the school and from the rest of the
faculty.... Trapped in the marginality they have sought, they seek resources to strengthen the specializations that confirm their irrelevance.
(p. 40)

Grumet is not alone in her criticism of specialist teachers. Small
(1998) claims that music education in the schools can lead to the
"demusicalization" of students: "Music teachers too often regard
themselves more as agents for the discovery and selection of talented potential professionals than as agents for the development of
the musicality that lies within each child" (p. 212). Others share
Small's belief.

While music teachers are generally accepted in secondary
schools (at least so far),[5] elementary schools are, for the most part,
losing their music teachers. The assault on specialists is evident in
elementary teacher education programs which, in many provinces,
prepare classroom teachers who are fortunate if they receive a minimal background in any of the arts, yet are expected, by policy if not
in practice, to deliver an arts curriculum which increasingly includes
art, dance, drama, and music.[6] Furthermore, fewer and fewer teacher
education programs in Canada provide options for elementary specialists in the arts. Ministries of education across the country have
developed arts curriculums (the good news — at least there is a recognition of the arts) to be delivered by classroom teachers (the not
so good news).[7] School boards and principals, meanwhile, hoping to
satisfy parents, at least "cover" the provincial curriculum, and present the annual concert, hire teachers who have "some" music to shore
up their music programs.[8] The upside of this trend is greater visibil-
ity for the arts, the joy of discovery and synergy as teachers from the
various arts disciplines work together, and the benefits to students
which result when they are engaged in something new. The downside
is that neither the time nor the budget allowances for the arts have
expanded to mirror the increased function — the contrary is true —
and there are not enough competent teachers to get the job done, thus
opening the door for arts organizations and other interested parties
to fill the resulting vacuum. Are there any reasons, beyond cost cutting, driving this change?

Indeed there are other reasons. At one level, faculties of education are driven by provincial policies which do not allow for specialist teachers, by school districts that return specialists to classrooms for budgetary reasons, and by too brief, post-degree teacher

education programs which do not allow time for preservice teachers to learn what they need to know, instead providing generic methodology courses which focus on social issues and generic pedagogy rather than content and content-specific pedagogy. What makes this generalist position attractive is the widely held (and to a considerable degree, valid) belief that specialists have a narrow understanding of what children need to learn and that they do not contribute to connection-making across subjects.

At a another level, the view that the classroom teacher can do everything is consistent with the earlier description of egalitarianism. It seems that, quality learning (helping children to be the best they can be) — which assumes quality teachers — is of little concern, certainly in music education. As Harris (1996) explains, teachers "are far too frequently given the responsibility of providing instruction in an area of the curriculum for which they have had little or no preparation" (p. 30). At the same time, egalitarianism is impacting on preservice student expectations of teacher education programs. In general, students receive more assistance and attention than in the past. Curiously, even though the study of music in Canada has historically been relinquished to the "talented," with the majority of the population convinced they cannot carry a tune in a bucket or have two left feet, many preservice teachers now expect that a single course should prepare them to teach music, with minimal effort or background on their parts. Is the myth of talent discussed by Harris (1996) being replaced by a myth of omniscience? Provincial policy, hiring practice, overspecialization, consequences of egalitarianism have all contributed to the near elimination of elementary music specialist teachers in many provinces.

Which brings us to the question of what is meant by "music specialist." Do we refer to someone with a degree in music? Someone who is a performing musician but also teaches? A recording artist who visits the schools? Perhaps someone who loves music and wants to teach it? While music advocates and music teachers lobby to keep music specialists in the schools, what do they really want? An instrumental program? What is a music specialist? What must music educators know and be able to do? Commenting on the British curriculum, Swanwick (1999) shows that the answer is not as obvious as it first appears: "Music teachers are inevitably specialists in one or two kinds of music but generalists in the much wider range of music required both by the National Curriculum and by our culturally diverse society" (p. 59). His remarks apply equally well to the Canadian context. Is there a problem with our definition of specialist?

Regrettably, more often than not, preservice students witness little meaningful music education in the elementary schools. It is the children who have the most to lose as music teaching is "dumbed down." This "dumbing down" appears in black and white in the following example from Ontario. Unlike for other curriculum subjects where the purpose is to meet the individual needs of students, the Ontario Ministry of Education and Training (1998) writes that "the arts curriculum is not intended to provide the intensive instruction that students with special abilities need. The abilities of such students can be developed through other means" (p. 5). Even more critically, how do teachers with a few meagre hours of study in music "help students develop the fundamental knowledge and skills that will enable them to appreciate artistic expression and to participate creatively in the arts" (Ontario Ministry of Education and Training, 1998, p. 5)? What do we expect students to learn? What level of achievement is good enough?

Unfortunately, the idea of excellence has been co-opted by those who link standards and excellence with a return to the basics. Our protests notwithstanding, the majority of the population do not consider music to be basic to schooling and do not believe an excellent education must include music. One result is fewer music education courses with fewer hours in elementary teacher education programs and a trend to dismantle existing programs regardless of their past records. Another consequence is that when budgets get tight, the entertaining (but not necessary) music program in the school is seen to be, albeit sometimes regretfully, expendable. The challenge, however, does not stop at elementary music programs.

Secondary music education programs (and to a lesser extent, elementary programs) have been accused of elitism — anathema to egalitarians.[9] The reason for this judgment is that only a small proportion of the student population, presumably the "talented," elect to take music classes. The typically performance-based nature of most music classes is seen to favour those with greater gifts.[10] While this approach has produced wonderful results, and performances are well received by the public, at the same time the perceived elitism is to some degree resented, in both the staff room and by members of the public.[11] Writers have pointed out the dangers of the construct we call talent, where talent means only a few can, and most cannot (Kingsbury, 1988; Small, 1998). Small (1998) points out that the "universal distribution of musicality is not a fantasy" (p. 208) and that it is Western beliefs which have produced the gap between the talented and those who cannot; Small claims that people have been taught to be unmusical. He offers a suggestion for teachers who contribute to the seeming unmusicality of their students: "In my opinion any music teacher caught doing such a thing or using the epithet tone-deaf of a pupil should be sacked on the spot" (p. 212). Harsh words, but words in keeping with the emancipating view that the Western population is, contrary to popular belief, musical. Where does Canadian music education as a whole stand in the move away from music for the talented few? Canadian music educators have absorbed a school of music or conservatory tradition which fosters excellence in production, a tradition that is perpetuated by graduates when they become teachers.

The musician identity of music teachers has been the subject of in-depth research (Mark, 1998; Roberts, 1991a, 1991b, 1993; White, 1996). That preservice music teachers typically see themselves first as performers, impacts on their reasons for teaching and their views of their role in the classroom: they seek excellence in performance, acting more like musicians than teachers. Teaching is seen to have less status than performance. White (1996) found the attitude persisted into at least the early years of teaching. Roberts (1991c) finds the definition of musician to be problematic and the difference between a teacher of music and a music teacher difficult to pin down. Do our students consider themselves musical; do we know what they think? Will music educators adapt to meet changing needs and social views or will we rest on our laurels? Is there a third alternative? Can we be excellent and equal too? (Zimmerman, 1997).

Perhaps the single most notable change and challenge in music education has been the rapid growth of technology. Computers make it possible for people who have little or no knowledge of traditional theory to compose music. Traditional notation and access to performers no longer appear to be the barriers to creativity they were in the past. Composing is no longer restricted to the genius but is accessible to all who wish to try. The potential is incredible, and music programs must now provide training in technology, or, possibly like the dinosaur, face extinction.

"Embracing" technology, while clearly empowering, has its costs. The time required to deliver technology courses leaves less time for more traditional courses. Technology eats a big hole in the music budget. Unless funding magically appears, some difficult choices will have to be made. What will go? There is also a heavy financial investment required to maintain and replace hardware and software, and partnerships with industry to be entertained — more choices to be made. Swanwick (1996) asks: "What are we to make of the power of the microchip? (perhaps the colonialization of music education by multi-national companies?). How do these technologies stand up to the test of our principles?" (p. 21). Indeed, how do they? Will we simply accept the new wonders unquestioningly or will we implement their usage with some understanding of the ramifications for the humanities. Will we mistake information for understanding (Roszak, 1994)? Will we surrender culture to technology as Postman fears in *Technopoly* (1993)? How can music teachers take advantage of technology in mindful ways which will enhance music education?

There are, it seems to me, reasons beyond budgetary concerns contributing to the threat to specialist music teachers in our schools: claims of elitism, the isolation of specialist teachers, the desire to empower teachers are other possibilities and help identify some of the challenges music teachers face in a society which values egalitarianism.

## Instrumentalism

The global economy has linked governments and parents into a shortsighted alliance to provide schools which prepare students for the world of work, an instrumental view of schooling which resurfaces when resources are scarce (Hanna, 1994). There is a fundamental disagreement over the purpose of education in Canada. Should the purpose of education be the examined life (Saul, 1995) or should it be preparation for the workplace, economic utility, and consumership? It seems that ministries of education across Canada have opted for the latter view, spurred on by the seductive lure of the lucrative global economy. Solway (1997) explores the consequences of the disintegration of the classical self in the instrumental view:

> In an increasingly utilitarian world dominated by economic anxieties and the pressing need to acquire new and profitable skills before they are rendered obsolete, the core-identity of the individual based on contemplation, conscience, inner leisure, productive solitude, and the patient acquisition of cultural and historical knowledge tends to atrophy with disuse and vanish entirely with contempt or neglect. (p. 63)

In *No More Teachers, No More Books*, Robertson (1998) presents a well-documented description of the "commercialization of Canada's schools": "If business is helping education, it is helping education to serve business better. The merger of private and public interests, like the merger of education and training, is not a synergistic, value-added collaboration. It is a capitulation" (p. 281). While schools hope to obtain more resources, in fact, they are selling out to business interests. Robertson provides an example of Mississauga's Gordon Graydon Memorial School whose business partnerships and entrepreneurial spirit are instructive. The school was built by business and benefited through receiving many resources, but, according to Robertson, the program's premise was "that the purpose of education is to teach students whatever their future employers want them to know" (p. 289). The possibilities for business partners shaping the direction of the school and for the formation of students as consumers are evident. Tudiver (1999) addresses the potential for funding to engender, at the very minimum, psychological obligations and sees an unhealthy end to the direction for commercialization and privatization: "If current trends continue, public education will become a branch of private industry" (p. 194). When the purpose of schooling is to produce workers, music educators are left with justifying the career opportunities of their students and delivering music programs with objectives that support employability rather than artistic and human values.

The arts community has nevertheless been quick to realize the immediate value of demonstrating how the arts contribute to the Canadian economy.[12] Latching on to the opportunity to develop a higher profile, the cultural industries have also been active in promoting advocacy initiatives in arts education.[13] Secondary music educators have little choice but to become involved in the career preparation which has become part of the curriculum. Advocacy arguments such as "Music makes you smarter" also support an instrumental view of music education in that the purpose of music education is to make you smarter — presumably in maths and science, not in music. Ironically, in focusing on the development of instrumental and vocal performers, music education has historically maintained an instrumental, vocational basis which has isolated it from the general education curriculum. Bumgarner (1994b) comments on the consequences of the development of technical proficiency as the goal of teacher education in the arts:

> Vocationally oriented arts teacher education programs constructed on the mastery of specific media and techniques and the application of the basic elements of each art form have failed to provide teachers with the kind

of education required to make the sorts of curricular connections and program advancements outlined above. (p. 26)

The extension of a vocation orientation to schools is not difficult to imagine.

Not all music educators, however, have adopted a solely vocational model. Other options include aesthetic music education, discipline-based music education, and comprehensive musicianship models which acknowledge the academic/cognitive as well as the artistic sides of a multifaceted music education. We have decisions to make. What kinds of music programs will we provide? Those that encourage our students to become proficient musicians or those that seek to develop an arts literate populace as described in *The State of the Art: Arts Literacy in Canada* (Hanley, McIntosh, Van Gyn, & Verriour, 1993) where the arts literate person:

- seeks out and attends to experience in one or more of the arts,
- perceives and responds to the qualities of art works where this is an appropriate cultural response,
- is knowledgeable about the specific code of one or more art forms (tradition, history, canon, vocabulary),
- has experience with the creative (doing) process in one or more of the arts, and
- exercises discernment (makes informed choices) in selecting arts experiences. (p. 103)

This description is written for all the arts but could easily be amended to apply just to music. When it comes to selecting an approach for teaching music is it a matter of either/or or something else?

The impact of instrumentalism on our schools should not be dismissed. The attraction of immediate benefits — such as free computers — could well blind us to the eventual costs of unlimited commercialization. Our choices will affect what and how we teach music in our schools and how and what our students learn.

## Postmodernism

*We are becoming a people of the ear…. Postmodern sound becomes insulation from society, as much as it reassures us that we are not alone.*
(Richard Rodriguez, *News Hour*, October 19, 1999)

In recent years, music educators have increasingly found themselves engaged in heated dialogue over fundamental issues such as "What is music?" "Who owns music?" "Is an art work an objective artifact or a construction by the beholder?" "Is music a noun or a verb?" The dialogue goes to the heart of the curriculum. What content will be selected? What and whose values will be espoused? What purposes does music serve? Is making music a political act? These ideas are at the heart of the debate between modernism and postmodernism.

Modernism originated in the European Renaissance and continues into the present. In a helpful article Fehr (1997) applied the belief system of modernism to arts education. Traditional arts education and its views are evident in the following belief statements:

- Western culture is supreme.
- Reason is a superior way of knowing.
- Science can explain the universe, and psychology can explain human behaviour.
- The art of different cultures can be ranked as a matter of aesthetic judgment.
- A line can be drawn between art and life.
- Truth is universal.
- High art is privileged over popular art. (pp. 27–28)

Modernism is being challenged by postmodernists who are critical of the scientific, rational world view attributed to modernists. Once again, Fehr (1997) provides a helpful synopsis of the characteristics of postmodernism. Postmodernism

- places an emphasis on the interconnectedness of world cultures and the need to tolerate conflicting views;
- allows a multiplicity of codes and conventions, including the popular arts;
- de-romanticizes the art work;
- removes borders between subjects;
- sees art as cultural critique as well as aesthetic experience; and
- questions Western cultural supremacy and privilege. (pp. 28–30)

Postmodernism also acknowledges the possibility of multiple narratives or realities: "We construct many realities, and do so from different intentions" (Bruner, 1986, p. 158). We experience a postmodern multiple perspective when we look a cubist painting by Picasso; read a novel where the point-of-view, instead of being the consistent "I" or omniscient third person, changes with sometimes bewildering frequency;[14] or listen to the bitonal music of Darius Milhaud and Charles Ives.

In my view, visual arts and drama teacher educators have largely accepted a postmodernist stance (see Duncum, 1989; Gablik, 1991;

Chalmers, 1992; Grumet, 1995); postmodernism poses the greatest challenge to music education (even though music educators acknowledge the multicultural nature of Canadian society). The deeply entrenched, traditional European music education based on the aesthetic principles of the 19$^{th}$ century is being challenged (Elliott, 1995; Small, 1998). Walker (1996) is an eloquent spokesman for the postmodern view of music education:

> Post-modern thought suggests a re-evaluation of both terminological signification and usage on both logical and socio-political grounds. In such things, the universal use of the term "music" means either we reject its connection with western musical theory through processes of semantic deconstruction, in which case its products become indistinguishable from sonic activities from other cultures, or we paternalistically bring these activities into the fold of music with all the built-in sense of superiority that involves. (pp. 9–10)

These views impact on the repertoire selected for music classes and the ways we think about music. Related issues are usually discussed under the heading of multiculturalism in education, although the latter term appears to be more limited in scope than the broader issues identified here. It is, for example no longer appropriate to talk of "high art" and "low art" or even "fine arts" (as the latter implies a devaluation of those arts not designated as "fine").

Postmodernism posits a contextualist conception of the music and the arts rather than accepting universal assumptions about the nature and value of music. If postmodern thought is accepted, a re-thinking of what constitutes music education may be required. For example, thinking of music as something people do rather than as an abstract object with its own existence changes the focus from the study of music to the doing of music. Certainly our valuing of music of other cultures where music is a community celebration changes from a curiosity about exotic things to an attempt to understand and respect. In a second example, Small (1998), working from within a postmodern framework, challenges time-honoured wisdom about practising:

> I cannot see the need to waste time and musicality practicing scales, exercises, and studies. When, for example, I work at my performance of material provided by J. S. Bach under the title *Italian Concerto* in F, it is amazing how my playing of the scales of F, B-flat, C major and D minor improves. (p. 215)

Many students would agree.

To live in the past is to die a slow death: "Teacher training [sic] programs may continue to produce teachers who view the world from one perspective, despite the increasing localization of global politics within the school" (Fehr, 1997, p. 27). It seems that many music teachers may need to expand their perspectives. But change does not come easily. Indeed, change in the music teaching profession with its proud record of achievement is not easily countenanced.

On the other hand, change, especially change for change's sake, can also be overrated. To deny the past and overlook its riches could be a grave error:

> Critics of Western cultural values see such values as emanating from the dominant and oppressive institutions of Western society; but it is just as appropriate and certainly more useful to emphasize the West's ideals of toleration, freedom of expression, and individual empowerment. (Smith, 1993, p. 13)

The emphasis on interconnectedness and the desire to counter the fragmentation and isolation of the modernist world has led many artists, educators, administrators, and writers to conceptualize the arts as a group, focusing on similarities, rather than on each art as a separate discipline. Provincial curriculum documents for elementary schools now have curriculum documents which usually encompass dance, drama, music, visual arts, and sometimes media under the umbrella of "the arts." There are benefits to this view. The maxim, "In numbers there is strength," applies. The arts have become more visible. But there is also the real danger that the uniqueness of each art and the necessary skills, knowledge, and understandings to appreciate and participate in each art form will be lost in a kind of soup. The question is whether the soup will be bland or flavourful.

Are music teachers willing to examine postmodernism and its implications for music education? Have some already done so? Will competing views contribute to tension among colleagues?

## Constructivism

Postmodernism addresses but does not deal specifically with epistemology. Teaching is undergoing a paradigm shift as constructivist approaches filter into professional development, the literature, and methods classes, producing learner-centred classrooms and new models for future classroom teachers. Constructivism is both a theory of learning and a theory of knowing which focuses on "how people construct their reality and make sense of their world" (Walker & Lambert, 1995, p. 16).[15] Walker and Lambert list the principles which distinguish constructivism from the "empty vessel" theories of learning which have dominated teaching in the past:

1. Knowledge and beliefs are formed within the learner.
2. Learners personally imbue experiences with meaning.
3. Learning activities should cause learners to gain access to their experiences, knowledge, and beliefs.
4. Learning is a social activity that is enhanced by shared inquiry.
5. Reflection and metacognition are essential aspects of constructing knowledge and meaning.
6. Learners play an essential role in assessing their own learning.
7. The outcomes of the learning process are varied and often unpredictable. (pp. 17–19)

Constructivist principles of learning are a challenge to the accountability seekers who wish to impose external standards of achievement and to many music teachers as well. The constructivist teacher does not provide their students with prepackaged content or a single "correct" set of procedures, choosing rather to provide them with alternatives and encourage thoughtful application and critique. Constructivist music teachers are willing to learn along with their students, encourage thinking (even if it is critical of the teacher), and provide opportunities for students to become aware of their own learning and thus engage in the assessment of their own progress.

Constructivism has an honourable pedigree including thinkers such as Vygotsky (1962, 1978), Bruner (1986, 1996), and Feuerstein (1990). Even though constructivism has its detractors (and has been and will continue to be misinterpreted and misrepresented, as have been most progressive movements in education), it has received strong support from the American Psychological Association in its adoption of a set of 12 learner-centred psychological principles (1994). A little elaboration about misrepresentation and misinterpretation of constructivism is in order. Although there is no single correct model, contrary to criticism and too frequently the implementation, neither the teacher's role nor learning outcomes or expectations become less important in the constructivist classroom. The teacher's role changes from that of source of all knowledge and decision maker to that of an observer, a helper, a listener. This role is more demanding than the traditional role because "one size does not fit all," and the teacher must always be thinking of how best to enhance the learning. The best way may even sometimes be the traditional way. Students are not left to drift and "rediscover the wheel."

There are serious and demanding learning expectations, but these exist at a broad level, allowing for individual learning profiles. Some teachers have already moved into this new role. Have music educators?

Our understanding of what constitutes knowledge, where it originates, and how we come to know is changing, as must our idea of pedagogy. In *The Culture of Education*, Bruner (1996) wrote: "Pedagogy is never innocent. It is a medium that carries its own message" (p. 63). Bruner discusses the impact of various models of mind on models of pedagogy. Whether we think of the child as willful and needing correction, as innocent and needing protection, as inept and needing skills, as empty vessels needing to be filled with adult knowledge, as egocentric and in need of socialization, as thinkers in need of intersubjective exchange, or as a combination of the above, our model will determine how we teach children. Bruner writes convincingly that we need to think explicitly about what he calls our folk psychological assumptions about teaching and learning.

Acknowledging the role of the learner leads to a different kind of classroom, one in which more than lip-service is given to the "hallmarks" of what Tomlinson (1999) calls the differentiated classroom:

- Teachers begin where the students are.
- Learners differ in important ways.
- Teachers must be ready to engage students in instruction through different learning modalities, by appealing to differing interests, and using varied rates of instruction, along with varied degrees of complexity.
- Teachers ensure that students compete against themselves more than against other students.
- Teachers provide ways for each individual to learn as deeply as possible and as quickly as possible.
- Students should be held to high standards.
- Learning involves effort, risk, and personal triumph. Success is likely to follow hard work.
- Teachers do not force-fit learners into a standard mold.
- Teachers are diagnosticians. (adapted, p. 2)

Each of these points can be used by teachers for personal report cards. My hunch is that, as a group, we music educators would do well on some points and rather poorly on others.

Tuning in more on the learners could inform teachers in new ways. A few examples will clarify what is meant. Ross (1995) provides a description of what students can accomplish when left to their own devices. Compare his story with that of the traditional music classes.

> Many teenagers...elect to teach themselves an instrument — the drums perhaps or the guitar. What do they do? They usually know already the kind of sound they are interested in. They insist upon the right equipment. They listen to their mentors and try to emulate them, running into problems of sound production and control, figuring their own way through them, comparing notes with fellow practitioners, following the example of preferred models. They work away tirelessly to master and perfect the speech act. They don't need to be composers, but they do need to feel in control and that means understanding and identifying with the thoughts and feelings embodied in the music they are playing. (p. 196)

A second example comes from *Songs in their Heads* in which Campbell (1998) reported on her study of the place of music in children's lives. This is her description of what the research team learned:

> [W]e discovered together that we may be most effective as teachers when we consider children less as blank slates to fill than as thoughtful minds — musical minds, already taking shape through the process of enculturation. We also learned together to view the children we teach less as some homogenized conglomerate whole than as musically inventive and expressive individuals. (p. xix)

Later in the book Campbell comments that although children are musical without teachers, the assistance of experts helps them become more musical: "I am campaigning not to 'deschool' music but, rather, to bring instruction in line with who the children musically are" (p. 196).

A third example comes from *The Mind Behind the Musical Ear*, Bamberger's (1991) ground-breaking study of how children develop musical intelligence. Her astute observations of children engaged in musical tasks contributed in a practical way to the realization that there is a gap between the way untrained and trained individuals process music. Bamberger noted a distinction between figural and metric ways of perceiving and understanding music (a figure/ground type of experience) that raises questions about traditional ways of teaching ear training and reading music notation. More and more educators are beginning to heed what their students have to say and show about how they learn. What of music educators?

Music educators are a practical lot, a quality which has been beneficial in the past when it was necessary to organize concerts and tours. (Ask a music teacher if you want to get something done.) When does virtue become a vice? Commenting on their focus on practical solutions Jorgensen (1997) said:

> Music educators typically value solutions to their questions more than the questions themselves. They are often more interested in positing practical answers to the issues they face than in raising questions about the underlying assumptions and methods they have espoused. Many have not learned to love the questions themselves. (p. x)

Teaching for Understanding (TfU) as opposed to teaching isolated facts or decontextualized skills (Wiske, 1998), while not a new idea, has been receiving considerable attention particularly in view of the need for problem solvers and creative thinkers.

> What's all the fuss about understanding? Isn't "teaching for understanding" what everyone tries to do in a classroom? Yes, dedicated teachers are trying every day to help students understand; but, unfortunately, it isn't so easy. Even successful students show lack of understanding when they try to apply what they have learned. (Hetland, Perkins, & Wilson, 1997, p. 13)

While TfU does not emanate from within the constructivist literature, the ideas certainly mesh with the constructivist goal of fostering thoughtful learners and have a "constructivist turn" (Perkins, 1998, p. 54). What does understanding mean? "Understanding...is being able to use knowledge in new ways" (p. 14). Understanding would seem to be a worthy goal for music education. Do we teach for musical understanding?

How can music teachers model a learner-centered pedagogy without abdicating their responsibilities and falling into the trap of lowered expectations? What are the consequences of constructivism for music education?

## Collaboration

One of the by-products of constructivism is a focus on community or working together. Collaboration was evident in many aspects of life in the 1990s, from the emphasis on cooperation rather than competition in learning (Covington, 1992) and in the business world (Senge, 1990),[16] from the establishment of communities of learners (Walker & Lambert, 1995), to the growing importance of interdisciplinary research. Given its tenacity to-date and the strong forces supporting it financially, the trend will continue well into the 21st century. I have rather arbitrarily separated collaboration from egalitarianism, instrumentalism, postmodernism, and constructivism and saved it as a final point because its impact on music education is a certainty; but there are overlaps. There are two aspects to this reality: One is internal to music education, while the second is external.

One outcome of collaboration is that the arts have banded together (or been put together) rather than be considered mainly as distinct disciplines or art forms. This lumping together has especially been the case in elementary programs where, as mentioned earlier, curriculum documents have been developed for "the arts" or "fine arts" (British Columbia). Since the merger, the fate of one art could be the fate of all so, in spite of misgivings, each art has a vested interest in supporting the others and, on the surface anyway, we are one happy family.

Collaboration among the arts is, of course, not new. Artists have worked together across the centuries to produce such works as operas and musical theatre productions at the same time as they have continued to develop their individual disciplines. Currently in arts education, at least external collaboration is evident in the person of arts coordinators (where we've managed to hold on to them), heads of fine arts in the secondary schools, and the arts curriculum personnel at provincial ministries of education. Working together is seen as essential to the survival of the arts in our schools, but there are tensions which we are reluctant to voice. How does this interdisciplinary approach work in practice? Will the honeymoon continue?

The concern is aggravated by recent events in arts education whereby arts partnerships (which have often excluded arts educators and music teachers or are designed to fill a perceived void) are celebrated and often generously funded whereas there does not seem to be funding to maintain current programs or hire music teachers. *Learning Through the Arts*, "a national approach to educational transformation through the arts" is a partnership undertaken by the Royal Conservatory of Music with educators, arts organizations, and corporate community leaders. The general idea is to use the arts to help children improve in aspects of the core curriculum — such as language literacy — and the prime "teachers" are artists who work with children and teachers. A promotional video which I viewed showed discussion with classroom teachers, conservatory personnel, and students, but no arts specialists; there weren't any at the schools in the video! Generously funded, *Learning Through the Arts* has generated considerable interest, and initial on-going external evaluation has been very positive (Wilkinson, 1996, 1997, 1998).[17]

Foundations are into the action also. Pitman (1998) provides the example of the Annenberg Foundation who invested $30 million dollars over five years with the cooperation of the Metropolitan Museum of Art, the Museum of Modern Art, and the New York Philharmonic "to take over from the Board of Education all responsibilities for arts education in New York City" (p. 196). Not much of a vote of confidence for arts educators! Or were there any in the schools?

These initiatives typically begin outside the schools (who can't afford them and haven't got time to apply for the grants) with arts organizations, conservatories of music, foundations, or university researchers, and schools — students and teachers — are seen to be the recipients.

Who gets to teach music in the schools is of considerable concern to me. Artists and arts educators have not always been sympathetic to each other's purposes and well-being (Bumgarner, 1994a, 1994b). Artists have denigrated teachers ("Those who can't, teach. And those who can't teach, teach teachers."), whereas teachers have sometimes neglected artists and not drawn upon their views or sought out expertise. In music education, there is even a disinterest on the part of too many music teachers in contemporary "serious" music and composers. Artists and teachers necessarily have different purposes, abilities, and perspectives: Artists make art; arts teachers seek to develop students' understanding and skills in the arts (Bumgarner, 1994a, 1994b). Yet, both groups are being propelled or propelling themselves into working partnerships (partially because such partnerships make sense in that both groups are purportedly working to serve the arts and promote arts education) with little dialogue about purpose and leaving unresolved the issue of who should be teaching the arts — qualified teachers or artists.

Some questions arise. Should artists replace arts educators, as is happening in some schools in Ontario where programs developed by visiting artists become the arts program and arts teacher are "returned" to the classroom, or should artists supplement well developed arts education in the schools? Artists, understandably, appreciate the additional income generated by working in the schools as well as the opportunity to nurture potential audiences. Should teacher education programs be providing an education component to artists-in-training to help prepare them for their future roles in the schools? Will teacher education in the arts be phased out in favour of an artist-educator model? (Dance education in British Columbia, for example, is being provided by professional dancers because, currently, there are few qualified dance educators.) Swanwick (1997) agrees with the artist or professional model for music teachers, suggesting "we have to think radically about the future." Will a professional model become the norm? Recall the problems which the musician identity creates for music teachers. Or should an explicit collaborative model of teacher education in the arts be promoted? The issue of the roles of arts teachers and artists will be addressed at "Sharing the Vision," the fourth National Symposium on Arts Education, to be held in Ottawa in July, 2000.[18]

The next area of collaboration is that of curriculum. In the context of curriculum, collaboration has been called integration. Integration, as it is explained in Canadian curriculum documents, is either (1) a merging of art, dance, drama, and music into *the arts*, as in the Ontario Core Curriculum (Ontario Ministry of Education and Training, 1995); (2) a suggestion that the individual arts should be used to enhance other subjects at the discretion of the teacher — the arts as decoration, what Morton (1996) describes as a colonialization of the arts; or (3) the provision for distinct arts disciplines with commonalities acknowledged, as in the arts curriculum documents from Saskatchewan (Saskatchewan Education, 1991), British Columbia (British Columbia Ministry of Education, 1998), and Nova Scotia (Nova Scotia Department of Education and Culture, 1998). The first two versions are more likely to be welcomed by elementary classroom teachers most of whom lack the skills and understanding to undertake more in-depth teaching of the arts and want to make other subjects more appealing. Grumet offers a comforting image of an integrated arts education, unfortunately with little acknowledgment of the learning required to achieve her vision. She writes:

> Arts education must emerge from the temple of the fine arts to join the curriculum. The ways of knowing the world that the arts present could make our kids smart. They could learn to dance what their bodies know, to draw the distinctions between ideas, to shape forms and shade colors to express relationships that they sense.... The arts need to appear in math class, in social studies, in physics, and in reading. (p. 41)

In advancing his vision for an arts-based integrated curriculum Pitman (1998) states that "[t]here must be the opportunity for teachers to prepare themselves to instruct not only in their own art discipline, but in the integrated arts style that perceives the connections that give meaning to the process of understanding" (p. 199). The vision is only a lovely dream unless there is the will to implement the vision and the time and money set aside for teacher development. That distribution does not reflect the reality, especially for elementary teachers who don't even receive adequate preparation in one, much less all the arts. Ironically, among specialist teachers, Pitman does not anticipate that it would be the humdrum teachers who would provide the biggest challenge to his vision:

> It will be the superb professional, well-trained, perhaps still a practicing artist, who knows all the best techniques, who is flexible and accountable, who cares deeply about every student but believes above all else that the specific single-discipline arts experience in her classroom is the most important moment in her students' day. (p. 211)

Sound like any one you know?

Music teachers need to take a stand. What kind of arts courses should elementary preservice teachers be receiving? Where should the diminishing resources be placed? On generalist or specialist programs? On integrated arts or on separate disciplines?

With the discussion of integration, I have moved beyond internal pressures to external ones. The integrated arts curriculum has been promoted not so much by arts educators (although some have been attracted by the idea) as by proponents of holistic education influenced by postmodern thinking (Laughlin & Street, 1992). While four arts are now officially recognized in provincial curricula, there has been no more time or funding allowed in the schools and no provisions made for the development of teachers. What is possible?

External pressures for collaboration come from students, the public, the government, arts communities, and, more recently the teaching profession and College of Teachers (in British Columbia and Ontario). Allow me to elaborate on a policy of the British Columbia College of Teachers whose recent decision regarding teacher certification in elementary programs has, in effect, wiped out specializations offered in the elementary program, including those in the arts in concurrent degrees.[19] This policy has impacted especially hard on the arts since many students enter faculties of education with little background in the arts and are unlikely to pick up courses in these areas before entering the faculty. The graduates move on to become the very classroom teachers responsible for implementing the arts curriculum! The British Columbia College of Teachers seems concerned solely with the need to address specified social issues[20] and a broad academic base (not usually including the arts) in future teachers. Similar or equally devastating forces have been eroding elementary programs across the country, usually through the elimination of consultants and specialist teachers. So far, secondary programs have escaped extinction.

I recently wrote an article arguing that music educators need to become more politically-minded:

> Typically, arts educators have avoided political involvement other than at the micropolitical level. Arts educators want to teach, not "waste their time" with what many construe as political chicanery. Engagement in advocacy initiatives, nevertheless, has belatedly been making music educators increasingly aware of the need to be heard by decision makers. (Hanley, 1998, p. 12)

It is pretty clear that there are a number of forces acting on music education and challenging our ideas about what it should be and who should be teaching it. Is it enough to simply carry on as we have valiantly in the past, letting our good work speak for itself? Should we become more aware of the larger issues, the players, and their goals? Should we do a better job of explaining what we do and why we do it? Who should be our audience? What are the merits of the arts education initiatives which seem to be flooding the literature and the web and earning considerable attention? Should the Canadian Music Educators Association be more involved in political action? Once again, we are left with a number of challenges.

## Conclusions

> *The enemy of reflection is the breakneck pace — the thousand pictures.*
> (Bruner, *The Culture of Education*, 1996, p. 129)

Music education is currently undergoing a time of change brought about by changing and conflicting cultural, social, and political ideas; quickly evolving technology; and financial pressures exacerbated by globalization. Criticisms of music education as it currently is delivered are numerous. Ross (1998) believes that "if music education — as instruction and assessment — cannot be reformed it should be allowed to die" (p. 261). Small (1998) challenges us further:

> The big challenge to music educators today seems to be not just how to produce more skilled professional musicians but how to provide that kind of social context for informal as well as formal music interaction that leads to real development and to the musicalizing of the society as a whole. (p. 208)

While I find considerable merit in some of the criticisms I have addressed in this chapter, it is my sincere hope that Canadian music education doesn't die. Nevertheless, there are many tensions which exist in the contemporary teaching context, and we must find ways of living with them and changing for the good of our students. I also think there is something valuable to be gained from using a constructivist approach in the music classroom, although such an approach challenges how we teach, especially our emphasis on sequence and use of whole class delivery for most of our teaching. In the final analysis, it will be, however, for you to decide whether the criticisms warrant action based on the evidence provided, your experience, and your thoughts about what is happening in our society.

In this chapter we have explored together the interrelationship and impact of five ideas on teacher education in the arts: egalitarianism, instrumentalism, postmodernism, constructivism, and collaboration. In the course of the discussion I have identified a number of challenges facing music education and music educators, not the least of which is the directive to do more with less. I pose the following summary of the challenges as questions rather than statements (in a constructivist manner) so that you can develop your own answers. As Bruner (1996) argues convincingly: "The art of raising challenging questions is easily as important as the art of giving clear answers" (p. 127). The answers, in my view, are critical to the well being of music education in the 21st century.

1.  Should music education serve the needs of some students or all students?
2.  Is the purpose of arts education to develop professionals or a literate populace (or both)?
3.  If they continue to exist, what should be the role of music specialists in the 21st century?
4.  Who should teach the music in our elementary schools — classroom teachers? specialists? artists?
5.  Who should teach the music in our secondary schools — classroom teachers? specialists? artists?
6.  Should music standards be developed for all students or some students? Is there a difference?
7.  How can music educators integrate technology into music classes in a humanistic way?

8. Should music educators stop thinking about music education and start thinking about arts education?
9. Should music educators re-examine their relationship with the other arts — pedagogically, artistically, and pragmatically?
10. What are our assumptions about teaching and learning in music education? Is revision or change needed?
11. What happens to the sequential structure of music programs if a constructivist pedagogy is applied?
12. What happens to the whole class approach if a constructivist pedagogy is applied?
13. Should music educators become more politically astute and active? [for example, being aware of the politicization of curriculum and taking a stand on the commercialization of Canadian schools]
14. Will music educators continue to foster parochial interests at the expense of the music education as a whole?

While these challenges are undeniable, you will probably have uncovered many more as you read these pages. Thoughtful deliberation and decision making about how to set a course for the future are the next steps.

What do I see as some of the implications of the 14 challenges identified in this chapter for music education? It will be necessary for us to:

- take a serious and critical look at what we do in our music classes and be able to explain convincingly why we do what we do,
- renew our commitment to music education so as not to become discouraged and overwhelmed by rapid and sometimes overpowering change,
- keep an open mind as we explore our options and attempt to go beyond what we know (without throwing away the past),P
- decide where the limited energy we possess and the diminishing resources coming our way should be placed,
- foster and engage in dialogues with teachers and artists, dialogues which are built on trust and mutual respect and whose purpose is seeking greater understanding and the best for students in a changing world, and

- work closely with others involved in arts education for the good of our students, the community, and Canada.

Although there are many challenges, there is also a great deal of hope and optimism. A graduate student recently reminded me that the Chinese word for crisis is made up of the words danger and opportunity. There are difficult decisions to be made. But if we don't provide leadership, someone else will make the decisions for us. Dealing with each of these challenges on our own would be overwhelming. Working together, who knows what we can accomplish?

## References

American Psychological Association. Presidential Task Force. (1994, March). *Learner-centered psychological principles: Guidelines for the teaching of educational psychology in teacher education programs.* Washington, DC: Author.

Bamberger, J. (1991). *The mind behind the musical ear: How children develop musical intelligence.* Cambridge, MA: Harvard University Press.

British Columbia Ministry of Education. (1998). *Integrated resource package — Fine arts K to 7.* Victoria. Author.

Bruner, J. (1986). *Actual minds: Possible worlds.* Cambridge, MS: Harvard University Press.

Bruner, J. (1996) *The culture of education.* Cambridge, MA: Harvard University Press.

Bumgarner, C. M. (1994a). Artists in the classroom: The impact and consequences of the National Endowment for the Arts' Artist Residency Program on K–12 arts education (Part 1). *Arts Education Policy Review, 95* (3), 14–29.

Bumgarner, C. M. (1994b). Artists in the classroom: The impact and consequences of the National Endowment for the Arts' Artist Residency Program on K–12 arts education (Part 2). *Arts Education Policy Review, 95* (4), 8–31.

Campbell, P. S. (1998). *Songs in their heads: Music and its meaning in children's lives.* New York: Oxford University Press.

Chalmers, F. G. (1992). The origins of racism in the public school art curriculum. *Studies in Art Education, 33* (3), 134–143.

Covington, M. V. (1992). *Making the grade: A self-worth perspective on motivation and school reform.* Cambridge: Cambridge University Press.

Cox, G. (1999). Secondary school music teachers talking. *Music Education Research, 1* (1), 37–45.

Cultural Human Resources Council. (1998). *Now hear this! Careers in music and sound recording.* Ottawa: Author.

Csikszentmihalyi, M., Rathunde, K., & Whalen, S. (1993). *Talented teenagers: The roots of success and failure.* Cambridge, MA: Cambridge University Press.

Cutietta, R., Hamann, D., & Walker, L. (1991). *Spin offs: The extra musical advantages of a music education.* Elkhart, IN: United Musical Instruments.

D'Souza, D. (1992). *Illiberal education: The politics of race and sex on campus.* New York: Vintage Books.

Doctorow, E. L. (1971). *The book of Daniel; A novel.* New York. Random House.

Doctorow, E. L. (1975). *Ragtime.* New York. Random House.

Duncum, P. (1989). Toward foundations for a socially critical art education. *The Journal of Social Theory, 9,* 12–25.

Eisner, E. (1997). Educating for tomorrow's jobs and life skills. In V. A. Marmillion (Ed.), *Arts education for life and work* (pp. 4–5). Los Angeles, CA: The Getty.

Elliott, D. J. (1995). *Music matter: A new philosophy of music education.* New York: Oxford University Press.

Elster, A., & Bell, N. (1999). Learning through the arts: A partnership in educational transformation. In B. Hanley (Ed.) *Leadership, advocacy, communication: A vision for arts education in Canada* (pp. 145–154). Victoria, BC: Canadian Music Educators Association.

Fehr, D. E. (1997). Clutching the lectern, or shouting from the back of the hall: A comparison of modern and postmodern arts education. *Arts Education Policy Review, 98* (4), 27–31.

Feuerstein, R. (1990). The theory of structural cognitive modifiability. In B. Z. Presseisen (Ed.), *Learning and thinking styles: Classroom interaction* (pp. 68–134). Washington, DC: National Education Association.

Gablik, S. (1991). *The reenchantment of art.* New York: Thames & Hudson.

Gardner, H. (1993). *Multiple intelligences: The theory and practice.* New York: Basic Books.

Goleman, D. (1996). *Emotional intelligence: Why it can matter more than IQ.* New York: Bantam Books.

Government of Canada: Communications. (1987). *Vital links: Canadian cultural industries.* Author.

Grumet, M. (1995). Somewhere under the rainbow: The postmodern politics of art education. *Educational Theory, 45* (1), 35–42.

Hanley, B. (1998). Creating a national vision for arts education in Canada. *Canadian Music Educator, 40* (1), 10–13.

Hanley, B., McIntosh, D., Van Gyn, G., & Verriour, P. (1993). *The state of the art: Arts literacy in Canada.* Victoria: Beach Holme Press.

Hanna, J. L. (1994). Arts education and the transition to work. *Arts Education Policy Review, 96* (2), 31–37.

Harris, C. E. (1996). Technology, rationalities, and experience in school music policy: Underlying myths. *Arts Education Policy Review, 97* (6), 23–32.

Hetland, L., Perkins, D., & Wilson, D. (1997). Teaching for understanding. In S. Veenema, L. Hetland, & K. Chalfen (Eds.) *The Project Zero classroom: New approaches to thinking and understanding* (pp. 11–60). Boston, MA: Harvard University.

Hoffer, C. R. (1986). Elitism and egalitarianism in arts education. *Design for Arts in Education, 87* (5), 24–27.

Jorgensen, E. R. (1997). *In search of music education.* Urbana & Chicago: University of Illinois Press.

Kingsbury, H. (1988). *Music, talent, & performance: A conservatory cultural system.* Philadelphia: Temple University Press.

Koroscik, J. S. (1997). The intellectualization of American arts education policy. *Arts Education Policy Review, 98* (4), 2–12.

Laughlin, M. K., & Street, T. P. (1992). *Literature-based art and music: Children's books & activities to enrich the K–5 curriculum.* Phoenix, AZ: Oryx Press.

Mark, D. (1998). The music teacher's dilemma — Musician or teacher? *International Journal of Music Education, 32,* 3–23.

Marshall, H. (Ed.). (1996). *Educational Psychologist, 31* (3/4).

Morton, C. (1996). *The "status problem": The feminized location of school music and the burden of justification.* Unpublished doctoral thesis, University of Toronto, Toronto, Ontario, Canada.

North, A. C., & Hargreaves, D. J. (1999). Music and adolescent identity. *Music Education Research, 1* (1), 75–92.

Nova Scotia Department of Education and Culture. (1998). *Foundations for arts education: Validation draft.* Halifax. Author.

Ontario Ministry of Education and Training. (1995). *The common curriculum: Policies and outcomes, Grades 1–9, The arts.* Toronto: Author.

Ontario Ministry of Education and Training. (1998). *The Ontario curriculum Grades 1–8: The arts.* Toronto: Author.

Perkins, D. (1998). What is understanding? In M. S. Wiske (Ed.), *Teaching for understanding: Linking research with practice.* San Francisco: Jossey-Bass.

Pitman, W. (1998). *Learning the arts in an age of uncertainty.* North York, ON: Arts Education Council for Ontario.

Postman, N. (1993). *Technopoly: The surrender of culture to technology.* New York: Vintage Books.

Roberts, B. A. (1991a). *A place to play: The social world of Canadian university schools of music.* St. John's, NF: Memorial University of Newfoundland.

Roberts, B. A. (1991b). *Musician: A process of labelling.* St. John's, NF: Memorial University of Newfoundland.

Roberts, B. A. (1991c). Music teacher education as identity construction. *International Journal of Music Education, 18,* 30–39.

Roberts, B. A. (1993). *I, musician: Towards a model of identity construction and maintenance by music education students as musicians.* St. John's, NF: Memorial University of Newfoundland.

Robertson, H.-J. (1998). *No more teachers, no more books: The commercialization of Canada's schools.* Toronto: McLelland & Stewart.

Rodriguez, R. (1999, October 19). White noise. *Newshour with Jim Lehrer* [transcript] [On-line]. Available http://www.pbs.org/newshour/essays/october99/rodriguez_10-19.html

Ross, M. (1995). What's wrong with school music? *British Journal of Music Education, 12,* 185–201.

Ross, M. (1998). Missing solemnis: Reforming music in schools. *British Journal of Music Education, 15* (3), 255–262.

Roszak, T. (1994). *The cult of information: A neo-Luddite treatise on high tech, artificial intelligence, and the true art of thinking.* Berkeley: University of California Press.

Saskatchewan Education. (1991). *Grade 5 Arts Education Curriculum Guide.* Regina: Author.

Saul, J. R. (1993). *Voltaire's Bastards.* Toronto: Penguin Group.

Saul, J. R. (1995). *The unconscious civilization.* Concord, ON: Anansi Press.

Senge, P. M. (1990)*The fifth discipline: The art and practice of the learning organization*. New York: Doubleday.

Small. C. (1998). *Musicking: The meanings of performing and listening*. Hanover, NH: Wesleyan University Press.

Smith, R. (1993). The question of multiculturalism. *Arts Education Policy Review, 94* (4), 2–18.

Solway, D. (1997). *Lying about the wolf: Essays in culture & education*. Kingston, ON: McGill-Queen's University Press.

Swanwick, K. (1996). Music education liberated from new praxis. *International Journal of Music Education, 28*, 16–24.

Swanwick, K. (1997, November 14). False notes. *Time Education Supplement*.

Swanwick, K. (1999). "Authentic" music and its effect on the attitudes and musical development of secondary school students. *Music Education research, 1* (1), 47–60.

Tomlinson, C. A. (1999). *The differentiated classroom: Responding to the needs of all learners*. Alexandria, VA: Association for Supervision and Curriculum Development.

Tudiver, N. (1999). *Universities for sale: Resisting corporate control over Canadian higher education*. Toronto: James Lorimer.

Vygotsky, L. S. (1962). *Thought and language*. Cambridge, MA: MIT Press.

Vygotsky, L. S. (1978). *Mind in society: The development of higher psychological processes* (M. Cole, V. J. Steiner, S. Scribner, & E. Souberman, Ed.s). Cambridge, MA: Harvard University Press.

Walker, D., & Lambert, L. (1995). Learning and leading theory: A century in the making. In L. Lambert, D. Walker, D. P. Zimmerman, J. E. Cooper, M. D. Lambert, M. E. Gardner, & P. J. Ford Slack (Eds.), *The constructivist reader* (pp. 1–27). New York: Teachers College Press.

Walker, R. (1996). Music education freed from colonialism: A new praxis. *International Journal for Music Education, 27*, 2–15.

White, D. (1996) *From performer-musician to teacher-musician*. Unpublished master's project, University of Victoria, Victoria, British Columbia, Canada.

Wilkinson, J. A. (1996). *Literacy, education and arts partnerships*. Unpublished interim report. (Available from The Royal Conservatory of Music, 273 Bloor Street West, Toronto, ON  M5S 1W2)

Wilkinson, J. A. (1997). *LLTA assessment report*. Unpublished interim report. (Available from The Royal Conservatory of Music, 273 Bloor Street West, Toronto, ON  M5S 1W2)

Wilkinson, J. A. (1998). *Learning through the arts, 1997–98*. Unpublished interim report. (Available from The Royal Conservatory of Music, 273 Bloor Street West, Toronto, ON  M5S 1W2)

Wiske, M. S. (Ed.). (1998). *Teaching for understanding: Linking research with practice*. San Francisco, CA: Jossey-Bass.

Zimmerman, E. (1997). Excellence and equity issues in art education: Can we be excellent and equal too? *Arts Education Policy Review, 98* (4), 20–26.

---

[1]I am grateful to the Canadian Music Educators Association and the University College of Cape Breton Press for permission to adapt "Challenges to Canadian

Teacher Education in the Arts" from *Connect, Combine, Communicate: Revitalizing the Arts in Canadian Schools* (1998) for this chapter.

[2] The Coalition for Music Education in Canada and provincial organizations such as the British Columbia Coalition for Music Education have shown leadership and initiative in advocacy initiatives, as have many stalwart individuals.

[3] There are other important issues — such as gender, racism, and poverty — which also need to be addressed by music educators. These topics have been widely discussed and, in fairness to the other authors in this book, I have limited my discussion to two issues at this time.

[4] See Dinesh D'Souza, *Illiberal Education: The Politics of Race and Sex on Campus* (1992) for a discussion of equality and liberal education.

[5] There are those who argue for a more interdisciplinary and holistic approach in secondary schools.

[6] but not language arts, in most places

[7] Having classroom teachers deliver music programs is a mixed blessing. On the one hand, music educators claim that music is for everyone, thus supporting the idea that classroom teachers should be able to teach music at the general level acceptable for other subjects. Job protection aside, we should perhaps feel gratified if our graduates can teach music. On the other hand, it is evident that most classroom teachers lack the expertise to teach music and have said so.

[8] "Some" music could mean playing the piano by number, one music course, or a music degree with minimal or no methods.

[9] Volume 87, number 5 of *Design for Arts in Education* (1986) is devoted to issues surrounding elitism and excellence in arts education.

[10] The source of this definition of "talented" is taken from *Talented Teenagers: The Roots of Success and Failure* by M. Csikszentmihalyi, K. Rathunde, & S. Whalen (1993, p. 21).

[11] There is a contradiction here. People don't really seem to know what they want. It is curious, for example, that what is rewarded at a professional level (consider the adulation and remuneration given National Hockey League stars) is not acceptable in the schools or the community.

[12] See *Vital Links: Canadian Cultural Industries* (Government of Canada: Communications, 1987) for an example of the arts community's perceived need to justify the arts on economic grounds. The Cultural Human Resources Council (CHRC) has developed a series of attractive and informative booklets called *Careers in Culture* to promote arts-related careers. The music title is *Now Hear This — Careers in Music and Sound Recording* (1998). The booklets are available from the CHRC.

[13] An example of this leadership is evident in the growth of the Coalition for Music Education in Canada.

[14] See for example Doctorow's *The Book of Daniel* (1971) and *Ragtime* (1975).

[15] For a discussion of the theoretical frameworks of arious forms of constructivism refer to Volume 31, numbers 3/4 of the *Educational Psychologist* (1996) a special issue edited by Hermine Marshall.

[16] This collaboration co-exists uneasily with the competitive global economy.

[17] See (Elster & Bell, 1999) for more information or contact the Royal Conservatory of Music.

[18] Symposium I was held in Cape Breton (1997), Symposium II in Victoria (1998), and Symposium III in Regina (1999). For information on the NSAE check out its web site at http://www.artsed.ca. The NSAE was originally an initiative of the CMEA.

[19] The decision is more complex, but this is not the place to go into details. For more information about the impact of this decision, contact the author.

[20] These issues currently include equity, special needs, First Nations, second language, and racism. These issues are important, but they are becoming a decontextualized focus of school curriculum and teacher education programs.

# Chapter Two

# Changing Attitudes, Changing Practice

*Eric Favaro*

The 1990s can be characterized as a time of reflection and a time to question the values that have helped shape our identity, our attitudes, and our beliefs. The Canadian identity, by its very history, has been influenced by a melding of cultures, and each region of Canada draws on the ethos of its citizens to help establish a unique identity that is reflected in all aspects of life. In education this melding has particular significance as we try to meet the challenges that continue to face us and try to cope with the trends and ideas that often infiltrate this country from south of the border and beyond.

It is ironic that the arts, which historically have identified and preserved culture, have not always had the recognition, respect, and support that Canadian artists and arts educators have sought. The outside influences of globalization, the economy, and politics have affected the attitude towards the arts. Moreover, in Canada we have learned that we cannot count on public or private sector support for the arts and arts education, whether measured in terms of funding, participation, research and development, or sales. Thompson, Director of the Canada Council for the Arts, during her address at 1998 National Symposium on Arts Education in Victoria, summed up the problem:

> At the end of the second millennium we are fighting a new barbarism, not of dark ignorance but of information glut and too many diversions. As ignorance is overcome by education, so will we learn to handle what I see as the perilous multiplication of entertainment gutted of content. Arts education is essential to discernment and judgement, and in the

41

broadest sense, arts advocacy is the fight for the return of the life of the spirit to the centre of our existence. (1999, p. 139)

Although this chapter will deal specifically with music education, it is inappropriate in view of current educational practice to isolate music from the other arts disciplines when establishing its place within the school curriculum. Alliances that have been established and continue to evolve provide strong evidence that all the arts — performing arts, visual arts, literary arts, and media arts — share commonalties and that, together, the arts could provide education with a focal point which would place them at the centre of the curriculum rather than on the periphery. To isolate one arts discipline or to make a stronger case for music over drama, or visual arts over dance, for example, merely marginalizes the arts in general and pushes them to the edge of educational priorities.

The past few decades have seen a profusion of research on the value of arts education in the schools, to such an extent that we could probably fill a library on the topic. Most often the research supports quality arts experiences in and out of schools, and yet this abundant research seems to go unheeded when decision makers are establishing priorities and setting new directions for education. There are many reasons for this state of affairs, but despite all that we know about the value and nature of the arts, the basic problem remains: the research has not changed attitudes. We could hypothesize and blame the economy for the lack of support for the arts. Yet we see an overwhelming amount of money directed to technology. So, there truly is money. We could blame the lack of support on the "Back to Basics" movement that has placed a tremendous emphasis on literacy, numeracy, science, and technology. Yet we know this direction contradicts the research of the past twenty years on teaching and learning. What has become obvious is that the research has not made a significant impact on curriculum, on teaching practice, or on administrative decision making.

If the arts matter, we should be able to say so clearly and confidently without being drawn into a kind of rhetoric which is often more destructive than helpful. More importantly, we must avoid at all costs the tendency of getting caught up in a special pleading for the arts, or even more harmfully, a pleading for one arts discipline over another. Instead we must make a case for education as a whole — for a conception of education that shows the importance of the arts in general. We want to show that the arts fit into the firmament of educational priorities and concerns, some of which are political, some economic, and some vocational. Unless we can make a case for the arts in relation to the whole agenda for education, we are bound to be marginalized. As Montgomery (1997) explains: "Perhaps it is time to go beyond just explaining the value of arts education as a separate entity and extend the justifications to include statements about its role in relation to the bigger picture: the entire educational structure" (p. 55).

In the spring of 1997 the Halifax City School Board announced the elimination of six teaching jobs, four in music and two in visual arts. A rally was quickly organized, with three hundred parents, a band, and a choir protesting the cuts. The board reconsidered and cut three visual arts teachers and a librarian instead. The message was clear. Some arts are more important than others!

To some extent three main factors have prejudiced the position of the arts in schools — the economy, the return to the "basics" trend, and the development of science and technology. These elements prejudice our case more if we succumb to their pressures or if we defend our position in hostility to them. The case for arts education is often based on the notions that the arts balance other subjects or that they develop skills and competencies that other subjects are incapable of developing. The argument is flawed. If we are to change attitudes towards the arts, this misconceived agenda must be replaced by one in which the place of the arts becomes more clear.

Education in the developed world is facing unprecedented challenges as we begin the new millennium. We tend to think that the problems we have now are ones that have always existed. They are not, and throughout the world situations are developing proving the urgency for new sorts of education that will meet the needs of students in the next century.

The economic landscape of the world is transforming itself at a rapid pace as new axes of trade and new economic relationships are formed. These developments are placing unique demands on education and the skills and attitudes that curriculum helps to promote. In addition, the new economy has increased substantially the debt load of many governments, and the burdens placed on tax payers have forced reductions in budgets to the extent that basic and necessary services are threatened.

Tied to the global changes in the economy is the restructuring of the political landscape. During the past decade the world has witnessed a political transformation, particularly in Eastern Europe,

Russia, South Africa, and Asia, that is leading to new sorts of political dependencies and interdependencies. Because the next generation will be faced with unprecedented challenges, schools today must provide students with the knowledge, skill, and attitudes that will prepare them to address these challenges effectively.

A third challenge to education is the emerging pattern of relationships developing around the world in terms of cultural interest and development. Through technology, migration, changes within and between national communities, we are witnessing changes in cultural production and cultural identity. It is impossible to talk about distinctive cultures which are not affected by world cultures. Education in the 21$^{st}$ century will be challenged to deal with these issues.

The arts all have fundamental contributions to make in meeting these challenges. It is critical therefore that we make our case for arts education in terms of the changing world and the skills, attitudes, and knowledge that will be required of our future citizens. More importantly, it is essential that teaching practice demonstrate a willingness to change and adapt to authentic learning experiences for students, and not merely perpetuate arts education as training "artists" or achieving aesthetic goals. These considerations are critical for changing the attitudes of those who view the arts and arts education as a fragmented part of a student's learning experience rather than the keyhole to learning.

It is often said that the arts have no status in schools. They don't! This may seem like a paradox to those in the community who view the arts affectionately and support them fully. In many communities the arts have high status with the artist a respected individual who achieves certain honours for community involvement. Moreover, knowledge of the arts is a sign of a "cultured" person, and arts institutions are valued for their prestige. Why then are they not so highly rated in schools?

To a certain extent, the lack of status for the arts in schools is due to political ambivalence. In the community, this ambivalence is one consequence of the high status the products of the arts have been given, while the processes that led to the achievements have been of little social interest. When one attends a symphony concert it is the performance that receives acclaim. The hours of rehearsal, the refinement process, and the skill development are of little consequence to the audience, and thus have a low status. Likewise for an exhibition. The finished work of art is recognized for its value (or lack of value), while the studio hours that were necessary to create the work are of little significance.

The public's view of the arts is quite different from what happens in schools where we stress the importance of process, which is of low status in the public's eye, over product, which enjoys high status. Thus, curriculum theorists continually criticize music programs that place the greatest emphasis on the spring concert or the festival performance over the learning taking place. Yet, these public performances appear to serve public expectations of music programs. Richards and Milligan (1997) explain:

> [T]he cuts have forced the music program to focus on the band program, because the band is a tangible and impressive product which gives parents feedback and something for which to fight. It is largely skills-oriented and delivers only one component of musical education. An unfortunate byproduct of this circumstance is that cuts are being directed at the lower grades which do not produce such impressive public displays. (p. 75)

In *The Challenge of Art to Psychology*, Sarason (1994) describes the US culture as one that does not recognize the true value of artistic activity in schools. Children bring artistic excitement to the first years of their elementary education, but soon the emphasis on realistic representations in visual arts and polished performances in music establish negative feelings that last through to adulthood. Students' artistic potentials are suppressed, and feelings of inadequacy prevail, until as adults (mostly in retirement) they turn their attention to drawing, painting, photography, and drama. Not unlike in the United States, Canadian schools are also guilty of these contradictions in their arts curricula. Could this not be one of the reasons for the marginalization of the arts in our public schools?

Even while the arts have been placed in jeopardy as school districts across Canada establish educational priorities, we have seen within ministries of education a move to revise arts curricula based on a changing philosophy that identifies the arts as central to education. Recently published curricula from British Columbia (British Columbia Ministry of Education, 1998), Saskatchewan (Saskatchewan Education, 1991) and Nova Scotia (Nova Scotia Department of Education and Culture, 1998) clearly identify dance, drama, music, and the visual arts within the core program, thus demonstrating a strong commitment to arts education. These documents describe the arts in terms of understandings and processes that include creative/productive, critical/responsive, and cultural/historical processes. Moreover, the curricula stress the interconnectedness of the arts to each other and to other areas of the curriculum. For arts administrators, this direction is encouraging as it demonstrates a willingness on the part of policymakers to value the arts by including them in the core program.

Problems still exist however in the transference and implementation of curriculum from the ministry office to the school district level. On a school timetable, each arts discipline has a place, isolated to a great degree from the rest of the curriculum. In many cases, particularly at the secondary level, the arts compete with each other and with other disciplines for students, time, and resources. This fragmentation pushes the arts once again to the periphery, jeopardizing their very existence. Pitman (1998) states: "Only the integration of the arts with an enlarged and globally conceived mandate, that involves every other discipline, can save the arts from gradual abandonment in our schools" (p. 206).

Clearly, there is a need for reform within arts education, including curricula, delivery, leadership, and training, which in turn will change attitudes towards the role of the arts in schools. This reform movement must articulate the purposes served by arts education based on conceptual research that identifies the nature of the arts and their roles in human experience. However, the challenges to reforming arts education seem almost insurmountable because of pressures both within and outside the arts education world.

When we refer to the arts we speak of several disciplines, including dance, drama, music, visual arts, literary arts, and media arts. Each has its own history, content, skills, traditions and most importantly, status within schools. Therefore, reform in each arts discipline, while acknowledging commonalities, must also acknowledge and respect the individual differences between the disciplines.

Another challenge to changing attitudes towards arts education is the inconsistency of roles within education of both specialist and generalist teachers, professional artists, arts institutions, and organizations. From province to province, and even within provinces, we see such variation in the delivery of programs. In many parts of Canada, music and other arts programs are delivered by classroom teachers with little or no training. Nationally there have been a number of initiatives that link professional artists and arts organizations to schools. While these may provide quality arts experiences for students, they cannot replace a sequential arts education provided most effectively by a trained specialist.

Yet another challenge is the balance between process and product, between production and reflection, between history and aesthetics, and on and on. In making a comparison between the approach of European (Austrian) music educators to those of North America, Mark (1998) states:

> Music education should make the young person aware of music as an essential part of human existence, widen its horizon of experience, provide access to the beauty of art and awaken the joy of music making.... In Austria, music making is only one of four approximately equivalent elements, which primarily does not include appearance in public, indicated implicitly in the term performance. (p. 3)

Coincidentally, we often look to the arts in European countries as having much higher status than in Canada and the United States.

A fourth challenge to changing attitudes is the lack of understanding of the arts as demonstrated by educational leaders, primarily at the school and district levels. Compounding the issue is the disappearance in recent years of arts education administrators who have traditionally been in positions where they can affect change at the decision-making level. The administration's commitment to arts education, therefore, becomes weaker as pressures mount to return to the "basics" — a language which administrators seem to understand.

Parents place an added challenge to the reform of arts education, viewing it as less "vocational" than maths and science, languages, technology and other areas of curriculum that will surely provide necessary skills for future employment. The fear of unemployment following their education is a primary concern for students in secondary and post-secondary institutions. Pitman (1998) describes a horizontal or integrated arts-based curriculum that:

> must prepare them to participate in an economy unlike any that has existed in the past, one that is "job poor," unable to heal the festering sores of enormous disparities of rich and poor, both between nations and within national boundaries. Unless integrated arts-based learning can succeed in addressing the issue of employment, there can be little hope of attracting the attention of teachers, parents, or students. (p. 91)

The arts community and government agencies dealing with the arts provide yet another challenge to the reform of arts education. Despite very well-intentioned efforts on the part of these groups, often their agenda is in conflict with that of arts educators and the school system. Although the relationship between the arts and arts education communities appears to be improving, there continue to be misconceptions of the roles that school- and community-based programs can play in delivering sequential programs to all students in all schools.

Finally, the complexity of the arts and arts education presents a significant challenge to reform and subsequently to changing attitudes towards the place of the arts in schools. The need for policy development, shaped by all the partners, must be recognized and promoted by arts advocates. Advocacy for arts education should deal with the implementation of policy changes, but without clearly articulated policies, advocacy activities become disjointed and inconsequential.

Changing attitudes in arts education are dependent to a great extent on a change in teaching practice. Furthermore, both attitudinal change and change in delivery methods are often influenced by personal and organizational agendas, including those of teachers, administrators, professional artists, arts organizations, and politicians. At a recent gathering of arts educators from around the world at the International Conference on the Future of Arts Education (New York, 1999), it became abundantly clear that unless we work together to establish a common agenda, the arts will continue to be marginalized and will remain on the periphery of the school curriculum.

There appear to be two distinct agendas which penetrate the debate on education and complicate the current problems of attitude. The first is academicism in which attainment bears the highest priority: higher test scores, increased standards, back to basics. In this agenda, arts education is not considered central because the arts are not perceived to be drawing on forms of intelligence. When we hear of abilities and success in the arts, the emphasis is not placed on intelligence but rather on talent. Herein lies a basic attitudinal problem.

Western education appears to be devoted to the development of academic ability, downplaying the role of the arts. In academic education emphasis is placed on logical, deductive reasoning which is evident in mathematics and language development. Because the arts are not viewed as central to the development of academic ability, the assumption is that they are less important.

The arts recognize, represent, and address the reality that intelligence is multifaceted. Perkins (1994) in his book, *The Intelligent Eye: Learning To Think by Looking at Art*, describes how children construct their own meaning, body of knowledge, and skill while participating actively in their learning and not by sitting passively listening, reading, and figuring. He argues that the arts play an important role in the development of the reflective intelligence, guiding students through the assimilation of experiences and knowledge.

Gardner (1993) described at least seven forms of intelligence, and despite an abundance of research over the past ten years, his theories have had little effect on elevating the arts within the school curriculum. Students possess a variety of abilities, many of which are neglected because teachers are not looking for them. There are many children who spend their years in school bursting with potential and intellectual capacity, and schools fail to recognize them. As they go through school these students are judged against a standard that does not apply to them and they go through life with a sense of failure. Arts education can make a difference for these students.

The second agenda is specialization. This is the tendency to think of the world in terms of our own particular subject. The difficulty with this approach is not only the expansion of knowledge and the burgeoning of subjects with their many forms and digressions but also the breakdown of barriers between subjects.

Recently published ministry documents on arts curricula have distinguished between learning in the arts and learning through the arts. Learning in the arts focuses on the individual arts discipline with its own skills and concepts, styles of procedures, and analysis of thought. Discipline-Based Arts Education (DBAE, Getty Center, 1985), an approach that started in the United States, stresses a sequential program that includes four areas: production, history, criticism, and aesthetics. In Canada, Saskatchewan has led the way in the development of arts curricula that follows a similar philosophy. This curriculum was developed in response to six main guidelines:

- the four strands of dance, drama, music, and visual arts should be developed as discreet strands (50 minutes each per week);
- each strand should include three components — the creative/productive, the cultural/historical and the critical/responsive;
- the curriculum should be developed for use by both the generalist classroom teacher and the classroom teachers;
- the curriculum should include Indian, Métis, and Inuit content perspectives;
- the required curriculum should include knowledge, skills, and attitudes; and.
- the curriculum should be based on a 200 minute per week time allotment. (Hanson, Bush, & Brown, 1997, p. 48)

Other provinces (British Columbia and Nova Scotia) have used the Saskatchewan curriculum as a model for their own curriculum development.

What do these developments mean for music? Kuzmich (1997) states that DBAE studies in music encourage:

- the making of expressive images, whether interpretive or creative;
- increasing aural perception, hence, a greater receptivity to different, complex, or important forms of human achievement;
- the viewing of a composition as a product of a particular time, place and culture; and
- the practising of arts criticism; i.e. giving reasons — interpretive and evaluative — to support judgements about quality. (p. 26)

An effective music program must include all aspects of the learning and must have goals arranged sequentially. Assessment is vital as both students, and teachers measure the attainment of these goals.

Learning through the arts is an integrative approach that allows connections to be made between the arts disciplines and between the arts and other disciplines and fields of study. Pitman (1997) in quoting the Arts, Culture, and Technology Initiative in New York City, 1995, states:

One of the most powerful ways to keep children motivated to learn and raise their levels of academic achievements is to use the arts and technology as tools for learning. Children are fully engaged when music, drama, visual arts, literature, and the full range of media and communications technology are integrated into all aspects of teaching and learning. (p. 195)

In 1995, the Royal Conservatory of Music developed a program in the Toronto schools called *Learning Through The Arts* ™ based on the research of Gardner and others. This program, which in 1999 was implemented in six sites across the country, reinforces the arts as a tool for the teaching and learning of many skills and concepts beyond the arts themselves. Elster and Bell (1998) state:

An arts based education can:

- facilitate the development of analytical and problem-solving skills that students have to learn;
- make learning relevant for students of the many diverse cultural backgrounds that exist in today's schools;
- facilitate the connections that need to be made among academic areas and events outside the classrooms; and

- enhance skills like teamwork, the ability to use and acquire information, and the mastery of different types of symbol systems and technology. (p.147)

Learning both in and through the arts are valuable experiences for students and provide the philosophical basis for the centrality of the arts in the curriculum. In learning in the arts, dance, drama, music, and visual arts are recognized as forms of intelligence, each with their own unique characteristics. In learning through the arts, the disciplines are recognized as forms of intelligence that facilitate and enhance student learning in all areas of the curriculum.

The specialization agenda recognizes the importance of having specially trained arts educators delivering the arts curricula. It also recognizes the value of classroom teachers in achieving curriculum outcomes through the arts provided sufficient training, planning time, and resources are available.

The last half of the 20$^{th}$ century can be characterized as a time of unrest, discovery, and change. Advancements in technology have transformed the way we think, work, and live. Moreover, our relationship to the environment has caused us to re-examine our very existence on earth, and plan for a future that is fraught with uncertainty.

Education, in its traditional sense, has been challenged to address the individual needs of students. The arts have a vital contribution to make to the reclamation of an education that prepares our students for their adult roles in society. As stated at the beginning, there exists a library of research on the importance of the arts in the curriculum, but there is little evidence to indicate that it has had a substantial influence on the attitude of most decision makers when they plan and implement programs.

Arts educators, including music educators, must consider ways to bring the research alive by examining their teaching practice and ensuring that their methodologies reflect current thought on the nature of teaching and learning. We can no longer satisfy the outcomes of new curricula using an outdated mode of delivery that shows little regard for individual creativity and lifelong learning. As importantly, we must recognize pluralism and value cultural diversity through an historical perspective. As we look forward, meeting the challenges to Canadian music education, we must feel confident in our abilities to establish priorities within education that place the arts at the centre of curriculum.

To quote Pitman (1998):

Seeking "the ultimate purpose of human life" and acquiring "the virtue of wisdom" must surely be restored as the central role of the school.... This will not happen simply through teaching children to conquer the various technologies that surround them, nor through a total preoccupation with skill training for vocational purposes. Rather, it will be the result of integrating all forms of knowledge in a cultural thrust that stresses the centrality of dealing with the basic problems facing our civilization, that emphasizes the interaction of all forms of wisdom identified over the centuries of human activity, and that perceives the artistic as the connecting tissue which can give coherence and intelligibility while emphasizing the human values that will sustain the planet. (p. 247)

## References

British Columbia Ministry of Education. (1998). *Integrated resource package — Fine arts K to 7.* Victoria: Author.

Elster, A., & Bell, N. (1998). Learning through the arts: A partnership in educational transformation. In B. Hanley (Ed.), *Leadership, Advocacy, Communication: A vision for arts education in Canada* (pp. 145-154). Victoria, BC: Canadian Music Educators Association.

Gardner, H. (1993). *Frames of mind: Theory of multiple intelligences.* New York: Basic Books.

Getty Center for Education in the Arts. (1985). *Beyond creating: The place for art in America's schools.* Los Angeles, CA: Author.

Hanson, E., Bush, J., & Brown, N. (1997). Saskatchewan's arts education curriculum: History and implementation. In B. Roberts (Ed.), *Connect, Combine, Communicate: Revitalizing the arts in Canadian schools* (pp. 45–53). Sydney, NS: University College of Cape Breton Press.

Kuzmich, N. (1997). Music education: A paradox. *Canadian Music Educator, 38* (3), 25–29.

Mark, D. (1998). The music teacher's dilemma — Musician or Teacher? *International Journal of Music Education, 32,* 3–22.

Montgomery, A. (1997). Music in the primary grades: The natural link to literacy. In B. Roberts (Ed.), *Connect, Combine, Communicate: Revitalizing the arts in Canadian schools* (pp. 55-63). Sydney: University College of Cape Breton Press.

Nova Scotia Department of Education and Culture. (1998). *Foundation for arts education.* Halifax: Author.

Perkins, D. (1994). *The Intelligent Eye: Learning to think by looking at art.* Santa Monica, CA: The Getty Center for Education in the Arts.

Pitman, W. (1998). *Learning the arts in an age of uncertainty.* North York, ON: Arts Education Council of Ontario.

Richards, P., & Milligan, D. (1997). The case for a multidisciplinary arts education curriculum. In B. Roberts (Ed.), *Connect, Combine, Communicate: Revitalizing the arts in Canadian schools* (pp. 75–88). Sydney, NS: University College of Cape Breton Press.

Sarason, S. (1994). *The challenge of art to psychology.* New York: Yale University Press.

Saskatchewan Education. (1991). *Grade 5 Arts Education Curriculum Guide.* Regina, SK: Author.

Thompson, S. (1998). Advocacy in the arts: A Canada Council perspective. In B. Hanley (Ed.), *Leadership, Advocacy, Communication: A vision for arts education in Canada* (pp. 137–144). 154). Victoria, BC: Canadian Music Educators Association.

# Chapter Three

# Nouveaux défis en éducation musicale chez la population francophone du Nouveau-Brunswick

*Anne S. Lowe*

## Introduction

L'éducation musicale francophone au Nouveau-Brunswick fait face, à l'heure actuelle, à des changements majeurs.[1] Ces changements sont les résultats de réflexions profondes sur la raison d'être et le rôle de l'éducation musicale dans l'éducation globale de la personne, et plus important encore, sur la pédagogie et le processus d'apprentissage qui sous-tendent la discipline. Les propos de ces réflexions ont été considérés pour l'élaboration d'un nouveau programme d'étude qui fera l'objet principal de ce chapitre. Ce programme sera adopté par le Ministère de l'Éducation du Nouveau-Brunswick (MENB), secteur francophone, en l'an 2000.

Afin de mieux comprendre les enjeux qui ont encouragé la réforme en éducation musicale, ce chapitre débutera par un bref aperçu de l'histoire de l'éducation musicale francophone au Nouveau-Brunswick. Ensuite suivra la description du cadre théorique du nouveau programme et une discussion des défis que rencontreront les musiciens éducateurs pour l'implantation de ce programme dans les écoles de la province.

✳ ✳ ✳

## Historique

Même si le premier document du Ministère de l'Éducation s'adressant à l'enseignement de la musique dans les écoles du Nouveau-Brunswick n'a été implanté qu'en 1965 (MENB, 1988), le chant a toujours eu une place privilégiée dans la vie familiale religieuse et sociale des francophones du Nouveau-Brunswick, surtout ceux de descendance acadienne. La musique vocale était pour eux le moyen par excellence d'expression culturelle (Green & Vogan, 1991). D'ailleurs, à travers le temps, plusieurs chorales se sont formées et se sont perfectionnées avec l'arrivée de gens spécialisés en musique. Au milieu du 20ᵉ siècle, même si les fanfares ont fleuri au Nouveau-Brunswick, les chorales demeuraient le moyen d'expression musicale privilégiée des acadiens. De fait, plusieurs chorales acadiennes, telles la chorale de l'Université St-Joseph et de Notre-Dame d'Acadie, ont été reconnues parmi les meilleures du Canada (Green & Vogan, 1991). De plus, avec la venue de l'éducation systématique de la musique dans les écoles publiques de Moncton, Frédériction, et Saint-John, les chorales d'écoles, quelques-unes de renommée nationale et internationale (ex., Chorale Beauséjour), se sont répandues très vite dans ces régions.

Dans les années '60, à la lumière du rapport du Tanglewood Symposium et de celui de la Commission d'enquête sur l'enseignement des arts au Québec (Conseil supérieur de l'éducation, 1988), l'enseignement de la musique, qui avait été axé sur le solfège et la théorie musicale, a subit une transformation profonde.

> On a remis en question la pertinence éducative des activités musicales traditionnelles — la chorale, la fanfare et le festival; on s'est interrogé sur la signification des contenus de solfège et de théorie étudiés; on a mis en doute l'efficacité des méthodes d'enseignement et la valeur éducative des manuels scolaires. (MENB, 1988, p. 3)

Ces remises en question et la mise en application des changements qui s'imposaient n'ont pas été toujours bien accueillies dans le milieu scolaire surtout compte tenu de l'insuffisance de matériel didactique en français. Par contre, malgré les controverses, un premier programme d'éducation musicale en langue française a été conçu en 1988 dans le contexte d'une restructuration du Ministère de l'Éducation, secteur francophone, en 1978. Ce programme 1988 proposait une éducation musicale en français pour tous les élèves du primaire indépendamment de leurs aptitudes musicales: une période de 50 minutes par semaine, enseignée par un spécialiste et 15 minutes par jour, enseignée par la titulaire de classe. Le programme, axé sur l'éducation esthétique, avait comme objectifs de

> permettre à l'élève, par des expériences d'audition, d'interprétation et de création, d'apprécier l'univers sonore et la musique de tous genres, formes et styles, quelle qu'en soit l'origine historique et culturelle, et quels qu'en soient les médiums de production et d'habiliter l'élève à participer aux diverses activités musicales individuelles et collectives. (MENB, 1988, p. 11)

Le processus d'apprentissage comprenait trois zones représentant: (1) les paramètres expressifs de la musique où l'élève, au début de l'année scolaire, perçoit et réagit à la musique (zone A); (2) les composantes expressives de la musique où l'élève, motivé par l'expérience vécue en zone A, s'engage à comprendre et à s'approprier les composantes du langage musical (zone B); (3) la structure expressive de la musique où l'élève, suite à l'apprentissage à la zone B, fera l'expérience de la création et de l'interprétation musicale. La communication musicale par l'entremise d'une manifestation musicale quelconque était encouragée qu'à la fin des expériences vécues à l'étape de la zone C. Les contenus pour chaque niveau scolaire (1–6) étaient décrits avec très peu de direction quant aux moyens pédagogiques nécessaires pour l'actualisation de ce programme. De plus, plusieurs musiciens éducateurs ont questionné la logique des 3 zones et ont souvent mis sur les étagères le programme pour y faire place à leur pédagogie et à leurs méthodes d'enseignement, d'une part influencées par la forme traditionnelle de l'enseignement axé sur l'enseignant, encourageant d'abord la lecture et l'interprétation musicale, et d'autre part, influencées par une pédagogie renouvelée axée sur l'élève, mettant l'emphase sur l'apprentissage des concepts musicaux par l'audition et l'interprétation. Quoiqu'une importance accordée dans le programme 1988 à la création musicale, très peu de musiciens et éducateurs ont incorporé ce moyen d'expression à leur salle de classe dû principalement à l'insécurité personnelle et au manque de formation. Malgré ces problèmes, l'éducation musicale a eu sa place parmi les sujets académiques et est enseignée, à l'heure actuelle, par un spécialiste[2] dans toutes les écoles primaires francophones du Nouveau-Brunswick.

Au début des années '90, la Commission Downey-Landry proposait une "remise en question de l'organisation pédagogique et administrative des écoles publiques de la maternelle à la 12ᵉ année" (MENB, 1995, p. 1). De nouveaux programmes d'études ont été élaborés apportant des améliorations pédagogiques importantes. Les renouveaux au niveau des structures et des approches pédagogiques encourageaient une importance accordée aux habiletés intellectuelles, telles la résolution de problème, la pensée critique, la prise de décision et la métacognition, et aux habiletés personnelles et sociales. Donc, il ne suffisait pas d'atteindre des résultats d'apprentissage au niveau des savoirs, mais aussi aux niveaux des savoir-faire et des savoir-être. Cette "école renouvelée" valorisant les savoirs, les savoir-faire, et les savoir-être a nécessité une élaboration de nouveaux programmes d'étude, d'où vient celui de l'éducation musicale qui sera piloté dans les écoles de la province en l'an 2000.

## Description du cadre théorique du nouveau programme d'étude en éducation musicale (M–12)

En plus de la description des fondements et des objectifs de l'éducation musicale, les renouveaux demandés par le MENB en 1995 ont exigé une élaboration claire et précise de l'orientation et des composantes pédagogiques de la discipline, très peu discutées dans le programme 1988. De plus, ces dimensions pédagogiques, tout comme les programmes d'études développés pour les autres matières scolaires, devaient refléter la pédagogie de "l'école renouvelée" prescrite par le MENB (1995). Les sections suivantes sont tirées directement du cadre théorique du nouveau programme d'éducation musicale (document de travail) basé sur la pédagogie de "l'école renouvelée" (MENB, 1999, pp. 9–39).

---

### Orientation à la discipline

*But et résultats d'apprentissage généraux de la discipline.* Le but de l'éducation musicale est de développer le potentiel musical et global de chaque élève en lui permettant d'acquérir l'autonomie pour qu'il puisse découvrir le plaisir et le bien-être qui lui procure l'expression musicale comme source continue d'expériences esthétiques, personnelles, sociales, et culturelles. Pour atteindre ce but, l'élève devra être en mesure de:

I. *Savoirs*

    A. démontrer sa connaissance des différentes composantes théoriques et techniques de la musique;

    B. acquérir des compétences en lecture et en écriture musicales;

II. *Savoir-faire*

    A. connaître et interpréter diverses pièces du répertoire vocal et instrumental d'ici, d'ailleurs, d'hier, et d'aujourd'hui;

    B. faire la discrimination auditive afin qu'il puisse comprendre, analyser et porter un jugement critique concernant le choix d'éléments musicaux faisant partie de pièces musicales d'ici, d'ailleurs, d'hier, et d'aujourd'hui;

    C. faire la synthèse de ses savoirs musicaux par l'expression personnelle et de pouvoir les transférer dans des activités d'improvisation et de création;

III. *Savoir-être*

    A. réagir de façon expressive, authentique, et personnelle à l'expérience musicale en démontrant ses dimensions affectives et esthétiques;

    B. comprendre l'importance du rôle de la musique dans la vie sociale et culturelle d'ici, d'ailleurs, d'hier, et d'aujourd'hui;

    C. encourager la vie musicale et culturelle de l'école et de la communauté;

    D. continuer, d'une façon autonome, de vivre des expériences esthétiques musicales pendant toute la vie.

*Progression de la discipline.* Dans le présent programme d'étude, les résultats d'apprentissage généraux et les composantes décrites ci-dessous sont les mêmes pour tous les niveaux M–12. Cependant, les apprentissages découlant de ces résultats doivent tenir compte du degré des savoirs antérieurs et du stade de développement cognitif, psychomoteur et affectif de l'élève. Les résultats d'apprentissage, regroupés en fonction du savoirs, du savoir-faire, et du savoir-être, font partie de la formation globale en éducation musicale. Toutes ces composantes doivent faire partie intégrante du processus d'apprentissage pour chaque niveau scolaire et ce dans le but d'assurer l'autonomie de l'élève afin qu'il puisse continuer de vivre des expériences musicales esthétiques la vie durant.

Les parties qui suivent élaborent les caractéristiques du savoir, du savoir-faire et du savoir-être musicaux.

### A. *Savoir*

Le contenu de tout domaine d'apprentissage comprend les concepts qui forment la structure de la matière enseignée, c'est-à-dire les concepts qui la distingue des autres domaines d'apprentissage. Puisque la musique est une forme d'art auditive, les concepts musicaux sont fondés sur les composantes orales de la musique. Ces concepts comprennent ceux reliés aux attributs du son (le *rythme*, la *mélodie*, le *timbre)* qui, combinés, produisent de l'*harmonie* avec une *texture* propre et qui peuvent être modifiés par un changement d'*intensité* sonore ou d'*articulation*. Les sons sont organisés en une *forme* musicale selon le *style* et l'*expression* du contexte historique et culturel.

Or, en éducation musicale, l'élève doit intérioriser les concepts reliés aux:

| | |
|---|---|
| **Attributs du son** | rythme |
| | mélodie |
| | timbre |
| **Combinaisons du son** | harmonie |
| | texture |
| **Modifications du son** | intensité |
| | articulation |
| **Organisations du son** | forme |
| | style |
| | expression |

### B. *Savoir-faire*

L'élève perçoit, réagit et s'engage dans des interactions avec le monde sonore par l'appréciation, l'interprétation et la création musicale.

Dans une activité d'*appréciation* ou d'écoute active de la musique, l'élève est appelé à décrire sa perception musicale par l'expression corporelle, l'image et la communication orale. En vivant des expériences diverses d'écoute musicale active, l'élève augmentera ses habiletés psychomotrices, cognitives, et affectives. Ceci lui permettra d'alimenter l'appréciation musicale par une analyse et une critique de l'oeuvre dans son contexte historique et culturel.

L'élève s'engage dans l'expression musicale par des activités d'*interprétation* et de création. C'est en chantant et en jouant des instruments que l'élève interprétera une oeuvre musicale. Ces deux formes d'expression musicale devraient occuper une place importante dans l'apprentissage intégral de la musique à tous les niveaux scolaires.

La *création musicale* se concrétise par l'improvisation et la composition. Dans les activités de création musicale, l'élève exprime l'essence de son être en faisant appel aux concepts musicaux appris. Tout élève, selon son stade et son rythme de développement musical, peut démontrer la synthèse de ses apprentissages dans l'improvisation ou la création musicale.

## C. Savoir-être

À travers toute expérience musicale, l'élève apprend à exprimer ses pensées et ses émotions dans un contexte personnel, social, historique et culturel. C'est par l'expression et l'évocation de pensées, d'images et d'émotions que la musique prend une signification.

Puisque la musique contribue à l'épanouissement de la personne au sein d'une société, l'élève doit avoir l'occasion de participer à de multiples activités qui développeront son sens d'appartenance et sa perception du rôle de la musique dans la vie communautaire et sociale. Il sera un consommateur de musique averti capable de faire de la discrimination auditive et de donner à l'art et à la musique une place de choix dans sa vie. De plus, la musique interprétée, créée et perçue dans des contextes historiques et culturels permettra à l'élève de découvrir la richesse et la diversité de l'âme humaine afin de se sentir solidaire avec tous les peuples de la terre. L'élève aura développé l'autonomie musicale nécessaire lui permettant de faire des choix qui l'amèneront à être fier de sa culture et confiant de sa place en société.

*Relation de la musique avec les autres disciplines.* L'apprentissage de la musique, comme celui des arts en général, est un moyen privilégié pour l'élève d'approfondir ses connaissances par rapport aux autres disciplines et de poser un regard différent face aux réalités de la vie humaine.

Sans enlever de l'importance à la spécialisation, l'élève doit être capable de relier ses nouvelles connaissances musicales à celles apprises antérieurement et de puiser des idées et des renseignements dans divers domaines lors de la résolution de problèmes.

Le programme d'éducation musicale doit offrir de nombreuses occasions d'apprentissage holistique en y intégrant le contenu provenant d'autres disciplines. De plus, l'élève doit avoir l'occasion de découvrir comment la musique se relie à sa vie personnelle, communautaire et sociale.

Ci-après sont décrits quelques exemples d'intégration du savoir, du savoir-faire et du savoir-être en musique transférables dans d'autres disciplines scolaires.

**A.**  **Musique**

- le rythme
- la mélodie
- la forme
- la communication expressive

**Français**

- le mètre en poésie
- le rythme naturel de la phrase grammaticale
- l'intonation naturelle de la prononciation de la phrase grammaticale
- l'unité, la variété, la répétition, l'accentuation et la structure d'un poème ou d'un énoncé grammatical
- capacité d'extérioriser ses émotions
- respect des autres
- rédaction des comptes-rendus et critiques
- compréhension du texte

**B.**  **Musique**

- le rythme
- la mélodie

**Mathématiques**

- les fractions
- les graphiques

**C.**  **Musique**

- le rythme
- la mélodie

**Arts plastiques**

- le mouvement
- la tension, le repos
- la répétition, le contraste
- l'utilisation de lignes, de patrons, et de motifs

- la forme

- la texture

- l'intensité sonore

- les éléments expressifs
  (style)

- le thème et la variation
- l'équilibre

- la densité

- l'utilisation d'une variété de
  textures

- les couleurs

- les éléments expressifs
  (style)

**D.**    **Musique**                **Sciences**
- la mélodie                     • les propiétés du son

**E.**    **Musique**                **Sciences humaines**
- tous les éléments              • les évènements historiques où
  musicaux                         culturels reliés à la musique
                                   d'une culture particulière

**F.**    **Musique**                **Formation personelle
                                   et socialle**
- tous les éléments musicaux     • l'estime de soi
                                 • la discipline personelle
                                 • la connaissance de soi et des
                                   autres
                                 • l'acquisition des valeurs
                                 • l'expression personelle
                                 • l'esprit innovateur
                                 • le sens critique

Ces composantes du développement humain favorisent l'apprentissage et sont essentielles à l'actualisation intégrale de chaque personne.

L'importance accordée à un engagement communautaire et social nécessite un changement philosophique et pédagogique de la part du musicien éducateur. Le cadre théorique spécifie les composantes pédagogiques qui favorisent l'atteinte de ces objectifs.

## Composantes pédagogiques du programme

### *Principes directeurs*

Le programme d'éducation musicale repose sur les principes directeurs d'ordre pédagogique découlant des buts et objectifs de la discipline.

1. L'éducation musicale contribue au développement global de l'élève en touchant de façon particulière à la dimension esthétique. C'est par le biais d'expériences musicales que l'élève prendra conscience de ses émotions et de ses sentiments.

2. L'éducation musicale est axée sur une approche socio-constructiviste à l'apprentissage. L'élève construit son savoir à partir de ses expériences antérieures. Par des expériences sensorielles, l'élève génère sa compréhension du concept musical qui s'approfondit continuellement selon ses expériences d'interaction avec le monde sonore. La démarche pédagogique exige donc le passage du connu (connaissances antérieures) vers l'inconnu (résultat d'apprentissage) pour enfin aboutir au nouveau connu (connaissances fiables, durables, et transférables).

   La construction des savoirs en musique se fait par l'interaction avec les autres dans une atmosphère où l'expression de soi et le respect des autres sont valorisés. Dans un esprit de collaboration, l'élève fait part de ses expériences, structure ses idées, résout des problèmes et fait l'analyse et la synthèse. C'est par l'interprétation d'oeuvres vocales et instrumentales collectives que l'élève reconnaît l'unité dans les diversités musicales et humaines comme une composante essentielle à la valeur esthétique de l'oeuvre musicale.

3. L'apprentissage musical s'effectue à travers une multitude d'activités musicales de diverses formes (interprétation, création, appréciation) afin de respecter les modes de représentation des connaissances (exploratoire, iconique, et symbolique) ainsi que le rythme et le style d'apprentissage de tous les élèves.

4. L'éducation musicale amène l'élève à développer sa créativité et son sens d'expression personnelle. À travers des

expériences pratiques qui incitent une participation active, l'élève aura l'occasion de s'exprimer par l'interprétation, l'appréciation, et la création musicale. Aussi, en favorisant une approche de découverte, l'élève pourra, par la pensée réflexive et critique, développer davantage sa créativité en situation de résolution de problèmes.

5. L'éducation musicale donne l'occasion aux élèves de vivre leur patrimoine. Elle contribue à la connaissance et à la fierté du patrimoine francophone acadien et canadien. Par l'expérience d'oeuvres musicales d'ici, d'ailleurs, d'hier, et d'aujourd'hui l'élève aura l'occasion à s'ouvrir à d'autres cultures.

6. L'éducation doit permettre à l'élève de devenir un consommateur capable de porter un jugement sur ses productions musicales et celles des autres. L'élève a des occasions d'exercer sa pensée réflexive et critique dans des activités d'auto-évaluation et de critiques constructives des réalisations collectives et individuelles musicales en salle de classe ou à l'écoute de musique enregistrée.

7. L'évaluation fera partie intégrante du programme d'éducation musicale. Les modes d'évaluation seront adaptés aux types d'évaluation recherchés et se rapporteront aux connaissances, aux habiletés, et aux attitudes des élèves d'après les résultats d'apprentissage visés. Les évaluations diagnostique, formative, sommative, et l'auto-évaluation seront les modes les plus couramment utilisés.

8. Les attitudes, les dispositions et les valeurs guident les activités du programme d'éducation musicale et les perceptions de l'élève. Un climat qui favorise une approche de découverte permet de développer sa dimension affective. La curiosité, l'objectivité, la prudence, l'esprit critique, la créativité, la patience, la discipline personnelle, l'ouverture d'esprit, la coopération, le respect, ne sont que quelques-unes des attitudes et dispositions visées.

### Démarche d'apprentissage et démarche pédagogique

*Définition de l'apprentissage.* Dans le programme d'éducation musicale, l'apprentissage est conçu comme un processus où l'élève acquiert une nouvelle connaissance de lui-même et modifie ses anciennes perceptions de lui-même. Le but premier de l'apprentissage est donc de générer de nouveaux apprentissages. Tout au long du processus, l'élève regroupe les informations similaires dans une structure bien définie pour leur donner un sens. L'élève chemine donc du connu vers l'inconnu pour arriver à un nouveau connu, donc de réaliser des apprentissages fiables, durables, et transférables.

*L'apprenant.* L'apprentissage est un phénomène complexe qui se réalise à l'intérieur d'une personne elle-même complexe. L'élève, bénéficiant de tout son potentiel cognitif, affectif, et physique, arrive au lieu d'apprentissage avec l'unicité de son champ perceptuel composé de plusieurs facteurs intrinsèques (perception, expérience, et motivation) et extrinsèques (culture et environnement personnel et éducatif) qui interviennent constamment avec le processus d'apprentissage.

Le rôle du musicien éducateur est d'organiser un environnement éducatif où l'élève est au centre de l'apprentissage. Puisque le processus qui nécessite l'organisation de l'information sensorielle est unique pour chacun, l'enseignant doit, dans un premier temps, aider l'élève à *percevoir* l'élément musical à l'étude et le guider vers la conception de cette notion musicale. Étant donné que l'élève est influencé par ses *expériences* antérieures, l'enseignant peut, par la suite, l'aider à construire ses apprentissages en faisant appel à ses expériences musicales antérieures. Enfin, puisque la *motivation*, caractérisée par le désir intrinsèque d'apprendre et d'agir est à la source du processus d'apprentissage, l'enseignant doit s'assurer que l'élève voit clairement les problèmes musicaux à résoudre et les résultats d'apprentissage à atteindre. L'environnement musical devra donc favoriser l'exploration et la résolution de problèmes pour que l'élève puisse exprimer ses représentations et ses connaissances personnelles du monde sonore. Puisque la musique créée et interprétée par les médias électroniques occupe une place centrale dans la vie culturelle de nos jeunes d'aujourd'hui, un effort d'intégrer les technologies en information et en communication doit être encouragée. C'est un "moyen" pédagogique qui permet à l'apprenant d'utiliser les outils de sa génération et de sa culture pour développer une compréhension des éléments structurels communs à la musique de tous les genres. La technologie favorise une approche de participation active et d'interaction directe de l'élève avec l'exemple musical dans une situation de résolution de problème. Cependant, pour permettre le transfert des connaissances, l'enseignant doit encourager des situations d'apprentissage variées où l'élève aura l'occasion d'appliquer ses nouvelles connaissances dans de nouveaux contextes.

L'élève est aussi profondément marqué par sa *culture* et *son environnement personnel* (parents, famille, amis), et ces facteurs ont un effet sur le processus d'apprentissage. De plus, l'*environnement éducatif,* c'est-à-dire la salle de classe et la qualité du matériel didactique et des équipements ainsi que le contexte ou la situation d'apprentissage qui donne le goût d'apprendre, influence l'apprentissage.

L'apprentissage est donc un processus qui doit tenir compte de la personne globale dans ses aspects cognitif, physique, et émotif en constante interaction avec son environnement personnel, culturel, et social.

*Démarche pédagogique.* Le programme d'éducation musicale part du principe que l'élève construit ses connaissances en reliant l'information nouvelle aux connaissances antérieures. C'est donc par l'apprentissage d'un concept que l'élève acquiert les compétences et habiletés nécessaires pour généraliser et transférer ses connaissances d'une situation à l'autre. Les concepts en musique sont les éléments qui forment la structure de la matière. A l'élève en éducation musicale construit sa définition ou sa compréhension d'un concept musical en catégorisant et en organisant l'information reçue des sens. Pour former, par exemple, le concept de mélodie, l'élève fait l'expérience de sons qui bougent vers le haut, vers le bas, de façon conjointe ou disjointe, et organisés en relation ou non avec un centre tonal. L'élève formera progressivement le concept de la mélodie par des interactions avec le contexte musical qui illustre clairement ce concept. Le musicien éducateur organise donc les situations d'apprentissage où le concept est présenté d'une façon significative pour l'élève, selon son stade de développement, et qui permettra le développement d'une fondation solide pour faciliter les apprentissages plus complexes. La compréhension d'un concept est donc génératrice de nouveaux apprentissages.

Il y a lieu maintenant de rappeler certaines caractéristiques de la formation d'un concept.

1. *Le concept se forme en passant du concret à l'abstrait.*
Pour intérioriser un concept, l'élève doit avoir l'occasion de découvrir, d'une façon autonome, le sens du concept par des expériences concrètes du monde sonore. Pour explorer, par exemple, la mélodie ascendante et descendante, l'élève pourrait découvrir les principes théoriques de la mélodie en manipulant les instruments de musique qui démontrent clairement la relation spatiale des sons (métallophone en escalier ou les blocs sonores). Ou encore, pour former le concept de la gamme majeure, l'élève pourrait explorer les sons musicaux afin de découvrir par lui-même les éléments théoriques propres à la formation d'une gamme majeure. Le symbole théorique de la formation d'une gamme majeure est présenté seulement après l'expérience musicale afin que le symbole représente le concept vécu et non une simple donnée théorique.

2. *La formation du concept est un processus graduel.*
Comme le mouvement du concret à l'abstrait est un processus graduel, la formation du concept est un long processus où l'élève passe de l'ambiguïté à la clarté et de l'incertitude à la certitude.

Il doit donc avoir l'occasion de découvrir le concept par des expériences multiples à long terme avec le contexte musical et d'apprendre par essais et erreurs.

3. *La formation du concept dépend de l'habileté à percevoir les caractéristiques du concept.*
Pour percevoir les caractéristiques du concept à l'étude, l'élève participera activement à une variété d'expériences sensorielles où les oreilles, les yeux, le toucher, et le corps entier sont en interaction avec le contexte musical. Pour ce faire, le musicien éducateur organise des activités d'apprentissage diverses comme le chant, l'interprétation instrumentale, l'écoute, et la danse qui répondent aux différents styles d'apprentissage et engagent la participation musicale active de l'élève.

4. *La formation d'un concept dépend du niveau de la complexité des exemples.*
Au début de la formation musicale, l'élève fait l'expérience d'un concept dans un contexte musical qui

démontre clairement les caractéristiques de celui-là. Au fur et à mesure que l'élève approfondit le concept, il sera appelé à le décrire à partir d'exemples plus complexes du répertoire musical. Puisque la musique est une forme d'art complexe, la compréhension des concepts de la mélodie, du rythme, de l'harmonie et ainsi de suite à l'intérieur du contexte musical global est souvent difficile. Il est donc parfois nécessaire, pendant les premières étapes de l'acquisition d'un concept, d'isoler les éléments précis de l'exemple musical qui illustre le concept visé. Par contre, cet isolement doit être suivi immédiatement de la découverte du concept dans son contexte global musical.

En guise de résumé, la formation d'un concept musical se construit en faisant des expériences musicales allant du concret à l'abstrait, de l'ambiguïté à la clarté, et de l'incertitude à la certitude.

*Stades de représentation des connaissances.* La recherche indique que le développement conceptuel passe par trois stades de représentation des connaissances: le stade exploratoire (représentation du concept par l'expérimentation), le stade iconique (représentation du concept par l'imagerie mentale) et le stade symbolique (représentation du concept par le symbole traditionnel approprié). Chaque stade est relié au degré d'expérience d'interaction avec le concept musical. À mesure que l'élève développe sa perception d'un concept, il représente sa compréhension dans un mode ou stade de représentation, commençant habituellement par le stade exploratoire, se dirigeant graduellement vers le stade iconique pour enfin atteindre le stade symbolique. Toutefois, ces stades ne sont pas précisément reliés à l'âge chronologique ou au niveau de maturité intellectuelle. Cependant, les expériences antérieures et la maîtrise de concepts similaires facilitent et accélèrent le processus de passage d'un stade à l'autre.

Le rôle du musicien éducateur dans ce processus d'apprentissage est d'abord d'être sensible aux stades dans lesquels les élèves représentent leurs connaissances. Par après, il prépare des activités pédagogiques où l'élève pourra démontrer sa compréhension du concept selon son niveau de développement. La séquence logique de ces

activités permet à l'élève de s'engager d'une façon autonome dans
des expériences d'apprentissage. Il est néanmoins important de
noter que certains concepts ne peuvent être représentés par le symbole traditionnel. La musique, qui exprime l'invisible, contient, de
par sa nature, certains concepts qui seront représentés seulement au
mode exploratoire ou iconique.

*Stratégies cognitives.* Les stratégies cognitives ou les processus
mentaux vécus par l'élève ont une conséquence directe sur
l'apprentissage. Le musicien éducateur planifie donc des activités
pédagogiques où l'élève pourra faire appel aux stratégies cognitives
adéquates pour traiter l'information reçue par les sens. Dans ce processus, l'élève découvre quelle stratégie cognitive il devra choisir
pour résoudre le problème énoncé. Il apprend donc à apprendre et
développe le processus métacognitif. Pour ce faire, le musicien éducateur devra continuellement décider à quelle stratégie faire appel,
pour quel contenu, pour quels élèves, et à quel moment cette
stratégie sera le plus efficace pendant l'intervention éducative.

Par exemple, à l'intérieur d'un cours d'éducation musicale où le
musicien éducateur concentre toute la leçon sur un concept, utilise
seulement un exemple musical et demande aux élèves de représenter
leurs connaissances seulement au mode exploratoire où celui-ci
démontre par un mouvement ou un geste sa compréhension du concept musical, l'élève utilise une stratégie cognitive inférieure
comme l'imitation ou le rappel dans des situations de résolution de
problèmes. Il imite les mouvements de l'enseignant, répond aux
questions par un simple "oui" ou "non" ou répète de mémoire la
définition du concept vu dans la leçon précédente. Lorsque l'élève
est appelé à faire le transfert de ses connaissances à un nouveau contexte musical (nouvel exemple musical) ou à un nouveau mode de
représentation des connaissances, une stratégie cognitive moyenne
comme l'application, la divergence, ou le transfert est exigée. Les
stratégies cognitives d'ordre supérieur telles que l'analyse et la synthèse sont utilisées lorsque les connaissances sont appliquées à un
nouveau concept, un nouveau contexte musical, un nouveau mode de
représentation des connaissances, et à une nouvelle expression musicale telle l'interprétation, la création, ou l'appréciation.

Afin d'assurer un engagement de la pensée critique et créative de
l'élève dans la résolution de problèmes et pour permettre le mouvement du connu vers l'inconnu au nouveau connu, le musicien-

éducateur doit poser des questions qui incitent l'élève à utiliser une variété de stratégies cognitives pertinentes tout en encourageant davantage les stratégies cognitives d'ordre supérieur comme l'analyse et la synthèse.

*Formes d'expression musicale.* En résumé, l'élève en formation musicale apprend en intériorisant les concepts, en représentant ses connaissances par le mouvement des stades exploratoires, iconiques, et symboliques et en utilisant des stratégies cognitives variées. De plus, l'élève participe à l'apprentissage en s'engageant dans une forme d'expression musicale reflétant le bien-fondé de la matière apprise. En musique, cette forme d'expression peut se diviser en trois catégories: l'interprétation (le chant ou la performance instrumentale), l'appréciation (l'écoute active et la description gestuelle, visuelle ou verbale de l'oeuvre musicale), et la création (la composition ou l'improvisation).

Le processus de création musicale peut respecter les étapes suivantes:

1. La mise en situation. C'est le moment où l'élève fait l'expérience du concept musical, découvre dans cette expérience une signification personnelle et ressent une motivation à prolonger son expérience par la création d'une forme expressive.
2. La découverte et l'exploration. L'élève écoute plusieurs exemples du répertoire musical qui démontrent clairement le concept à l'étude et découvre comment l'artiste a manipulé les sons pour produire l'oeuvre. Par la suite, il explore lui-même les diverses possibilités d'organiser ses sons.
3. La matérialisation de la composition musicale. C'est la phase où s'effectue la synthèse des sensations personnelles et des perceptions musicales en une composition musicale originale et cohérente.
4. L'objectivation. C'est le moment où l'élève valorise et évalue sa création musicale.

Dans une démarche d'apprentissage, les étapes de création peuvent être planifiées. Par contre, à mesure que l'élève gagne de l'expérience et de l'autonomie musicale, il importe de lui offrir l'occasion de réaliser ses compositions dans une démarche plus libre. Par l'appréciation, l'interprétation, et la création musicale, l'élève révèle sa compréhension intellectuelle, physique, affective, esthétique, sociale, et culturelle des concepts musicaux. Le musicien-éducateur voit à ce que les activités d'apprentissage engagent l'élève dans les trois formes d'expression musicale afin de respecter le style et le mode d'apprentissage préférés de chacun.

L'apprentissage musical se réalisera si toutes les composantes du modèle sont considérées. Il se déroule en forme de spirale suivant une séquence déterminée par l'expérience de l'élève. L'apprentissage musical comprend toutes les composantes de l'activité musicale, c'est-à-dire, le contexte (exemple), le contenu (concept), la forme d'expression (interprétation, création, appréciation), les modes de représentation des connaissances (exploratoire, iconique et symbolique), et les stratégies cognitives. Toutes ces composantes, en interaction continuelle entre elles et en conjonction avec le champ perceptuel de l'élève, activent le processus d'apprentissage. Si le musicien éducateur considère ces forces interactives complexes, le résultat de l'apprentissage sera de générer de nouveaux apprentissages.

## L'évaluation et l'éducation musicale

La fonction primordiale de l'évaluation en éducation musicale est d'encourager, par l'auto-évaluation et par les rétroactions constructives et fondées de la part de l'enseignant et des pairs, la qualité des savoirs, savoir-être, savoir-faire, et savoir-devenir musicaux. L'évaluation est un aspect naturel de la résolution de problèmes en éducation musicale et fait partie intégrante du processus d'apprentissage.

Puisque la manifestation artistique est subjective de nature et que la priorité devrait être sur le développement musical de la personne plutôt qu'au produit musical, il est important de minimiser l'évaluation du produit musical en soi et de promouvoir, par diverses formes, l'évaluation du cheminement de l'élève dans ses expériences d'appréciation, d'interprétation et de création musicale. "C'est le souci de guider le cheminement 'musical' de chaque élève qui prédomine dans l'évaluation des apprentissages" (Programme d'études d'art plastique, MENB, 1996 p. 49).

L'évaluation musicale se fera dans un contexte individuel et collectif qui favorise la libre expression dans un climat de confiance et de respect. L'élève pourra donc manifester, en toute liberté, ses connaissances, ses habiletés techniques, ses attitudes et ses émotions dans des expériences concrètes de création, d'interprétation et d'appréciation musicales. L'évaluation dans ce contexte d'apprentissage valorise la pensée divergente, innovatrice, originale, et flexible.

Les techniques d'évaluation peuvent servir à l'évaluation des habiletés, connaissances, et attitudes envers la musique. Par contre, il est primordial de choisir le moyen d'évaluation approprié au contenu évalué.

Ci-dessous se trouve une description de quelques techniques d'évaluation propices à l'éducation musicale.

*a) La grille d'observation.* La grille d'observation sert à évaluer les élèves au cours d'activités musicales individuelles ou collectives. C'est un moyen de faire le point sur les étapes du processus d'apprentissage de l'élève. Puisque c'est impossible d'évaluer toutes les composantes de l'activité musicale à la fois, l'enseignant peut sélectionner quelques attributs pour chaque évaluation.

La liste d'éléments musicaux pertinents à l'évaluation permet un coup d'oeil rapide et donne des renseignements particuliers par rapport aux attitudes, les connaissances et les compétences de l'élève. Elle sert aussi à l'établissement d'un profil d'apprentissage qui indique le progrès de l'élève sur une période donnée.

*b) La grille pour évaluer l'interprétation musicale.* L'interprétation musicale fait appel à une facette d'expression de la personne et touche aux aspects cognitif, psychomoteur, affectif, et esthétique. Par conséquent, toutes ces dimensions font partie intégrante de l'évaluation.

La grille peut donc contenir des éléments (1) par rapport aux *connaissances* rythmiques, mélodiques, harmoniques, stylistiques et formelles de la pièce musicale interprétée, (2) par rapport aux *habiletés psychomotrices* démontrées par l'intonation, l'articulation, et la clarté des sons produits, (3) dans le domaine *affectif* et *esthétique*, par rapport aux émotions et la sensibilité personnelles exprimées par les éléments expressifs de la musique comme l'intensité et le sens du phrasé musical. Puisque le *pro-*

*cessus* d'apprentissage est priorisé dans la formation en éducation musicale, l'évaluation finale de l'interprétation musicale dépend des stades de développement et de l'évolution graduelle de l'élève vers l'atteinte des résultats d'apprentissage prescrits par le programme d'étude.

*c) La grille pour évaluer la création musicale.* "Les critères pour l'évaluation de toutes formes de création artistique sont l'authenticité, l'autonomie et la créativité" *(Programme d'études d'art plastique,* MENB, 1996, p. 50).

L'*authenticité* représente la capacité de l'élève à exprimer sa composition d'après des critères précis.

L'*autonomie* se caractérise par la capacité de l'élève à s'exprimer en démontrant une compréhension globale des éléments musicaux étudiés.

La *créativité* est la réponse originale aux exigences de l'apprentissage visé.

L'évaluation créatrice est dépendante du développement de l'enfant et de sa capacité personnelle de faire la synthèse de ses apprentissages au moment de l'évaluation.

*d) Le journal de bord.* Le journal de bord est un outil très efficace pour encourager l'élève à réfléchir sur ses situations d'apprentissage. Il peut prendre plusieurs formes selon le stade de développement de l'élève. Le journal peut contenir un dessin, un petit commentaire ou un paragraphe plus détaillé sur une activité ou un sujet particulier vu en classe. L'élève peut y noter des questions, des succès ou définir les domaines pour lesquels il a besoin d'une aide additionnelle pour continuer le développement de son potentiel musical. Le journal sera donc l'outil de communication entre l'élève et l'enseignant.

Les activités de rédaction du journal peuvent être orientées vers des questions posées par l'enseignant en situation d'apprentissage. Par exemple:

- Qu'avons-nous fait en salle de classe aujourd'hui?
- Qu'avons-nous appris grâce à ces activités?
- Qu'avons-nous appris sur nous-mêmes?
- Quelles stratégies avons-nous utilisées pour solutionner les problèmes?

- Quelles images ou émotions ont été évoquées au cours des activités d'aujourd'hui?
- Comment pouvons-nous appliquer dans nos activités musicales futures ce que nous avons appris aujourd'hui?

Ces réflexions pourront se faire à l'oral ou à l'écrit selon le développement individuel de l'élève.

*e) Le portfolio.* Le portfolio est un recueil des travaux de l'élève qui démontre son cheminement relativement aux savoirs, savoir-faire, et savoir-être musicaux. Il peut servir à motiver l'élève et à donner à l'enseignant et aux parents une idée du profil du progrès graduel de l'élève.

L'élève et l'enseignant peuvent déterminer et clarifier ensemble l'objet, la conception, et la réalisation du portfolio musical. Celui-ci peut contenir:

- des annotations de musique apprises ou créées;
- un poème qui décrit le sentiment de l'élève à la suite d'une écoute active;
- des analyses et critiques de musique enregistrée, de musique jouée en concert, ou en spectacle;
- de l'information générale sur le style, le genre, et les compositeurs de musique d'ici, d'ailleurs, d'hier, et d'aujourd'hui;
- des enregistrements d'interprétations et de créations musicales personnelles;
- des auto-évaluations;
- des évaluations par les pairs;
- des réflexions personnelles sur les contributions de la musique au bien-être personnel, culturel, et social.

L'évaluation musicale valorise, avant tout, l'élève dans ses moments de succès. Par conséquent, l'élève est continuellement encouragé dans son cheminement musical personnel et est stimulé à progresser par des activités d'évaluation musicales adaptées à son stade de développement et à son rythme, style, et mode d'apprentissage personnel.

De plus, si le rôle principal de l'éducation musicale est d'amener l'élève à découvrir la joie profonde de l'expression musicale, l'évaluation se fera dans une ambiance positive qui favorise la confiance, le respect, la communication, le dialogue et la collaboration. La bibliographie utilisée pour écrire ce document se trouve à l'Annexe A.

## Discussion

Pour la première fois dans son histoire, ce nouveau cadre théorique élabore d'une façon précise l'orientation et les composantes pédagogiques de l'éducation musicale. Basée sur le document cadre de tous les programmes d'étude de la province (MENB, 1995), il rejoint les principes directeurs et l'approche pédagogique socio-constructiviste communs à toutes les matières scolaires. Tout en gardant la spécificité de chaque matière, l'uniformité de la structure et de la philosophie de base des programmes d'études permettra aux directeurs d'écoles, aux agents pédagogiques, et au public non-musicien de comprendre et de valoriser le rôle de l'éducation musicale dans le développement global de l'apprenant. De plus, l'éducation musicale au même titre que les autres matières scolaires, sera reconnu officiellement comme une matière qui contribue au développement des habiletés intellectuelles d'ordre supérieur ainsi qu'aux habiletés personnelles et sociales nécessaire pour faire face aux réalités du 21$^e$ siècle. Espérons que cet effort aura un effet positif sur la sauvegarde de l'éducation musicale dans nos écoles!

Alors, quels sont les nouveaux défis du musicien éducateur? Premièrement, celui-ci ne pourra plus se tenir à l'écart et enseigner d'une façon isolée et plus ou moins engagée face aux renouveaux pédagogiques inhérents au domaine de l'éducation. Il devra, par la formation continue, se tenir à jour en éducation tout comme en éducation musicale. De plus, il devra, au sein de son école, de son district scolaire, et du MENB, participer aux équipes d'enseignants qui travaillent à l'amélioration du système d'éducation local, régional, et provincial. À l'intérieur de son école, il pourrait aussi être demandé de participer à la construction de projets interdisciplinaires comprenant une collaboration étroite entre ce qui se réalise dans la salle de musique et la salle de classe.

Deuxièmement, tout en valorisant comme dans l'ancien programme, les savoirs et savoir-faire musicaux, le musicien éducateur devra trouver des moyens pédagogiques pour développer le savoir-être musical. De plus, puisque la création et l'improvisation musicale sont encore mentionnées comme composantes indispensables au savoir-faire musical, le musicien éducateur devra incorporer ces formes d'expression à ses plans de cours, que ce soit au niveau du primaire ou du secondaire.

Troisièmement, le musicien éducateur devra s'approprier la démarche d'apprentissage et pédagogique prescrite par le programme d'étude. Il se préoccupera premièrement de l'élève dans une approche socio-constructiviste de l'apprentissage. Donc, ses plans de cours devraient refléter la démarche d'apprentissage qui commence par le connu de l'élève allant vers l'inconnu pour enfin arriver au nouveau connu, l'apprentissage graduel du concept musical, le respect des stades de représentation des connaissances de tous les élèves, et l'utilisation de stratégies cognitives d'ordre supérieur à travers toutes les formes d'expression musicale (interprétation, création, et appréciation). L'élaboration de ces plans de cours nécessitera donc une réflexion profonde et une recherche ardue de matériaux propices à l'atteinte des objectifs visés.

Quatrièmement, le musicien éducateur devra respecter le rythme et le style d'apprentissage de tous les apprenants y compris les élèves en difficulté et les surdoués. Les stratégies d'apprentissages devront donc rejoindre l'unicité de tous dans leurs forces d'apprentissage individuelles.

Cinquièmement, l'évaluation musicale devra faire partie du processus d'apprentissage. L'éducation musicale sera incluse au bulletin scolaire et sera évaluée selon la même grille d'évaluation que les autres matières. Le musicien éducateur devra donc établir des critères bien définis qui mesureront les savoirs, savoir-faire, et savoir-être musicaux. Son plus grand défi sera d'incorporer l'évaluation dans le processus d'apprentissage et de trouver les moyens d'évaluation efficaces pour sa réalité professionnelle. Il devra rendre compte à l'élève, aux parents, et aux administrateurs du progrès de chacun et de son rendement face à l'atteinte des objectifs du programme.

Ces défis sont exigeants, mais réalisables si le musicien éducateur est passionné de son rôle en société et de l'importance de l'éducation musicale dans la vie de tous les apprenants. D'ailleurs, les rétroactions des musiciens éducateurs suite à deux sessions de formation (été 1998 et 1999) et à l'application du cadre théorique dans leur enseignement sont positives. Malgré ceci, l'influence de ce programme sur l'éducation musicale au Nouveau-Brunswick se verra seulement dans les années qui suivront son implantation systématique en l'an 2000.

La prochaine étape consiste à l'élaboration du contenu du programme d'étude. De fait, une équipe travaille, à l'heure actuelle, à préciser les résultats d'apprentissage spécifiques pour chaque programme (musique générale et musique instrumentale) et pour chaque niveau scolaire. La première ébauche est terminée et sera étudiée par une équipe de musiciens éducateurs de toutes les régions de la province en l'an 2000. Il est prévu que le contenu soit piloté dans toutes les écoles francophones de la province en l'an 2001.

Pour conclure, nous constatons que l'éducation musicale dans le secteur francophone du Nouveau-Brunswick est "vivante" et "vibrante" et qu'elle prend de plus en plus sa place dans l'éducation globale de l'apprenant. Nous sommes enthousiastes face à l'avenir de l'éducation musicale au Nouveau-Brunswick. C'est en ayant une vision commune du rôle de l'éducation musicale dans la vie et l'éducation globale de chaque personne que nous garderons l'éducation musicale dans les écoles. Continuons à travailler vers ce but qui nous tiens tous à coeur.

## Références

Choate, R. A. (Ed.). (1968). *Documentary report of the Tanglewood symposium.* Washington, DC: Music Educators National Conference.

Conseil supérieur de l'éducation (1988). *L'éducation artistique à l'école, Avis au Ministre de l'Éducation.* Gouvernement du Québec.

Green, J. P., & Vogan, N. (1991). *Music education in Canada: A historical account.* Toronto: University Press of Toronto.

Ministère de l'Éducation du *Nouveau-Brunswick (MENB). (1988). Musique,* programme d'études. Frédéricton, NB: Auteur.

Ministère de l'Éducation du Nouveau-Brunswick (MENB). (1995). *Excellence en éducation: l'école primaire.* Frédéricton, NB: Auteur.

MENB (1996). *Programme d'études des arts plastiques — 9ᵉ année (provisoire).* Frédéricton, NB: Auteur.

Ministère de l'Éducation du Nouveau-Brunswick (MENB). (1999). *Programme d'éducation musicale. Cadre théorique (document de travail).* Frédéricton, NB: Auteur.

## Annexe A

### Bibliographie

Abeles, H., Hoffer, C., & Klotman, R. (1994). *Foundations of music education.* Toronto: Maxwell MacMillan, Canada.

Barth, B. M. (1993). *Le savoir en construction: former à une pédagogie de la compréhension.* Paris: Ed. Retz.

Bergethon, B., Boardman, E., & Montgomery, J. (1997). *Musical growth in the elementary school* (2nd ed.). Montréal, PQ: Harcourt Brace College.

Bigge, M., & Shermis, S. (1992). *Learning theories for teachers.* New York: Harper Collins.

Boardman, E., Pautz, M., Andress, B., & Willman, F. (1988). *Holt music.* Toronto: Holt, Rinehart & Winston.

Boardman, E. (Ed.). (1989). *Dimensions of musical thinking.* Reston, VA: Music Educators National Conference.

Boardman, E. (1996). *Fifty years of elementary general music: One person's perspective.* Communication présentée à Kansas City, MO: Music Educators National Conference.

Boyle, D., & Radocy, R. (1987). *Measurement and evaluation of musical experiences.* New York: Shirmer Books.

Brummet, V., & Haywood, J. (1997). Authentic assessment in school music. *General Music Today, 2* (1), 4–10.

Bruner, J. (1966). *Toward a theory of instruction.* Cambridge, MA: Harvard University Press.

Bruner, J. (1990). *Acts of meaning.* Cambridge, MA: Harvard University Press.

Bruner, J. (1996). *The culture of education.* Cambridge, MA: Harvard University Press.

Claxton, G. (1988). Growth points in cognition. London: Routledge .

Colwell, R. (Ed.). (1991). *Basic concepts in music education II.* Niwot, CO: University Press of Colorado.

Dubé, L. (1994*). Psychologie de l'apprentissage.* Québec, PQ: Presses de l'Université du Québec.

Elliott, D. (1995). *Music matters: A new philosophy of music education.* New York: Oxford University Press.

Gardner, H. (1983). *Frames of mind.* New York: Basic Books.

Legendre, R. (1993). *Dictionnaire actuel de l'éducation,* (2ᵉ éd.). Montréal, PQ: Guérin.

Lehman, P. (1990). *Music in today's schools: Rationale and commentary.* Reston, VA: Music Educators National Conference.

Levi, A. W., & Smith, R. (1991). *Art education: A critical necessity.* Urbana, IL: University of Illinois Press.

McLaughlin, J. (Ed.). (1988). *Toward a new era in arts education.* New York: American Council for the Arts.

Ministère de l'Éducation de la Colombie Britannique (MEBC). (1996). Musique de la 8ᵉ à la 10ᵉ année. Vancouver, CB: Auteur.

MENB (Ministère de l'Éducation du Nouveau-Brunswick) (1993*). La mission de l'éducation publique au Nouveau-Brunswick.* Frédéricton, NB: Auteur.

MENB (1995). *Excellence en éducation: L'école primaire.* Frédéricton, NB: Auteur.

MENB (1995*). Vers une école primaire renouvelée: Référenciel de mise en oeuvre.* Frédéricton, NB: Auteur.

MENB (1995). *Programme d'études Sciences au primaire (provisoire).* Frédéricton, NB: Auteur.

MENB (1996). Programme de français au primaire. Frédéricton, NB: Auteur.

MENB (1996). Vers une école primaire renouvelée: Le nouveau quotidien de l'école primaire. Frédéricton, NB: Auteur.

MEO (Ministère de l'Éducation de l'Ontario) (1995). *Le programme d'études commun: politiques et résultats d'apprentissage de la 1re à la 9e année*. Toronto, ON: Author.

MEQ (Ministère de l'Éducation du Québec) (1988). *Éléments de docimologie, fascicule 4 : l'évaluation sommative*. Québec, PQ: Publications du Québec.

MEQ (1988). *Éléments de docimologie: L'évaluation formative*. Québec, PQ: Publications du Québec.

MEQ (1996). *Programmes d'études Musique 1re et 2e secondaire*. Québec, PQ.

Paquette, C. (1984). *Des pratiques évaluatives*. Victoriaville, PQ: Éditions NHP.

Reimer, B. (1976). *Une philosophie de l'éducation musicale* (Y. Bédard, Trans.). Québec: Les Presses de l'Université Laval.

Reimer, B., & Wright, J. (1992). *On the nature of musical experience*. Niwot, CO: University Press of Colorado.

Smith, R., & Simpson, A. (E (1990). *Asthetics and arts education*. Urbana, IL: University of Illinois Press.

Stauffer, S. (Ed.). (1995). *Toward tomorrow: New visions for general music*. Reston, VA: Music Educators National Conference.

Tardif, J. (1992). *Pour un enseignement stratégique*. Montréal, PQ: Éditions Logiques.

West, C. I., Farmer, T. A., & Wolff, P. M. (1991). *Instructional design*. New York: Prentice-Hall.

*Why We Need the Arts*. (1988). Communication présentée à l'American Council for the Arts.

---

[1] La province du Nouveau-Brunswick, la seule province officiellement bilingue au Canada, a adopté en 1978 une restructuration du Ministère de l'Éducation qui a consisté en une division linguistique, c'est-à-dire un secteur francophone et un secteur anglophone du Ministère géré par un ministre et deux sous-ministres (un associé à chaque groupe linguistique. Chaque secteur fonctionne indépendamment l'un de l'autre et, par conséquent, a ses propres programmes d'études pour l'enseignement au primaire et au secondaire des écoles publiques de la province. Il est donc important de noter que ce chapitre traite seulement de l'éducation musicale du secteur francophone des écoles du Nouveau-Brunswick.

[2] Dans le but d'alléger le texte, lorsque le contexte de rédaction l'exige, le genre masculin est utilisé à titre épicène.

# Chapter Four

# Language, Culture, and Religion in Quebec Society and Their Impact on Music Education

*Joan Russell*

## Introduction

At the beginning of the 21$^{st}$ century, music education and music teacher education in the province of Québec are undergoing significant changes in terms of who teaches music, who receives instruction in music, and how music teachers will be prepared to meet the challenges of a changing society. In the last three decades of the 20$^{th}$ century, schools in the English Protestant sector have seen a reduction of music specialist teachers at the elementary level and the reduction of music programs at the secondary level. At the same time, schools in the French sector have seen an increase. Schools with a music specialist in the English Catholic sector have been rare in the past and continue to be rare in the present. However, I am optimistic about the future of music education and in this essay I propose to explain why.

This discussion of music education and music teacher education in Québec focuses on that small part of the population that is English-speaking because that is where my personal experience and professional interests lie. The discussion is organized in three parts: Part One gives a brief overview of the sociocultural contexts of Québec education prior to the 1960s and the social revolution dubbed the "Quiet Revolution"; Part Two describes some present social realities in Québec as these relate to music education[1] and outlines briefly two major restructuring initiatives relevant to the

81

organization of Québec society at the end of the 20<sup>th</sup> century: the reorganization of school boards from division along religious lines to division along linguistic lines; and a proposal to eliminate religious instruction in public schools and replace it with instruction in moral education and the study of religion-as-culture. Part Three describes McGill's music teacher education program designed in response to policy initiatives of the Ministry of Education of Québec (MEQ) (Ministère d'Éducation du Québec, 1997). Finally, I offer some predictions about the future of music education in the English sector schools of Québec.

I write from the perspective of an English-speaking Québecer who grew up in Montréal as a member of the Protestant minority culture in a majority French Catholic province during periods of both stability and great social upheaval and who has chosen to live and work in a place that I love. I have lived in various urban and suburban communities, attended many English Protestant public schools, played in my high school band and orchestra, taught elementary and secondary music in the private and the public sectors, taught university level music courses, and became a professor of music education at McGill's Faculty of Education. I have been responsible for the development and implementation of a new program, the Bachelor of Education in Music at McGill University, a program designed in response to new MEQ requirements (Ministère d'Éducation du Québec, 1997). I also teach graduate and undergraduate music education courses to preservice generalist and music specialist teachers, supervise student music teachers, and enjoy the friendship of many music teachers in English sector private and public schools.

I have been witness to massive changes in Québec society, including the supremacy of the Catholic Church over the education of French and English Catholic students, and the sudden and dramatic loss of that supremacy during the social revolution that began in the 1960s, the formation in the '60s of a Ministry of Education and the subsequent standardization of curriculum, teachers' salaries, and the establishment province-wide of modern, fully equipped comprehensive high schools (*polyvalentes*) aimed at the standardization of educational opportunities for all citizens.

More recently I have witnessed the 1998 restructuring of the educational system along linguistic lines and subsequently the debates over a proposal, known as the Proulx Report (1999), to eliminate religious instruction from schools. There have also been dramatic changes in the cultural makeup of Montréal that have occurred with the arrival of large numbers of people of different cultural and linguistic backgrounds, especially from Asia, the Caribbean, and Latin America. These societal changes reflect rapidly changing social realities and value systems in Québec. The struggle to meet these realities is reflected in changes in teacher education programs, in the restructuring of school boards, and in a profound examination by French Québecers of the values that they want to have as the foundation of what the MEQ calls the "school project." These experiences have given me an insider's view of music education in the English sector.

## Part One: Sociocultural Historical Contexts

In Québec, budget constraints and support for music education are linked to issues of language, culture, and religion. Knowledge of the sociocultural and historical factors, what Bresler (1998) calls the "macro" contexts, that have shaped the evolution of Québec education helps to frame our understanding of how music education and music teacher education have evolved. Three historical contexts are particularly relevant to music education in Québec: the period prior to the 1960s, the period of the 1960s until 1998, and the present, our entry into the 21$^{st}$ century. Education in each province has evolved in a unique way, but Québec's uniqueness surely lies in the part that language and religion have played in Québec life since the establishment of the colony. In Québec, there coexist two distinct macro cultures separated by language — of which only one, French, is official — each culture having prominence in different aspects of public life. In addition, the Catholic church until the 1960s reigned supreme over matters of health and education for the French-speaking majority, while the small English-speaking minority maintained its public institutions through government and private support.

Education in Québec is unique in another way. Unlike in many provinces, Catholic and Protestant schools (that is, schools serving anyone who is not Catholic) have always been public sector schools. The rights of these two groups were enshrined in the British North America Act of 1867 which gave Catholics and Protestants the right to have access to confessional schools. The Protestants established and administered schools that promoted Protestant ideals and values, and the Catholics did likewise. While the division of the two school communities was based on religion, there has been a *de facto* division in Québec by language and thus, also by culture.

The French-speaking population, a minority in Canada but a majority in Québec, has always had control over their own education, first, from the time of the first French colony by the Catholic church and later, in 1964, with the creation of the Ministry of Education (MEQ), by the state. With the exception of a few French-speaking Protestants, to be French was to be Catholic. Everyone else — English speakers, non-Catholics, non-English, and non-French speakers — formed a culturally diverse English-speaking community as individuals from many ethnic and linguistic backgrounds, mostly from Great Britain and western Europe, joined the English-speaking Protestants who dominated educational and other public institutions. This group was linked by language and, through schooling, also by culture.

French Protestants, forced to choose between their language and their religion chose religion, lost their language, and became assimilated into the English-speaking community and the Protestant culture. Immigrants who did not speak French and who were not Catholic were directed to the English school systems, bringing a cultural diversity to the English system that was unknown in the French system. These divisions along religious and linguistic lines, made up of cultural groups with different musical traditions, created a social dynamic in this province that have had, and continue to have, implications for music education.

### Traditions in the English sector

English Protestant schools[2] in Québec, originally drawing heavily on the model of Scottish education, inherited a tradition of ensemble singing, and many schools had choirs. Choral festivals, with massed choirs and adjudication of performances, were a regular annual feature of school life in Montréal. Graduates of Baron Byng High School[3] who are now in their '70s and '80s still gather together every few years to sing the songs they learned under Dr. Herbert, their music teacher. In that school every student had classroom singing experience, and each class was expected to prepare a piece to sing at concerts. Many elementary schools had ensemble singing as a regular feature of the day, often taking the form of hymns or other songs at daily assembly at the start of their classes and at special gatherings.

Using the American model as a guide, many English high schools in Montréal started up bands and orchestras in the 1940s and 1950s. These musical activities were taken by students as a regular part of the school curriculum; students could get credit by sitting high school leaving examinations in music. In my school, band class was held for one period each day, all through Grades 7, 8, and 9. An annual band festival attended by all of the bands in the English sector and by bands in the northern United States was held each year at the Town of Mount Royal High School. The English Catholic system did not provide such experiences for its students. Unlike in many other provinces, instrumental music instruction in Québec schools — English or French — seldom begins before Grade 7, and band but rarely orchestra have replaced choral music in many English schools that once supported choral singing.[4]

A tradition of schooling in music provides the foundation for its continuation. Students in the English Catholic system have been especially denied the benefits of music education, and few students in English Catholic high schools have had opportunities to pursue the study of music in a serious way. The reality for this group is that their numbers have not been large enough to warrant the hiring of music specialist teachers, nor has there been a tradition of singing or instrumental performance in these schools that would create pressure on the system to provide music education for subsequent generations. Moreover, in the era prior to the1960s this group, bound together by religion as well as language, had little experience of singing in church because congregational singing, unlike the Protestant services, was not a feature of the Catholic mass. Because they did not have a tradition of music education, few students from the English Catholic system expressed a desire to become music teachers, therefore few music teachers were available to penetrate the system and create musical traditions.

## Music teacher education in Québec prior to 1999

In the early 1970s the Ministry of Education built modern, comprehensive high schools all across the province and outfitted them with band and orchestral instruments. McGill's Education Faculty established a music department, created permanent and part-time teaching positions, and furnished it with space, pianos, teaching materials, and small instruments for elementary teacher education in music and for music graduates taking the Diploma in Education.

Since the late '60s the pathway to becoming a music teacher for the Protestant schools in Québec was first to complete a Bachelor of Music degree and then to apply to the nine-month Diploma in Education program. Upon completion of the Diploma program graduates received a temporary permit to teach and could apply for certification after the completion of the equivalent of two years of teaching. Graduates of this program sought positions teaching music in the public or private sector, in elementary or secondary schools, but they were limited to teaching music.

As director of the Diploma in Education program for the three years before its termination in 1998, I learned that applicants were accepted if they had 35 music credits and a minimum of a B average. No distinction was made as to the types of courses represented by those 35 credits, and some candidates were woefully unprepared for the musical demands of the classroom. During those three years I found that applicants could be loosely classified into five groups in terms of their motivation for entering the program:

1. I'll go into teaching in case I can't make it as a performer.
2. I always wanted to be a singer but my parents insisted that I take this Diploma so I'll have something to fall back on.
3. I've always loved kids and have wanted to be a teacher ever since....
4. I have a B. Mus., and I've been a performing musician for some time. Now I'm excited at the idea of becoming a teacher.
5. I have a B. Mus. and have been teaching for several years without certification; my board is now insisting I become certified.

While groups 3, 4, and 5 seemed to be the candidates most likely to adapt well to the profession, those from group 1 and 2 were often less desirable material for the profession because of their lack of motivation.

In the French (Catholic) sector, certificate programs of music specialist teacher training in instrumental music teaching were hurriedly implemented in the late 1960s and early '70s. Candidates were piano teachers or instrumental performers who were interested in a teaching career. Graduates of these programs formed the first generation of instrumental music teachers in the French high schools and established the tradition of band programs.

✳ ✳ ✳

# Part Two: Recent and Present Social Realities

Québec society, particularly outside the city of Montréal, is a fairly homogeneous society in terms of language (French) and religious traditions (Catholic).[5] In the mid-19th century, Montréal was a city whose majority language was English, the language of commerce, if not of law or government. Today Québec is an officially unilingual French province. At the same time Montréal is a *de facto* multilingual city. The majority of its residents are French-speaking; English is the second most widely used language; and Spanish is rapidly becoming the third. Most residents of Montréal speak French and English, and many speak three or more languages. The French language is predominant at the official, public level, and the civil service. Although the English-speaking community is dynamic, has influence due to its historical position within Québec, and is tied to cultural, political, and business institutions across Canada, the public use of English is restricted by law.

More recently, due to a perception of a decline in the use of French, laws were passed by the Assemblée Nationale du Québec which led to the restriction of access to English schools to children of parents one of whom received education in English in Québec. These regulations, coupled with a large-scale exodus of English-speaking residents from the province, have resulted in reduced school enrolments and fewer schools in the English sector. Reduced population is thought to be a factor implicated in reduced budgetary support for English schools. Another factor is the requirement to teach French as a second language.

## *The impact of second language teaching*

At the close of the 20th century there appears to be inequality between French and English schools in terms of music instruction, and at least part of the reason for this inequity has to do with the need for second-language instruction. English-speaking students educated in the province of Québec are generally perceived to be functionally bilingual by the time they leave high school, while French-speaking students are thought to be less fluent in English. This inequality is probably due to the fact that English instruction in French schools begins later in the school life of the child, occupies less time in the schedule than French instruction in English schools, and is considered a less urgent priority. As a result of resources devoted to ensuring that high school graduates can function in French, and because of the lower enrolments referred to earlier,[6] English schools today are likely to have less money available for expenses such as music specialist teachers. Education in art, music, and physical education, and resources for libraries have been reduced or eliminated in English schools. In contrast, students in the French sector may now expect to have music classes delivered by a teacher who has been trained as a music specialist and are more likely to benefit from art teaching and a librarian. The present situation appears to be a reversal of how things stood in the two systems prior to the social revolution in Québec when English-language Protestant schools had lively singing and instrumental music programs, and the French and English Catholic schools did not.

## Parental response to the absence of music education

Music teaching in some English elementary schools is provided in or out of school time by certified and uncertified music teachers and is financed either by special Ministry funds designated for special assistance to needy schools or, in middle class communities, by parents' groups. Music teachers who teach in these circumstances are usually paid by the hour, receive no health, pension, or vacation benefits; they enjoy no job security or seniority, and the hours that they put in do not count in any ministry calculations of service. The parents in one of the schools in my neighbourhood raise money to pay for a music teacher who comes to the school two full days each week. "Melanie," a certified teacher whom one of her colleagues calls "The Pied Piper," is a cooperating teacher for McGill's program of music teacher education who generates great enthusiasm among my student teachers. She serves two schools during school hours by transporting her keyboard, xylophone, and percussion instruments in her van. Because the law requires that a "board" teacher be present during her classes, many of these teachers, catching the children's enthusiasm, participate along with their students. When preparations for concerts are under way, some of the teachers help Melanie by rehearsing the children, as they are familiar with the concert materials and they have observed some of her her rehearsal techniques. This seems to me to be a fine collaboration between a specialist and classroom teachers.

However, Melanie receives none of the benefits that an experienced, certified teacher has a right to expect. After university training as specialists, graduates who obtain such positions find themselves in the same position they might have been in had they not attended university. Some teachers may be contented with such working conditions because it suits their life situations. I am not in favour of such arrangements because I believe that they devalue the worth of professional, educated teachers and relieve the government of its responsibility to provide education in music to children of all socioeconomic groups.

### The contribution of private schools to music teacher education

Many private schools in Montréal have music specialists at the elementary and secondary levels. The teachers in these schools play an important role in training student music teachers because the schools are situated in the city, are easy to reach by public transportation, classes tend to be relatively small, and they are unaffected by labour strife. It seems ironic that a public institution such as McGill, whose primary mission is to train music teachers for the English public schools of Québec, has had to rely so heavily on the private sector to provide field experience for its student teachers.

### Traditions and values: Culture and religion

Whereas teachers in the English system once worked within a framework of Protestant ideals and values, this framework is under pressure as teachers in the Montréal area today, where most of the population resides, are expected to know, respect, and accommodate a wide range of cultural values, beliefs, and practices. One example of this accommodation arises at school concerts, where musical traditions of different cultures can be presented.

Mention of Christmas at December concerts and the use of traditional Christmas music have been eliminated in some public and private schools and have been replaced by themes. In two December concerts that I attended recently, one had "self-esteem" and the other had "the circus" as their themes. These decisions created, in my view, a musical problem because the repertoire for these themes is limited, and students were deprived of musical experiences that have their roots in antiquity. In other schools, also with a diverse population, the teachers told me that there is no objection to using musical materials from the Christian repertoire, which has, in a sense, become public property. Teachers tell me that parents know when they send their children to that school that the music of Christmas is part of the school's heritage and represents its value system. From an aesthetic standpoint, what criteria inform a teacher's decision when choosing between "I Saw Mommy Kissing Santa Claus" and "Silent Night"?

In an interesting turn of events, some of the most organized and vocal objections to the use of Christmas music in school concerts comes from the teachers and parents in the French sector, two groups that are about one generation removed from the church-dominated school system and society of an earlier era. These and other societal changes make demands on music teachers that they did not previously have to think about.

### Devolution of responsibility for elementary music teaching to classroom teachers

The decline in the hiring of music specialist teachers at the elementary level coupled with the Ministry's requirement for schools to provide 2 hours of instruction per week in art and music have resulted in increased pressure on classroom teachers. Studies[7] have shown that classroom teachers tend to lack confidence in their ability to teach music. As a result of this lack of confidence, many students emerge from elementary school with little or no "school" musical experience. Classroom teachers also feel pressured at being expected to teach "everything" in a curriculum that they feel is already tightly packed. Their program of teacher preparation at McGill requires that they take 3 credits (1 course of 39 hours) in one of the arts.[8] They can choose among music, visual art, drama, and movement. While it is possible for students to take more than 3 credits in music, and some do, some students take no courses at all in music.

Once in the workplace, teachers help each other by exchanging their strengths, one taking a colleague's class in science, for example, in exchange for music or art. At December and May concerts I see classroom performances of great ingenuity and imagination as classroom teachers prepare sometimes visually stunning and thematically coherent presentations. The weakest link, in my experience, is usually the quality of the singing. While many teachers are perfectly comfortable teaching the words to a song, they usually do not have the experience it takes to produce tuneful singing or to manipulate the materials of music in ways that make the singing experience more interesting, beyond a literal rendition. Few classroom teachers have the skills to get students singing in harmony, or to shape a phrase, or use musical devices such as accent or changes of tempo and dynamics to produce a more musically expressive performance. Without a musically trained teacher, or a classroom teacher who has received more in-depth training than one course can provide, students' experiences of music may be *socially* satisfying, but the possibilities of children being engaged with new and more sophisticated worlds of *musical* experience will be limited. The fact that we are part of a society that is concerned about illiteracy in language, math, and computer skills, but is content to tolerate it in music, challenges us constantly to explain the difference between making music to pass the time or for sheer pleasure[9] and making music to learn something about music and about ourselves and each other through musical experience.

### Realignment of school boards according to language of instruction

In possibly the most dramatic move in education since the 19th century, the government of Québec passed legislation in 1998 that saw the restructuring of school boards along linguistic lines, rather than along religious lines and the consolidation of school boards in the province from 1,600 down to 69.[10] English-speaking students who previously were educated under Catholic or Protestant school boards are no longer separated by religion. The common denominator now is language. English-speaking Catholics and non-Catholics have opportunities to share resources. These two populations are in a minority in Québec, and their numbers have been shrinking especially since the political upheaval in Québec and the rise since the 1970s of the movement towards sovereignty. The English Protestant school population prospered as a linguistic and religious minority in what was once a bilingual province, and they were protected by the British North America Act. In contrast, as a linguistic minority within the French Catholic system, the English Catholic school population has suffered from lack of support. Being tied by religion rather than by language, it fell into an alliance with the French Catholics by religion rather than into an alliance with the English Protestants by language.

### Religious education: The Proulx Report

At present, trained instructors in Catholic and Protestant religion must be provided in schools for students who are adherents of those faiths, and instructors of moral education must be provided for all others where numbers warrant it. Students are sectioned off into separate classes for instruction according to their belief systems for 2 hours each week. A report by Jean-Pierre Proulx (1999) on the place of religious instruction in public schools was recently studied by the government of Québec. The Proulx report recommends the abolition of confessional schools and the replacement of religious instruction with the study of religion as culture. Teachers would be trained to teach moral education, and the principles of Catholicism and Protestantism would be treated as two among many belief systems.

### Ministry of Education requirements for education in the arts

Students from Kindergarten to Grade 8 must have 2 hours of instruction in "the arts" each week. In Grades 7 and 8 this requirement is usually met as a short-term (12 week) foray into each of music, art, and drama. In my classes for preservice generalist teachers some students, mainly those from the English Catholic system, report that they never had music in their elementary or secondary schools. Some have had opportunities to make music outside the system, in church or community choirs, or at camp, for example. Others claim to have had no experience of singing or playing an instrument. I consider such students to be deprived. In my opinion the system has failed to educate them. The new program now being implemented at McGill University and at the French universities and the restructuring of the school boards should help to correct this failure.

Changes in the ways in which schools are organized in terms of language and religion, ministry requirements for "arts" teaching, and the changing cultural makeup of the Province of Québec, but particularly the city of Montréal, are reflected in McGill's new program of music teacher education, implemented in September 1999.

## Part Three: Music teacher education for the 21st century

All music teachers in Québec must now possess a Bachelor of Education degree,[11] and McGill University is the primary institution in Québec offering certification as a music specialist teacher[12] for the English sector. The requirement that all teachers hold a Bachelor of Education attests to the value that Québec places on teaching. Whereas the Diploma in Education was a 9-month program, tacked on at the end of undergraduate studies in music, the new Bachelor of Education in Music program gives more equal weight to the knowledge, ability, and aptitude required to be a professional teacher. It integrates academic studies in music, studies in a second subject, professional studies, and field experience in each year of the 4-year program. Graduates are certified to teach at the end of program.[13] In addition to the integrated structure, an increase in the number of hours of field experience,[14] and the addition of four professional seminars, a significant change to the program is the requirement that music specialist teachers be prepared to teach a second academic subject. Students must complete seven courses[15] in a second teachable subject and must have field experience teaching that subject. In order to provide our graduates with additional depth in music — the additional requirements of the Bachelor of Education has resulted in a reduction in the number of music courses students can take — McGill offers the program concurrently with the Bachelor of Music (Music Education). Students have the opportunity of obtaining the two degrees after 5 years of study. The first graduates from a dramatically altered teacher education program designed to meet the demands of a changing society, will obtain certification early in the 21st century.

*Teaching in French.* All English schools have strong French programs, including full French immersion, and one of the ways in which some schools meet their quota of instruction in French is in the music class. When placing student music teachers McGill must ensure in such schools that the student has sufficient command of French to carry out the teaching tasks effectively. As McGill attracts many students from other provinces, not all of whom are confident speakers of French, their placements create challenges for the student teacher placement officers. At the same time, McGill attracts many French-speaking students who have to work extra hard at mastering their spoken and written English in order to be certified to teach in English. If French speakers wish after graduation to teach in the French system they must pass the same oral and written language test that graduates from the French universities must pass. English-speaking and French-speaking students tend to see these challenges as opportunities to learn another language and culture.

*Initial teacher training, lifelong learning, and reflection on practice.* MEQ policy statements emphasize that student teachers should not be seen as fully formed teachers upon graduation. Rather, their undergraduate years are to be perceived as the initial stage in a lifelong process of learning. Implicit in this stance is an acknowledgement of the value of the knowledge that is gained from a lifetime of practice. It makes a statement about the value of teachers' professional knowledge. "Initial teacher training" is also a phrase that helps cooperating teachers conceptualize student teachers as beginners and reminds them of the necessity of guiding and mentoring them during their field experiences.

Reflection on practice is an attitude, a habit, a frame of mind that is conceptualized as an ongoing activity throughout a teacher's professional life. Reflection encourages the development of habits of critical thinking, analysis, observation, and interpretation that strengthen the student's identity as a professional. The concept of a reflective stance and the techniques of reflection are introduced to student music teachers in the very first year. During their first year field experience students begin to assemble a professional portfolio that is developed throughout the four field experiences and the professional seminars held in each year of the program. In the 9-month Diploma program, it was difficult if not impossible to develop the habit of reflection and to learn its techniques.

*Isolation of music teachers.* Isolation has always been a feature of music teaching and is one of the factors that research has shown contributes to professional burnout. The Ministry insists that teachers learn how to work in teams in order that they may learn to share resources, knowledge, and skills. In the B.Ed. program, student music teachers will learn to share knowledge and skills both with other student music teachers and with student teachers of other subjects through small-group discussion and the preparation of projects for their professional courses. The ability to work as a team is a skill that they will be able to bring to their teaching. Although the McGill Office of Student Teaching tries to place two students with one teacher, team teaching has not been a feature of the music students' field experience in the past, and I have noted that music specialist student teachers are less experienced than classroom teachers at preparing and implementing projects that involve group work. In the new program music students will learn how to work as a team.

Music teachers can also be isolated physically. Their field experience teaching a second academic subject will help to get them out of the confines of the music room and more into the mainstream of teaching. This experience should help them to understand better the place of the music program in terms of the whole school and will help them grasp the similarities and differences in the teaching of different subjects.

*Balancing subject matter knowledge and professional knowledge.* In the sequential system of teacher preparation, students first learned subject matter, then had what amounted to a crash course in the professional knowledge base.[16] This body of professional theoretical knowledge was presented to students in 2 blocks of 35–40 days, each block followed by an intensive, full-time field experience lasting about 35–45 days. The effect on the student teacher was shock by total immersion. There was little time to reflect on the significance of what they were learning, and survival was often the primary mode.

The weight and distribution of the academic, professional, and practical components of any music teacher education program reveal the relative value placed on each set of components. In the new program the integration of professional courses, academic courses, and practica across the full length of a program provides a better balanced approach to music teacher education. In accordance with MEQ documents that emphasized the importance of the convergence of teachers' practical knowledge and subject matter knowledge, [17] the Bachelor of Education in Music was designed in such a way that student music teachers take professional courses, music and second academic subject courses, and field experience and a supporting professional seminar in each year of the program thus integrating theory and practice. We believe that the music teacher education program, structured in this way, will better prepare student teachers to take on their professional responsibilities.

*Versatility in the workplace.* In the past music specialist teachers were trained only in the teaching of music. While this gave them a certain competence in music it also limited their marketability because they could only apply for music specialist positions. If there was a shortage of positions, and there often was (and is), graduates would find themselves unemployed or accepting jobs that were not related to their training. Now prepared to teach music at the elementary and secondary levels and to teach a second academic subject either at the elementary or secondary, graduates bring additional skills to their job interviews.

*The multicultural classroom.* Students and their teachers address multicultural issues as a theoretical topic in a course called "Intercultural Education or The Multicultural Classroom." They also address the issues as they bear on practice in their Professional Seminar when they have opportunities to discuss actual situations that they may be immersed in during their field experiences. In these courses students will be required to address the issue of musical repertoire in a culturally diverse school. Questions will include: What should be the basis for musical decisions? Who should make the musical decisions? Is the choice of repertoire a musical or social issue? How do the two issues intersect, and how may they be reconciled so that musical needs are met in ways that music teachers, their students, school officials, and parents find acceptable?

*The case of the mature student.* Our program of music teacher training is ideal for the student graduating from CEGEP[18] or from high school, in the case of students from outside Québec. However, it is unrealistic to expect all young people to know, at the age of 18 or 19, what they want to do with their lives. Individuals who obtained undergraduate degrees in music, then pursued careers in some facet of the music world or in business, perhaps got married and started families, and now decide to enter the teaching profession face a period of training of at least 2–1/2 years of full-time study in order to become certified teachers. These mature students often bring a wealth of musical knowledge and life experience and a strong commitment to the teaching enterprise. My hope is that this group will not be unduly deterred from seeking certification by the length of the program, and that ways can be found to support their studies.

### Predictions and expectations

*Employment opportunities for music teachers.* I see little possibility of developing music education programs in schools if there is no individual on staff who can initiate and maintain some semblance of a program of systematic study and establish musical traditions.

A music specialist in a school brings to the school community special expertise that can provide structured musical experiences for students, act as a resource for classroom teachers who wish to incorporate musical activities into their daily routine, help to integrate music into other areas of the curriculum, and thereby create a musical subculture. A musical culture in a school is one in which music is not an isolated event for 30 minutes in the week but may occur routinely at various times of the day and is considered a regular practice. A music specialist can start a staff choir, get parents singing with their children at concerts, and initiate musical traditions that will come to be seen as a normal part of school life. Classroom teachers with musical training, such as the graduates of our B.Ed. program will receive, will have the possibility of weaving music throughout the fabric of the school day.

At the elementary level graduates may be hired not only for their ability to teach music but also for their ability to teach moral education, or education in visual art, drama, and movement. Once in their schools, depending on their skills and dispositions, our graduates will be able to increase the proportion of music in their schedule by trading off their skills with their colleagues who are less well trained or less confident about their ability to teach music. Abundant examples exist of teachers who were able to increase significantly the proportion of their music teaching and thus develop lively music programs that became an important feature of their schools. Similarly, at the secondary level our graduates are likely to be hired primarily for their ability to teach music and their chosen second academic subject. In the context of the secondary school, as in the elementary school, there is also a possibility for the motivated and skillful teacher to increase the proportion of music teaching. The first critical step is to obtain the teaching position.

*Second academic subject.* As any salesman knows, it is difficult to introduce a product if the door is closed. With a Bachelor of Education in Music degree, with 21 credits in a second teachable subject, with 4 years of integrated professional and academic courses and 700 hours of field experience behind them, with training at the elementary and secondary levels, graduates will be in a strong position to compete for teaching positions at both the elementary and secondary levels. I predict that over the long term, the new program will have an overall beneficial effect on music education in the schools of Québec because it will enable our graduates to get a foot in the door. The Ministry permits McGill to graduate approximately 15 music specialists per year. I predict that all of the graduates who want to teach will find teaching positions.

*Extensive field experience & diversity of experience.* The 700 hours of field experience that student music teachers will have had by the time they complete the Bachelor of Education in Music will result in graduates who will bring to the job market knowledge of the functioning and character of a variety of elementary and secondary schools and classrooms. The professional seminars that accompany the field experiences will have helped them to reflect on and interpret their classroom experiences and to make sense of it. I expect that our music education graduates will be much better prepared to handle the complex demands of teaching than they were under the previous system of teacher preparation. They will have more confidence in their ability to teach and more skills to offer their employers.

*The formation of a professional identity.* The identity issue is particularly poignant for student music teachers who experience a tension between their perception of themselves as musicians and their perception of themselves as teachers; I expect that this tension will be reduced in the future. Because of the new requirement that music specialist teachers must obtain a Bachelor of Education, candidates are more likely to be drawn from the group who are highly motivated to become music teachers rather than from the group who fall into teaching by chance. The systematic socialization of music teachers into the teaching profession and the formation of teacher identity are key features of the program, and I expect that the program's integrated design and professional seminars will help students to reconcile these tensions.

*The value of bilingualism.* As a consequence of intensive second-language programs in Québec, most of our student music teachers are bilingual. Our program also attracts French mother-tongue speakers. Those students who wish to teach in the French sector have the opportunity of sitting the French language test administered by the French school boards. The ability to teach in French or English will give these students additional employment opportunities in the French and the English sectors.

*Realignment of school boards along linguistic lines.* One of the consequences of being a linguistic minority within the French Catholic system is that English Catholics have not had access to the same resources and services as English Protestants. With the restructuring of boards along linguistic lines, the possibility arises that English Catholic children will benefit from being part of a larger pool. One Catholic elementary school principal with whom I had several conversations on the topic of music education for English Catholic children expressed the expectation that the restructuring would allow the children in his school to have access to a music teacher.

*The Proulx Report.* Should the Proulx report be adopted, schools would no longer be required to provide as many as three or four different religion and moral education teachers[19] within a sin-

gle school. The potential practical impact on music education if
the Proulx report's recommendations are adopted cannot be
known,[20] but I am hopeful that they would result in the release of
funds and time that could be used for more music teaching in the
schools.

## Looking Ahead

I expect that graduates of the new Bachelor of Education in Music
program will have enhanced employment opportunities because
their possession of a Bachelor of Education with a strong background
in music and studies in one other subject will make them eligible
for teaching positions and because of the confidence they will bring
to their interviews. That confidence will come from the skills, versatility, experience, and sense of professional identity that their
program has given them. I expect that graduates who are motivated
to introduce musical experiences into their classrooms and schools
and are creative about implementing their ideas will do so. I also
expect to see more, not less music in the schools. Only systematic
studies carried out some years hence will be able to assess adequately the impact of these changes.

Technological and societal changes taking place at this time in
our country's history and their effects on classroom life remind us of
the importance of musical experience in the lives of children and of
the need for music educators to continue to promote the presence of
music in the classroom, in the school and in the community. The
intersection of repertoire choice and cultural diversity in the classrooms of the 21st century will challenge music teachers to be creative in their approaches to repertoire selection. The growing pressure
to integrate music across the curriculum will challenge teachers to
devise strategies that will permit integration to be achieved without
sacrificing music educational objectives. Teachers will be challenged to find ways to create musical traditions in schools where
they did not previously exist, so that school communities will come
to expect music making as a regular and significant activity as playing an integral role in the education of their children. The Ministry
of Education's new curriculum dictum that students in K–8 receive 2
hours of instruction each week in music and art will challenge
teacher education programs to provide teachers with the musical
skills and resources needed to carry out the task and will challenge
schools to ensure that this musical expertise is available to students.
We at the universities will need to continue to help our students find

ways of meeting these challenges at the philosophical, theoretical, conceptual, and applied levels. Our teacher education programs, for both classroom teachers and music specialist teachers, are responding to these challenges by listening to education students and professional teachers and through ongoing internal discussions aimed at refining and improving program design, curriculum content, and methods of implementation.

## References

Boudreau, S. (1990). *Catholic education: The Québec experience.* Calgary, AB: Detselig Enterprises.

Bresler, L. (1998). The genre of school music and its shaping by meso, micro, and macro contexts. *Research Studies in Music Education, 11,* 2–18.

Green, J. P., & Vogan, N. F. (1991). *Music education in Canada: A historical account.* Toronto: University of Toronto Press.

Mills, J. (1989). The generalist primary teacher of music: A problem of confidence. *British Journal of Education, 6* (2), 125–138.

Ministère d'Éducation du Québec. (1997). Teacher training: The arts, physical education and second language education. Orientations and competencies. Québec, PQ: Author.

Proulx, J.-P. (1999). Le rapport du groupe de travail sur la place de la religion à l'école.

Regelski, T. (1994, April). *Action research and critical theory: Empowering music teachers to professionalize praxis.* Paper presented at the Qualitative Methodology in Music education Conference, University of Illinois, Urbana-Champaign.

Richler, M. (1971). *St. Urbain's horseman: A novel.* Toronto: McLelland & Stewart.

Richler. M. (1984). *The apprenticeship of Duddy Kravitz.* Scarborough, ON: Prentice-Hall Canada.

Russell, J. (1996). Musical knowledge, musical identity, and the generalist teacher: Vicki's story. *McGill Journal of Education, 31* (3), 247–260.

Stake, R., Bresler, L., & Mabry, L. (1991). *Custom and Cherishing: The arts in elementary schools.* Urbana Champaign, IL: Council for Research in Education.

---

[1] Green & Vogan's (1991) *Music Education in Canada* is a fine source of information about the kinds of music education that was provided to French-speaking students from the earliest years of the French colony. Until the 1960s in the French sector, music education consisted largely of the study of solfège and/or piano or violin. Music programs as we have come to know them today as large group participation in choirs, bands, and orchestras are the models that I am thinking of when I talk about the development of music education in the public system. These are the models that developed since the 1940s in the English sector, and have developed so strongly since the 1970s in the French sector.

[2] "English Protestants" was a term that embraced all who were not French or English Catholic.

[3] Baron Byng High School was thinly disguised as Fletcher's Field High School in Mordecai Richler's *The Apprenticeship of Duddy Kravitz* (1984) and in *St. Urbain's Horseman* (1971).

[4] Although some band directors get their students to sing, the focus of the program is instrumental, not choral.

[5] Whether individuals are practising Catholics or not, the tradition is nevertheless a cultural inheritance.

[6] not to mention general cuts in base budgets

[7] See for example Stake, Bresler, & Mabry (1991), *Custom and Cherishing: The Arts in Elementary Schools* and also Mills (1989), "The Generalist Primary Teacher of Music: A Problem of Confidence" and Russell (1996), "Musical Knowledge, Musical Identity, and the Generalist Teacher: Vicki's Story."

[8] Elementary teachers were once obliged to take four courses in the arts as part of their program. Today that number has been reduced to one course to make room in their program for other requirements. Although it is possible for a generalist teacher to choose music as an area of concentration, few do so, for a variety of reasons including the belief that having music as a concentration will not contribute to their chances of gaining a teaching position. There are, however, ongoing discussions at the Faculty of Education about the wisdom of providing student teachers with so little experience with the arts.

[9] I don't mean to suggest that these are not worthwhile experiences, only that they are not academic pursuits.

[10] plus three boards serving the northern and native populations

[11] All music specialist teacher training programs in Québec must meet the same criteria for accreditation.

[12] This year Bishop's University in the town of Lennoxville, some 90 miles south of Montréal, has approximately 3 students in a music specialist program.

[13] The certificate is recognized in all provinces.

[14] 700 hours in the schools

[15] 273 classroom hours

[16] Professional courses include "Philosophical Foundations of Education," "The Multicultural Classroom," "Educational Psychology, Measurement and Evaluation," "Exceptional Children," and "Music Curriculum and Instruction."

[17] Regelski refers to this convergence as "praxis." He explained the concept of praxis in a paper titled "Action Research and Critical Theory: Empowering Music Teachers to Professionalize Praxis."

[18] Collège d'Enseignant Général et Professionel — a postsecondary institution designed to prepare students for university or provide them with technical training

[19] Catholic, Protestant, Moral Education.

[20] The National Assembly of Québec decided before the end of the fall session, 1999, to proceed with changes to the confessional system gradually rather than to make radical sweeping changes and shelved the Proulx Report.

# Chapter Five

# Who is Teaching
# The Next Generation of Teachers?
## Implications for Music Education in the New Millennium

*Carol Beynon*

## Introduction

> *Given the apparent esteem accorded student teaching, one might assume that it is grounded in a sound theoretical foundation, with general agreement concerning its structure and activities.... [It] has not developed a sound theoretical basis, and has no uniform standard or structure.... The fragmentation and lack of articulation within student teaching mirrors a similar dilemma throughout [the content of] most teacher education programs.*
> (Guyton and McIntyre, 1990, pp. 514–515)

The practicum component is consistently valued and rated as the most important component of teacher education by preservice teachers not only throughout Canada but across the entire North American continent (McIntyre & Byrd, 1996; Pinnegar, 1995). According to the teacher education literature, there are no obvious links between the curriculum provided by the university instructors in teacher education courses — be it music education or any other curriculum area — and the practicum assignments that the cooperating teachers design (Britzman, 1991; Feiman-Nemser & Buchmann, 1987; Guyton & McIntyre):

> As teacher educators, we recognize student teaching as the most salient experience in the education of teachers. We are often frustrated that material taught in university courses does not appear to survive student

teaching and seldom seems to become part of the practice of the teachers we educate. (Pinnegar, 1995, p. 56)

All professionals realize the nature of the dependence — between student teachers and those who seek to influence them — as riddled with contradictions because there is no simple correspondence between what any professional thinks should happen during student teaching, what exactly the student teacher should do to realize these ideas, and what actually occurs. (Britzman, 1991, p. 175)

From these comments, it appears that the practicum in preservice teacher education is highly contested terrain. It is in the practicum that student teachers say they learn the most about teaching, and it is in the practicum that university teacher educators worry that their students will become merely socialized into practice without analysing the underlying assumptions of their practice (Britzman, 1991; Feiman-Nemser & Buchmann, 1987).

Metcalf and Kahlich (1996) discuss the negative effects that student teaching placements have on student teachers' attitudes, knowledge, and classroom practice, and, they note that the longer the field experience, the worse it is for student teachers' future practice. They also note that there are too few exemplary sites where student teachers can be placed to rectify the negative effects of the practicum experience.

The student teacher practicum is supervised almost exclusively by cooperating teachers who receive student teachers into their classes for a period of time ranging from a few days to several months, depending on the program. The purpose of the experience is literally to *practise teaching*. Cooperating teachers generally volunteer for the task, take on this responsibility in addition to their full-time teaching duties, have little or no professional preparation for becoming a teacher-supervisor, and assume the role for a variety of reasons ranging from the altruistic to the selfish. Research shows that cooperating teachers generally have little understanding or knowledge of the expectations of the teacher education institution and conceptualize their role in isolation (Enz, Freeman & Wallin, 1996; Guyton & McIntyre, 1990; Knowles & Cole with Presswood, 1994). However, at the same time, they are influential teacher educators who have a dramatic and intense effect on the future practice of student teachers (Feiman-Nemser & Buchmann, 1987; Lortie, 1975). In speaking about the power of the practicum experience and the role of the cooperating teacher, The Holmes Group in its report, *Tomorrow's Teachers* (1986), describes the relationship between student teacher and cooperating teacher as one that seeks conformity and replication:

> Most student teachers quickly conform to the practices of their supervising teacher and rarely put into practice a novel technique or risk failure.... The emphasis is on imitation of and subservience to the supervising teacher, not upon investigation, reflection, and solving novel problems. (p. 55)

As the new millennium unfolds and the past becomes viewed as outmoded and even primitive, we find ourselves in a world that is undergoing complex and massive societal change in culture, education, politics, and in the economy. Our world is becoming increasingly diverse and complex. Boundaries — both real and invisible — are being altered or dissolved, and our newest teachers who will become our decision and policymakers within the next ten years must to be able to accommodate and thrive within those changes in order to further an effective educational system in general and viable arts programs in particular.

With this perspective from the literature about the role of the cooperating teacher in mind, I embarked on this study at the turn of the millennium by interviewing and visiting the classrooms of six cooperating teachers with whom several of my student teachers in music education are placed each year, in an attempt to ferret out their values, beliefs, and ideologies about teaching, learning, and learning to teach. These are the classrooms where our newest music teachers — the ostensible leaders in music education in Canada in 10 to 20 years — observe current pedagogy and practice, cut their teeth in issues of teaching and learning, and develop formative concepts about their own teaching practice for the future. Through the findings of this study, I explore the cooperating teachers' belief systems to understand the impact that their beliefs and practices as school-based teacher educators have on their student teachers' development in the preservice program. I begin with the premise (from the earlier research presented) that cooperating teachers, through their intensive one-on-one contact and direct communication with their student teachers during the practicum sessions, have a great impact on student teachers' representations of teaching and their ideologies of teaching and learning.

✳ ✳ ✳

## Meeting the Cooperating Teachers

All six cooperating teachers work for the same medium-sized urban school district in different but fairly typical elementary and secondary schools. Their teaching experience ranges from six to thirty years. Five of the six have acted as cooperating teachers for several years, and only one had any formal preparation for taking on the role as school-based teacher educator. (The one teacher is voluntarily enrolled in an 80-hour additional qualifications course, called *The Cooperating Teachers' Course* offered through this Faculty of Education.)

The parameters for the role of the cooperating teacher are laid out in the teacher education institution's handbook for cooperating teachers, and each cooperating teacher receives a copy of *The Practicum Handbook* prior to the first term of the academic year. The guidelines are instrumental in nature and allow a certain amount of flexibility and ownership to cooperating teachers as to how they carry out their role. There are no specific guidelines for music teachers, or for elementary versus secondary teachers; all cooperating teachers follow the same set of general guidelines.

The data gathered from the observations of and interviews with the six cooperating teachers were interesting and informative. In spite of their gender difference, contrasting school settings, the ages of pupils they taught, their range of experience, and varying approaches to teaching, five themes that characterized their values, beliefs, and ideologies about the role of the cooperating teacher as an important teacher educator in learning to teach emerged from their conversations. These five themes, formed as questions, are explained in the next section of the paper. They are:

What does it mean to be a teacher?
Why be a cooperating teacher?
How do theory and practice intersect in student teaching?
How are student teachers evaluated?
What does it mean for student teachers to take risks?

## Learning to Teach: What Does it Mean to be a Teacher?

The question — How do student teachers learn to teach? — provided a beginning and focal point for the interviews with the cooperating teachers. It was both interesting and surprising to note that almost all of these teacher educators were taken aback by the question and admitted that they had few ideas about how novices learn to teach, nor — even though they see themselves as teachers of teachers — had they given the question much thought. When pressed, they tended to use their own experience as a guide in answering the question and described an apprenticeship as the best way to learn to teach. Their responses about learning to teach could be summarized into the following four points that differentiate subtly between learning *to* teach and learning *about* teaching. (These points are not ordered by importance, rather by the sequence in which they were normally discussed by the cooperating teachers.)

1. Passion for the role is paramount to becoming a teacher.
2. A teacher personality is required.
3. Real learning about teaching occurs only after years of experience in teaching.
4. Knowledge of subject matter is important.

These four points are used to introduce and then illustrate the role that cooperating teachers play in helping student teachers negotiate their identity in learning to teach and identifying what it means to be a teacher.

### The importance of passion in learning to teach

Raghav[1] had 30 years of teaching experience and was the cooperating teacher with whom Richardo, one of my student teachers, was placed in his second practicum assignment. Raghav spoke earnestly about the need for student teachers to have a passion for teaching:

> How do people learn to teach? It starts with a natural desire that they indicate to become a teacher.... They see teaching as something they "have" to do in their lives. It may almost be instinct too. I mean that there are lots of people who want to teach, but can't.... There's no potential there, no deep desire and unless that comes to the surface, I believe that they can't be successful teachers.

This concept of desire and instinct was reinforced by Laura, an elementary music teacher, who noted how important it is for student teachers:

> to get inspired, to keep yourself motivated because this is what it is all about. Teaching, especially music, is exhausting work day after day, year after year and you have to be totally consumed with enthusiasm and passion to be a good music teacher.

The issue raised here has to do with the relationship between self-motivation to be a teacher and success as a teacher. The cooperating teachers were convinced that passion was a prerequisite for teaching, and that if passion to do the job was clearly evident, then success in being a teacher — perhaps longevity in one's teaching career — was more likely. It was assumed that student teachers who had passion for teaching had the necessary background and belief systems to be a teacher, or at least, the motivation to learn what one would need to be successful. With passion, these cooperating teachers believed that their student teachers could and would want to develop the competence to be able to plan appropriate learning activities, carry them out successfully, and evaluate the learning effectively.

In discussing teaching, student teachers frequently talk about their dreams and desires to become good music teachers. They see themselves fitting into the same role as the teachers they remember from their own schooling and they look forward to carrying out the same kinds of practices they had experienced as pupils.[2] Their representations of teaching are based on their recollections as pupils, and their passion is consonant with the *natural instinct* sought by their cooperating teachers. What is significant to note here is that passion for teaching likely emanates from student teachers' past recollections of schools and images of teachers and pupils — a recalled infatuation with past schooling that will likely be representative of student teachers' actions in classrooms in the present and future. According to the cooperating teachers in this study, student teachers are expected to carry past practices that will likely emulate and maintain the assumptions of the dominant society's vision of education into the future.

The value of passion in becoming a teacher, on the other hand, may not be the first criterion that university teacher educators identify as a necessity for becoming a teacher. Instead, university teacher educators tend to encourage their students to consider different (and developing) representations of teaching that challenge past and current norms. There is a realization, that while many student teachers come to teacher education with instinct and desire, novice teachers need to be enthusiastically open to new and different ways of looking at teaching — methods that may even subvert the norms of traditional forms of practice and view learning in a different form that would empower all pupils in their classes to engage in suitable learning activities.

The cooperating teachers pointed out that there is a difference between passion for becoming a teacher and a natural teaching personality. While passion is perceived to be important in becoming a teacher, it, alone, is not enough. A teaching personality is required, according to the cooperating teachers with whom I spoke.

### The importance of the "teacher personality" in becoming a teacher

In our discussions, the familiar question — Are teachers born or made? — kept creeping through the layers of conversation. All of the cooperating teachers spoke about working with the *naturals* in the profession and said that it was much easier to work with a student teacher who possesses a natural enthusiasm for teaching and pupils and an eagerness for learning. The development of the teaching personality was seen as a natural, spontaneous, and required trait in order to become a teacher. One who is identified by the cooperating teacher as having *sparkle* is assumed to be able to plan effective lessons and to engage pupils' minds and bodies in learning and making music. Laura told me that she believes that the personality needed to become a good teacher is inborn and cannot be taught in the process of learning to teach:

> *Right now, I have a student [teacher] who is a natural with the kids. She just knows how to interact with them, and that's something that you cannot teach someone to do or how to like children. She is a good teacher already. We can teach the mechanics of teaching, like lesson planning, punctuality, rules and regulations, but you cannot teach the natural things like personality. What we [cooperating teachers] are teaching is how to bring that natural personality out. And if it's not there, it's not there.*

Laura went on to talk about the competence of the student teachers she had this year and described them as naturals. She said, "I wondered if they need to be in the teacher education program at all because they were already so good. It certainly made my job a lot easier. It was like I had two extra teachers in the classroom." Laura was questioning the need for and the relevance of professional education for beginning teachers because it seems that she feels that all that is necessary is for student teachers to develop a teaching personality to be successful teachers. The rest of the details of learning about teaching can be taught in the classroom setting.

What is significant in this discussion is the reliance on the personality to play a dominant role in evaluating teaching potential. It seems that if the student teacher can engage the pupils then they are deemed successful, natural teachers.[3] For certain, classroom management problems are minimized. What was lacking from this discussion, however, was further discourse on what was taught, how it was taught, and what was learned and by whom. There was no analysis at all of the nature of the curriculum or its pedagogy in determining the effectiveness of the teaching and learning of the pupils. It seems that student teachers who have a naturally engaging manner with pupils may not be evaluated on their abilities to plan effectively or be required to teach in such a way that pupils are engaged specifically in learning. These facets are taken for granted, and student teachers could be rewarded for being entertainers, not teachers. The sparkle of the teaching personality seems to mask the critical components of teaching through the assumption that if one is able to engage pupils, the content must be relevant and important.

### *Real learning about teaching occurs only after years of experience*

Since teachers work mainly in isolated situations on their own, these cooperating teachers pointed out that learning to teach is largely a self-taught process. Warren noted:

> *It was just by doing that I've learned to teach, I'm afraid. Because I think that you learn by either seeing it or doing it…and by your own trial-and-error…. I mean, how you feel like a baseball player is by playing baseball. It's not by sitting in a classroom and learning about the mechanics of it. You don't feel like a baseball player until you've played ball, and you don't feel like a teacher unless you are actually teaching…. I am a classical guitarist and how I really felt like a musician was by performing. Teaching seems to me to be one of those things that you have to learn by doing it, by watching it done, and doing it some more.*

After seven years of teaching, Warren emphasized that he had really learned to teach only after years of experience, and he noted that he was learning much about teaching still, but on a deeper, more thoughtful level than previously. He said that would be how he assumed that his student teachers would learn to teach.

It appears that the cooperating teachers value the student teaching experience as the preliminary step in learning to teach but noted that learning about teaching takes time to develop. They seem to mean that initially one needs to learn to use one's personal desire and personality to gain confidence, and that competence only comes after some years of experience in the classroom. Years of practical and it seems, reflective, experience in the classroom are essential, they said. Warren added that he had gained preliminary understanding and confidence about teaching during his preservice year from talking to his cooperating teachers, his peers, and faculty members about his experiences while a student teacher. At that point, he valued and enjoyed his university courses, but it was only after a few years that he realized the importance of the university courses to his teaching and how to blend the theoretical overviews he had gained with his practice in the classroom:

> *The school setting is where everything comes together. You have to keep re-forming and refining your ideas. You need to have a place where you can look at different theories of curriculum delivery and I think the most effi-cient place to do that is right in the classroom setting. The student teachers have to be able to hear it, see it, and try it out for themselves in a guided set-ting so that they can carry on in their class.... That's how I learned about teaching.... Everything about teaching is frightening the first time through.... Terror is a good teacher, if you think about it. It somehow puts everything into focus for you when you realize that you have to do this or you fail the pupils in the classroom and as a teacher. That's when the observa-tion and discussion in the practicum classroom is so critical, but the deeper knowledge only comes after years of teaching.*

Warren and the others were explicit that their representations of teaching were unsophisticatedly formed in their own teacher education program and in their early years of experience. It was only after a few years of experience that they began to feel like teachers and had some confidence in their practice as teachers and began to understand their beliefs and practices.

Paradoxically, student teachers do not have time to truly practise teaching. The pressure is on to demonstrate teaching competence as quickly as possible in the practicum session since it is the observing cooperating teacher who makes the important evaluative judgement and writes the critical comments that will help the candidate find a teaching job. Demonstrating competence for the student teachers and cooperating teachers almost always means having well-behaved and attentive classes. Since there is no long-term opportunity for professional growth in a three- or four-week practicum session, everything which is to be accomplished or improved must be done immediately for the next class. Not only is the student teacher required to accommodate quickly, but the cooperating teacher must think of techniques and solutions that can be explained, transferred, learned, and adapted immediately. Student teachers often speak of being overwhelmed in the busy school setting as there is so much to absorb and they have little experience in observation.

But, it does not escape the student teachers that their cooperating teachers endure and cope with the same level of activity day after day. As Helen pointed out, "Everything is so immediate in the classroom that student teachers have to become accustomed to doing everything quickly." On the other hand, the cooperating teachers remembered the busyness of the practicum and the brevity of the teacher education program. They acknowledged their role in perpetuating the view that their student teachers need to demonstrate immediate competence. They constantly feel the pressure and responsibility to ensure that their own pupils cover the curriculum and they try to provide their student teachers with the techniques and means to teach competently as quickly as possible. Gerald said:

> *As I gain experience as a cooperating teacher, my expectations are changing. My intent is to have my student teachers involved in a lot more teaching activities, and I know it is really busy, but they have so little time and few school placements. So even though it is the first session, I like them to be more involved in pupil evaluation. It's easy for them to teach [a new piece], or to hand out papers for the kids to work away on, but the evaluation of that work is crucial and they need to do more of that. I try to have them teach as much as possible in a short time, just to give them the experience. And I try to remember to talk to them about the professional aspects of teaching, theory and practice, etc.*

The cooperating teachers in this study also remembered feeling pressured during the practicum to show their competence, and they recalled what it was like to return to the university after a practicum session. They said that they went back to enjoy a rest after surviving the busyness of three or four weeks in the classroom and they enjoyed sharing their stories of teaching with their friends. Their memories of the practicum during their teacher education program remained vivid, while their recall of the content of their university classes was hazy. In fact, most had difficulty remembering what it was they had studied in the university courses. Upon reflection and in retrospect, however, the cooperating teachers remarked that the content was likely quite important and would have been useful in their professional growth over the long term.

### Knowledge of subject matter

Each of the cooperating teachers in this study felt that subject matter knowledge was an essential qualification to be a music teacher and the fact that is mentioned last, highlights its necessity. They assumed that they would only ever work with student teachers who were already accomplished musicians with the requisite baccalaureate background in musicianship, performance, and conducting. Quite simply, these cooperating teachers firmly believe that novice teachers cannot be successful as music teachers unless they have these prerequisites and they are not interested in working with student teachers who are not university-trained musicians. Gerald pointed out:

> *I have been really lucky. In my six years as a cooperating teacher, I have always had good student teachers. They have been enthusiastic and have had a good subject knowledge. I have found that they are always keen to get up and conduct in front of my classes, even though they may be nervous at first and not really know what to teach. I couldn't work, or at least I don't want to work, with a student teacher who does not have that knowledge. The job of working with student teachers is hard enough without having to teach them subject content.*

Gerald alludes to the fact that having mastery of subject mastery is not enough. His job as a cooperating teacher is to help his student teachers take their background knowledge and transform it into useful information for pupil learning in the context of his classes. Gerald may be alluding to what Shulman (1987) refers to as *pedagogical content knowledge* in which he points out that subject matter knowledge and pedagogy cannot be isolated in teaching. They must intersect so that teachers can transform the subject content into accessible learning information for pupils through strategies or techniques that Shulman refers to as a teacher's pedagogical content knowledge.

## Summary

These four points — passion for teaching, having the requisite teacher personality, experience in teaching, and mastery of subject content — permeated the conversation with the six cooperating teachers in this study and have a major impact, in these cooperating teachers' minds, on how student teachers learn to teach, and in defining how cooperating teachers define their roles. At the same time, these teachers emphasized both the importance of their role as teacher educators and how it impacted on their busy day-to-day lives a classroom teachers. The interviews seemed to give them an opportunity to rethink why they have taken on such a significant role in addition to their classroom work.

## Why Be a Cooperating Teacher?

Being a school-based teacher educator is demanding and time-consuming. Why do cooperating teachers voluntarily take on this role? While a number of reasons were provided, two rather significant motives stood out:

1. The cooperating teachers appreciate having another adult to provide additional instructional help in their increasingly demanding classrooms — a second teacher or teacher assistant;
2. Having another adult in the class eases the isolation that comes with teaching.

Warren spoke about having another set of capable ears, eyes, and hands in the classroom:

*I enjoy having someone else to work with in the classroom. My classes are very busy, and having an extra set of hands around is very helpful to make sure that as many of the kids are getting one-on-one instruction where possible. It's helpful for marking, assessing pupils. With a good student teacher, I just get more things accomplished with my curriculum and with the pupils.*

With only one teacher normally in the classroom trying to monitor the learning and activities of 30 or so pupils, trying to cover the curriculum effectively with all of the pupils, and doing all of the marking, the extra help of a competent student teacher is appreciated.

Gerald, a senior elementary teacher, enjoyed having another adult in his classroom to talk about teaching:

*I find it so interesting to talk directly about teaching and my experiences in my classes with another adult. I rarely have an opportunity to do that. Teaching tends to be very isolated, I find, and by having another adult in the classroom I can talk about what I teach, the methods I use, and what I think is important in teaching. Teachers do not often get a chance to really talk about their work except in very general terms, and this helps me to review what I do. I seem to learn more about myself as a teacher through talking about my teaching with my student teachers, and it forces me to question what I do and why, something I might not do if I didn't need to explain my work to someone else in great detail.*

The isolation of teaching is a concept that has been discussed in the literature (see for example Lortie, 1975), and it appears that having student teachers not only eases the discomfort of detachment from other educators for these practising teachers but allows them opportunity to review and question their practice as they make it explicit to their student teachers.

The cooperating teachers' comments are congruent with what I observed in their classrooms. I watched in each case as the student teachers and cooperating teachers talked extensively about pupil learning and the events in that particular class during the class and after the class was over. In many cases, the conversation was directed and dominated by the cooperating teacher, but in others the conversation reflected questions that the student teachers had asked. In conversations with the student teachers, they told me that when they discussed their observations and experiences with their cooperating teachers; their cooperating teachers talked to them as co-teachers; and they valued the experience because it made them *feel* like teachers — something that did not seem to happen in the university-based classes, they added. The student teachers said that their cooperating teachers would ask them for their assessment of certain aspects of the program, would advise them regarding important information for their pupils, and observe attentively when they tried different techniques in the classroom, whereas in university classes, their status as student was reinforced as they sat in lectures and demonstrations, and completed assignments. The student teachers' comments confirmed that these cooperating teachers see their student teachers not so much as student teachers, but as co-teachers in their classrooms.

## How Do Theory and Practice Intersect in Student Teaching?

> *That knowledge has the capacity to appear both meaningless and meaningful is a dilemma that underscores the structure of teacher education and the lived experience of those who work there. The trivialization of knowledge becomes most evident when prospective teachers leave their university course work and attempt, through classroom teaching, to render this knowledge pedagogical and relevant. It is here that student teachers must not only make sense of theory but attempt to experience practice theoretically. The last form of fragmentation — between theory and practice — is most apparent when prospective teachers live the dramatic shift from learning about teaching in university settings to teaching in actual classrooms.*
>
> (Britzman, 1991, p. 46)

Warren's earlier comments about learning to teach after years of experience allude to Britzman's (1991) arguments about the link between theory and practice. For Warren the link is concrete and dramatic and happens for teachers only after years of experience in teaching. He says that the link between theory and practice is reciprocal — it is not necessarily just practice that is generated by theory, but, he believes, theory should be informed by good practice:

> *I think sometimes the student teachers believe that their university work is too theoretical and that their work in the classroom is much more important. I probably felt that way too as a student teacher, but my experience has taught me that it is not as simple as that. It works both ways. Sometimes I do things in my teaching that seems instinctive, not theoretically based, and it works very well. Real learning does occur. But then I think that I develop a theory out of that practice that becomes part of my way of teaching. At other times, I read about new ideas or theories and then I try to create relevant practice out of that.*

Laura's philosophy about the links between theory and practice were consonant with Warren's as she pointed out that she develops theory out of her own practice. Her work, like Warren's, is based on a sound understanding of the relation of practice and theory that comes after several years of experience. The cooperating teachers reminded me that classrooms should not be perceived as atheoretical venues for learning about teaching because the practice that occurs there is interrelated with theoretical constructs in a significant way. Laura said:

> *Our teaching practice is not just mindless practice. You know, as teachers we constantly develop our practice out of theory, but we also have to develop theory out of practice as we evaluate our own work on a daily basis.*

The issue of theory and practice needs to be paramount in teacher education as teacher educators try to help student teachers gain knowledge and understanding (or theories) about the process of teaching and learning. But the links are not always obvious to student teachers or to the cooperating teachers, and indeed I listen carefully as my own student teachers criticize the content of many of their classes at the teacher education institution. They see neither the relevance nor the rationale in their current situation for many of the issues they study. Fortunately, they feel they can raise their concerns, and some changes in their courses have occurred as a result. Their school-based teacher educators concur with the student teachers. While all of the cooperating teachers acknowledge that *some* learning about teaching did occur in the university setting when they were student teachers, all believed that it was in the classroom context where authentic learning about teaching occurred for them, and they openly relay that sense to their student teachers. Most rejected Britzman's (1991) notion that the university was the home of theory and the school the base of practice. Rather these cooperating teachers believed that theory and practice were interwoven in a significant way in their classroom practice, and the practicum provided an ideal setting where student teachers could observe both, try both, and reform and refine their ideas. Significantly, they expressed pride that they were *the* influential teacher educators of novice teachers.

## How Are Student Teachers Evaluated?

Cooperating teachers are required by teacher education institutions to complete and submit regular evaluation reports on their student teachers throughout the practicum session. Evaluative reports are the prime tools that student teachers use to find employment as a teacher, and cooperating teachers are well aware (as are their student teachers) of the power that their pens ultimately hold. We can assume from their earlier comments that passion, personality, and the best musicians would be the major criteria for an excellent report. One of the first things that Raghav looks for in evaluating student teachers is classroom management — or the student teachers' ability to engage the pupils and to be able to maintain a learning environment. Laura spoke of looking for a natural, comfortable teaching manner with the children in her classes. Both were observing their student teachers to ensure that they could develop and maintain an effective learning environment.

Demonstrating the ability to get pupils' interest and to keep them on task requires not only an enthusiastic presence but also the ability to organize and present activities to the pupils that keep them engaged and on task. So, the cooperating teachers reason, if the pupils were engaged (i.e., playing their instruments), they were likely involved in learning. As Helen said, "You cannot teach them [her pupils] anything unless you can make them pay attention. So classroom management is really important to me." Most student teachers sense immediately that a quiet, mannerly classroom of pupils is necessary to succeed as teachers (i.e., get a good report), and most use their personalities or whatever means they have to get their pupils' interest and keep them on task in order to secure that excellent evaluative report from their cooperating teacher. Their beliefs are confirmed by the earlier comments of their cooperating teachers, and their behaviour emphasizes the fact that student teacher evaluation may be weighted towards the ability to maintain a disciplined classroom — which does not always indicate a learning classroom — rather than evidence of student learning. All of this interaction works to hinder student teachers in taking risks in a situation which is intended to be safe and supportive for learning about teaching, rather than merely getting an excellent report for hiring purposes.

## What Does it Mean for Student Teachers to Take Risks?

Kate, an elementary music teacher with many years of experience, pointed out that following the established routines of cooperating teachers is in fact experimentation for student teachers. She notes:

> *Most student teachers haven't had much experience in teaching and so trying even the most traditional technique is new for them. When they try my old tried and true methods, they are taking risks, but at their own level. The routines in my primary classes are important to follow because the kids need the stability and consistency to feel comfortable and safe to be able to get to work. Yet the routines are new to my student teacher, such as entering the class, taking attendance with singing games, and so on. And she still makes small adjustments to what I normally do, which is just fine.*

Student teachers, on the other hand, often feel pressured to follow established routines for several reasons. They learn to respect the cooperating teachers' methods and feel they should try to emulate them because they can see that they are effective. Richardo, a student teacher, noted:

> *When I came into the teacher education program, I assumed I would just have to jump through the hoops to do what Gerald [my cooperating teacher] did to be successful. I promised myself that although I would follow what he did to get a good report, I would be my own teacher when I got out on my own and be a lot better than teachers nowadays. But he is great. The kids like him. And even though at first I didn't really like how he did things, I soon learned that they work for him and now they work for me. Why wouldn't I use them? He's a good teacher.*

On the other hand, each cooperating teacher commented that they expect the student teachers to bring new practices to the classroom from their study at the university. Several of the cooperating teachers noted the new *ideas,* and talk with their student teachers about them and then experiment with them in their own practice.

Helen, the novice cooperating teacher with 13 years of teaching experience, said:

> *I am amazed at how much I learned from my two student teachers. What they talk about in their observation and planning is like a review of teacher training for me — showing my student teacher how I plan for short- and long-term learning, thinking about pacing, searching for creative ways to do things to motivate the pupils and to help them learn, and on and on. But then they also bring new ideas from the Faculty that I hadn't thought about before, and this causes me to consider my own teaching in a different way.*

Laura also noted how receptive she is to new ideas which the student teachers bring from their university courses and said that she looked forward to finding things out from them when they came to her class. She referred to the learning during student teaching as a *two-way street* in which both she and her student teachers learn about teaching from each other. Laura noted that she has incorporated several ideas into her own teaching practice which she learned from her student teachers. Raghav noted:

> *Not only do they bring new ideas to me that I can use but I often change my own practice through my observations of the ways in which the student teachers do things. I find it going through my mind, "Now that student has taught that in a particular way that I have never thought of or heard about before. But it works well. Maybe it would be appropriate if I were to discuss that with him/her and to try that myself.*

It seems that the student teachers, in following established routines and in trying out a few new ideas, are actually experimenting, but with the traditional methods of their supervising teachers which are new to them because they are novices. It is the cooperating teachers who have the confidence, expertise, and experience who are looking for innovative ideas and who are willing to experiment with them in their classes during the practicum.

## Insights and Implications

The five themes that emerged from the observations and interviews in this study clearly describe the views of these cooperating teachers in particular and tend to support the findings in the literature about cooperating teachers' views of their role as teacher educators. There is no doubt in exploring the question — who is teaching the next generation of music teachers? — that school-based music teachers are influential teacher educators whose practices have a major impact on future practice of novice music teachers. In this section, I summarize the findings of this study in relation to the literature on teacher development and develop some implications for the cooperating teacher's role in teacher education.

Luke (1995) explains that "schools are charged with the problematic task of introducing children to the texts and discourses of official knowledge and practice" (p. 37). So too are cooperating teachers in their role with student teachers. In becoming cooperating teachers, experienced teachers assume the role of providing preliminary school-based preparation of the next generation of teachers through a learning method which is largely based on an apprenticeship model. Laura told me that, in the practicum, student teachers are expected to observe and replicate the work of their supervising teachers, to discuss the practice in relation to the activities of the classroom, and to appreciate the significance of that practice:

> *Student teachers learn so much in the classroom that they cannot learn in the Faculty, like being with the kids, and planning and teaching for a whole day, from early morning rehearsals through to team practices after school. I try to be very explicit about what I am doing so that I can explain to them what I am doing and why I am doing it. I expect them to follow my advice. But the ones [student teachers] I have had this year were just excellent and they fit right into my program. It was more like team-teaching.*

Since, as was noted at the beginning of this paper, the practicum experience has such a profound, long-term effect on student teachers' practices as beginning teachers, two questions arise:

1. What kind of practice is it that student teachers observe and emulate in their cooperating teachers' classrooms?
2. If cooperating teachers' practices have such a long-term effect and impact on the next generation of teachers, can change in music education ever occur?

The traditional school system has been described as one that acts in the best interests of the dominant, middle class, and values the cultural capital of that class (Apple, 1962; Bourdieu, 1977). Teachers implicitly contribute to the maintenance of those values through their curriculum and teaching methods and by collectively viewing their pupils as a generic, genderless mass in their speech and practice.

> Schools tend to render legitimate or illegitimate certain elements in the student's cultural capital. Since by tradition schools act in the inter-

ests of the dominant classes, then it is the cultural capital of ruling groups that is legitimized by schools.... The dominant sociocultural groups' cultural capital is an "academic" one, when compared with the culture of working class people and many minority groups. (Corson, 1995, pp. 148–149)

Student teachers are rewarded for complying with and adopting similar teaching behaviour to their cooperating teachers. For example, student teachers develop preconceived representations of teaching as pupils in schools which are generally traditional, generic, conservative, and value-laden (Lortie, 1975), and are likely consistent with the practice which they observe in their practicum classroom (Guyton & McIntyre, 1990). These representations become the academic cultural capital of teaching, and student teachers' replications become legitimated by their cooperating teachers in a very powerful way. Even though more critical views of education or even different insights shared may be discussed during university preservice classes, the activity and impact of the individualized practicum overshadows other learning.

In observing the classes of these cooperating teachers, I found all of the teachers to be dedicated, conservative professionals who teach using traditional, performance-based methods. All are recognized as highly successful and competent teachers; they are articulate about their practice and their beliefs; and all are perceived as highly successful leaders in music education in their schools and within the school district by pupils, school administrators, and the community. They seem to understand the importance of their roles as teacher educators in handing on their beliefs and practices to the next generation of teachers, and each approaches this responsibility with awareness, enthusiasm, and commitment. They seem confident in their personal, professional competence and talked to me about the accomplishments of their programs, their graduates, and even their student teachers with some pride. In the constant busyness of their jobs with pupils, in curriculum development, and in the evaluation of student progress, as teacher educators and also as family and community members, no one mentioned a concern for looking at different ways of doing things. These cooperating teachers express their beliefs about teaching practice with confidence, authority, and satisfaction, and they seem to remain largely uncritical in nature of current practices. Perhaps it is because there is too little time, need, or incentive for practising teachers to look at practice from an alternative framework or maybe it is because their work as teachers is validated by the student teachers who willingly and unquestioningly replicate their practice.

That cooperating teachers are satisfied with their practice comes as no surprise. They have been recognized for their beliefs, values, and practices by school administrators (who select them to be cooperating teachers), parents, pupils, and the community who provide daily feedback; they have been raised and found success in the structures of their social and educational environment; they have had experiences throughout their lives that reward their work as teachers. They work in the roles that are created for them within a limited range of narratives that they hear, see, and experience, and these seem to be the only future roles available to them (Corson, 1995). In developing intensive, professional relationships with their student teachers during the practicum, they pass on the traditional and accepted narratives.

The student teachers in this first class of the new millennium continue to come from traditional backgrounds (McIntyre & Byrd, 1996; Townsend, 1995) and traditional student teaching settings, and they seem to readily accept, participate, find success in, and value the traditional narratives of teaching that they experience in the schools. In developing a teacher identity, it is easiest for them to reproduce what they observe in their cooperating teachers because it relates to what they remember as pupils in schools. Their one-on-one intensive work with their cooperating teachers is an exceptionably powerful instructional tool. As one peels away the layers in learning to teach during the preservice program, one readily sees that the process of learning to teach becomes complicated by the varying and sometimes conflicting beliefs of a triumvirate of critical persons:

1. by the student teacher's recollections of teaching, their preconceptions of teaching, their current beliefs, and primarily by their powerful one-on-one experiences with their cooperating teachers;
2. by the university teacher educator's research into teaching, their emergent beliefs and the way in which they develop their curriculum in university pedagogy courses; and,

3. by the cooperating teacher's beliefs and practices, as well as the pervasive ideologies of the educational system.

The question to be asked is "Will these teachers of the new millennium merely replicate throughout their careers the teaching practices passed on to them, or will they practise these views of learning and then, with experience, confidence and some comfort, will they attend to seeking out the change that may be needed in the next generation of schooling?"

It seems apparent from this study that student teachers and cooperating teachers (and perhaps university faculty too) have similar entrenched beliefs and practices about teaching and learning, and these practices tend to be reinforced and legitimated in the practicum setting. It appears that the cooperating teachers' value systems outweigh and influence the developing values and concomitant emerging identities of student teachers as teachers and give weight to the long-held assumption that cooperating teachers have a great deal of influence or power over the practices of their student teachers and in reinforcing the beliefs that their student teachers bring to learning about teaching. These cooperating teachers were articulate about the role they play as significant teacher educators. They are aware of their importance in novice development and they are proud of the role they play in legitimizing and passing on the ways and means of schooling to the next generation of teachers. This legitimation provides a confirming sense of their authority in the educational system through their past practices and helps to ensure that this practice of experience will be taken up by the next generation of teachers.

Certainly the success of student teaching as a critical component of preservice teacher education in the past cannot be argued. But, what we have learned in this study certainly provides challenges for future teachers, policymakers, and teacher educators as we embark into a new millennium where we continue to experience radical and complex change. Such findings might lead us to believe that there is no hope for change in the educational system in general or for any change to be effected in developing state-of-the-art music education programs in schools in the next century. While this is probably more than less an accurate perception, we must realize that change is slow and time consuming and cannot be merely mandated. Eisner (1992) says that "one thing is clear. It is much easier to change educational policy than to change the ways in which schools function. Schools are robust institutions whose very robustness provides a source of social stability" (p. 610). But, we are left with hope if we recall comments made by teachers like Warren and Laura, who now see the significance of their earlier learning in teacher education that they had previously dismissed as unimportant and irrelevant. As long as teachers' minds are open to ongoing learning, perhaps it is unreasonable to place the weight of change in the new millennium immediately on the shoulders of the newest teachers. They must be allowed to try, become somewhat comfortable, then take some risks after a few years of experience if they are to develop and effect a changed system. Then, they might be most willing, able, and in the best position to recreate the educational system.

## References

Apple, M. (1982). *Education and power.* Boston, MA: Routledge.

Bourdieu, P. (1977). *Outline of theory and practice.* London: Cambridge University Press.

Britzman, D. P. (1991). *Practice makes practice.* Albany, NY: SUNY Press.

Corson, D. (1995). *Discourse and power in educational organizations.* Toronto: OISE Press.

Eisner, E. (1992). Educational reform and the ecology of schooling. *Teachers College Record, 93,* 610–627.

Enz, B. J., Freeman, D. J., & Wallin, M. B. (1996). Making sense of teaching and learning: A case study of mentor and beginning teacher problem solving. In D. J. McIntyre & D. M. Byrd (Eds.) *Preparing tomorrow's teachers: The field experience* (pp. 115–130). Thousand Oaks, CA: Corwin Press.

Feiman-Nemser, S., & Buchmann, M. (1987). When is student teaching teacher education? *Teaching and Teacher Education, 3,* 255–273.

Guyton, E., & McIntyre, D. J. (1990). Student teaching and school experiences. In W. R. Houston (Ed.), *A handbook of research on teacher education* (pp. 514–534). Toronto: Macmillan.

Holmes Group. (1986). *Tomorrow's teachers: A report of the Holmes group.* East Lansing, MI: The Holmes Group.

Knowles, G., & Cole, A., with Presswood, N. (1994). *Through preservice teachers' eyes: Exploring field experiences through narrative and inquiry.* Toronto: Macmillan.

Lortie, D. (1975). *Schoolteacher: A sociological study.* Chicago, IL: University of Chicago Press.

Luke, A. (1995). Text and discourse in education: An introduction to critical discourse analysis. In M. W. Apple (Ed.), *Review of Research in Education, 1995–1996,* (Vol. 21, pp. 3–48). Washington, DC: American Educational Research Association.

McIntyre, D. J., & Byrd, D. M. (Eds.). (1996). *Preparing tomorrow's teachers: The field experience.* Thousand Oaks, CA: Corwin Press.

Metcalf, K. K., & Kahlich, P. A. (1996). Laboratory experiences as transition form campus to field. In D. J. McIntyre & D. M. Byrd (Eds.) *Preparing tomorrow's teachers: The field experience* (pp. 97–114). Thousand Oaks, CA: Corwin Press.

Pinnegar, S. (1995). (Re)experiencing student teaching. In T. Russell & F. Korthagen (Eds.), *Teachers who teach teachers* (pp. 56-69). London: Falmer Press.

Shulman, L. S. (1987). Knowledge and teaching: Foundations of new reform. *Harvard Educational Review 57*, 1–22.

Townsend, R. G. (1995). How a few politicians and managers of education find policy success and happiness. In K. Leithwood (Ed.) *Effective school district leadership* (pp. 135–181). Albany, NY: SUNY Press.

---

[1]All names are pseudonyms.

[2] Each year in my first class with my aspiring secondary school music teachers, I ask them why they are taking my course — a compulsory music pedagogy course specifically designed to prepare them to become high school music teachers. Every year, at least half of the class reflects on their own high school music teachers and they comment emphatically about the impact that this one music teacher had on them in choosing their course of study in university and their career. They see themselves carrying on that tradition for their pupils.

[3]The question has to be asked: What does it mean to engage students? Does it mean that learning must be occurring or does it mean that student teachers have only to keep pupils' attention without attending to the learning at hand?

# Chapter Six

# Elementary School Music
## Reflections for the Future

*Amanda Montgomery*

Music education during the early years provides an important foundation for children's musical development. Much of the groundwork for musicianship is established in these years through experiences with rote singing, improvisation, movement response, instrumental play, and reading and writing of music notation. These early explorations stimulate the building of a personal musical framework through which children filter all musical encounters later in life.

For many Canadians, elementary school music serves as the only formal music education before entering adulthood. Quality music classes in the critical preschool years are limited across the country. In addition, school music in most provinces becomes an elective rather than a required subject in the curriculum after grade six. Although private music instruction attempts to fill the gap, its access is often restricted by the financial resources of individual families. Indeed by default, teachers of elementary school music often find themselves in the position of having to play a heightened role in the process of nurturing children's musical growth.

Historically, music instruction in Canada became a part of the elementary school curricula as early as 1846. Egerton Ryerson — first Superintendent of Education in Canada West prescribed vocal music as a subject for the elementary grades in the Common School Act (Ryerson, 1853). Justifications included comments regarding the social and moral benefits for students studying music, all extra-musical aims that had little to do with music's intrinsic value (Green & Vogan, 1991).

Such generalized explanations have continued far into the 20th century. During this period, elementary school music instruction evolved into a variety of formats. Ranging from general music classes to more performance-based experiences, teachers offered students a depth of instruction dependent upon the quality of their previous teacher training.

From the beginning, classroom teachers rather than music specialists were given the nod to teach music in Canadian public schools. As one administrator put it in British Columbia in the 1870s:

> It might be argued that all teachers have not a taste for vocal music, probably not, neither have all teachers a particular bias for English grammar or algebra, yet all are obliged to teach the former at least. With the requisite amount of application, the theory of vocal music can [also] be acquired and taught by all. (Green & Vogan, 1991, p. 95)

While the practice of using classroom teachers to teach music has not always been consistent between, or even within provinces, such teachers have continued to be responsible for much of the elementary music instruction in this country.

Unfortunately, fulfilling music requirements has not always been easy for classroom teachers. Indeed, minimal university preservice training in music has made many of them feel uncomfortable with the process of teaching music (Krehbiel, 1990; Barry, 1992; Brown, 1993; Vandenberg, 1993; Montgomery, 1994, 1995a, 1995b). As Bressler (1993) reported: "They [classroom teachers] perceived music instruction as requiring special skills, special language, and pedagogical practice they did not have" (p. 5). This feeling of inadequacy has only increased during the last 30 to 40 years as specialized approaches such as Kodály and Orff began to influence Canadian music education practice (Montgomery, 1995b).

Many classroom teachers have attempted to reconcile these challenges by offering modest music curricula consisting of a little singing with the piano or simply listening to recordings. Others have relegated music in their classrooms primarily to servicing other subject areas (Bresler, 1993), while some have gone to the extreme of offering only a token music curriculum of minimal time allotments each week (Amen 1982; Smith, 1985; Verrastro & Leglar, 1990). The unfortunate consequence for children has been the great discrepancy in music curricula that exists between elementary classrooms across Canada. Children have often been at the mercy of an individual teacher's psychological comfort regarding music. In addition, individual school's financially based decisions to place specialists only in the upper elementary grades has left a terrible musical void in the lives of many younger children. Given the critical role played by elementary music education in the artistic lives of children, this situation has become alarming.

A few classroom teachers have been lucky enough to teach in school boards where their discomfort and lack of preparation in music was enhanced through the support of specialized music consultants. These consultants have supplied a variety of services for the classroom teacher including supervising their music lessons on a weekly or monthly basis, facilitating curriculum design and evaluation, and supplying musical materials and resources to the classroom. Unfortunately, during the 1980s, many boards found it necessary due to financial restraints to drop music consultants from their support staff. As we enter the year 2000, such supervision is extremely rare in Canada and has left the classroom teacher with little if any auxiliary music assistance. It may be frightening to see what happens to elementary music education in the future if classroom teachers continue to shoulder the majority of the elementary music teaching while surviving with only minimal training and support for their music responsibilities.

Although some school boards in Canada have recognized the value of hiring trained music specialists to offer kindergarten to grade six music instruction in their elementary schools, this policy has not always been a guarantee for success. Certainly such elementary teachers have received more in-depth training in music and conceivably are prepared to offer a more comprehensive curricula in music education than their classroom teacher counterparts. One might conclude that such programs, delivered by music specialists, would include a variety of musical experiences that would engage children in a dynamic learning process.

In reality, such diversity and breadth in music curriculum has been limited. Research indicates the activity of singing tended to play the central role in many elementary music classes (Walter, 1969; Shand, 1982; Montgomery, 1990). Time allotments to the other activities have varied depending on a variety of factors including (1) grade level of the class, (2) years of teaching experience, (3) in-service training, (4) school location, (5) preservice education, or (6) methodological preference (Moore, 1981; Amen, 1982; Montgomery, 1990; Ratliff, 1991). In addition, specialist teachers surveyed in Alberta reported that pressures to give public performances were so great (e.g., from administrators, parents, etc.), that they had little choice but to concentrate on preparation of concert music during classroom time. This increase in performance preparation inevitably eroded curricular time that might have been spent developing a broad foundation for children's musicianship (Montgomery, 1995b).

Pedagogical competition between "Orff" and "Kodály" teachers may also have contributed to narrowness in practice. Many Canadian elementary music teachers in the last twenty years have found it all too comforting to label themselves according to their pedagogical preference. Rather than be guided by the inherent value of both influential teaching approaches, these teachers have been inclined to become "champions" of their own personal choice in the methodology war.

What this competitiveness has meant in classroom practice has of course been quite diverse, but the act of labeling has led many teachers into an unnecessary role of pedagogical defensiveness. Caught in the web of competition, some teachers were encouraged to reproduce learning structures intact with little or no modification to individual classroom situations. Although experience has indicated that both approaches offer extraordinary potential for nurturing children towards a distinct aspect of musical knowing, neither can be used in isolation without limiting the child's depth of musical encounters (Montgomery, 1997).

Ideally, elementary music education should help children develop personal meaning out of sound. Whether encountering a nursery song, a symphony movement, or a dirge played on a didgeridoo, children need to learn to think about, and understand, the musical sounds they encounter. Understanding, or musical knowing, comes from active engagement with music. Musical exploring, performing, improvising, reflecting, analyzing, and creating are all activities associated with such engagement. Each plays an important role in the curriculum process of helping children move towards strong musical growth.

Contemporary elementary music practice guided by such goals can be said to be grounded in three principles of instruction. Research suggests each as being critical for success in elementary music teaching and learning (Zimmerman, 1993). These principles are:

1. Music learning should proceed in a sound before symbol process.
2. Music learning should involve hands-on exploration of the structure of music through multiple perspectives.

3. Music learning proceeds most effectively when the content, activities, and skills are sequenced in an easy to complex learning order that matches students' cognitive, psychomotor, and socioemotional developmental levels.

These learning principles may be viewed as frameworks through which teachers develop individual instructional practice. Each serves as both a starting point and an evaluative lens through which quality elementary music education may be judged. As Eisner (1985) states: "[T]heory is not to be regarded as prescriptive but as suggestive. It is a framework, a tool, a means through which the world [of teaching] can be construed" (p. 178). Thus, teachers can make quite diverse pedagogical choices while still maintaining the integrity of these learning principles.

The first principle, sound before symbol, allows children to experience music aurally before labeling and reading its symbolic representation. In Canada, such emphasis can be traced back to Pestalozzi, a 19th century Swiss educator who advocated children's instruction beginning with stimulation of the senses and proceeding in step-by-step practice to theoretical understanding (Pestalozzi, 1800/1898). Pestalozzi's influence was brought to this country by early 19th century music teachers and their later 20th century counterparts. Similar to the way many cultures around the world start the music learning process, research indicates sound before symbol is a powerful tool for nurturing children towards musical understanding (Zimmerman, 1991).

Sound before symbol provides children with a developmentally appropriate three-step process for experiencing music: (1) aural encounter with music, (2) verbal and visual labeling of music, and (3) recognition of visual symbols and translation into appropriate musical response. Through this process, children develop an active knowledge of music and its parts which leads them closer to the goal of personal musical understanding. How long a teacher should spend on each of the three steps logically depends on the age and experience of the children. Younger children (K–2) need considerably more experiences organized around the aural stage of learning since most are at the beginning of their encounters with sound structures. Older elementary school children, building upon a larger repertoire of musical sounds, might need fewer aural experiences leaving more time for in-depth development during symbolic response.

The second learning principle suggests musical meaning comes from hands-on experience with music and its structural parts. Quality elementary music education, then, places musical concepts at the core of the musical learning process, utilizing a variety of musical activities through which to explore these concepts. According to many psychologists, concept formation involves organizing, categorizing, and labeling perceptions into meaningful cognitive structures. In music, these cognitive structures, or musical concepts, provide children with personalized mental organizational units needed to expand their knowledge and understanding of the complexities of musical elements (e.g., rhythm, melody, timbre, etc.). As children encounter new, similar, or different aspects of music, their existing concepts are stretched and modified into new mental units which are subsequently used to help make sense of music during future experiences.

Providing students with a variety of curricular experiences such as singing, improvising, moving, playing instruments, creating, analyzing, and reflecting places an emphasis on musical structure in the elementary music curricula that can help children make personal sense of the musical sounds in their world. As Davidson and Scripp (1992) suggest, "Through activity, discrimination, and thoughtful observation, multiple perspectives of the same event or object are generated, differentiated from one another, and during reconsideration, integrated into a new and more comprehensive understanding" (p. 400). Thus, multiple exploration with musical concepts is integral to the development of personal musical knowing.

The third principle indicates that developmentally appropriate choices in content, skills, and activities have tremendous impact on the whole child and therefore merit constant consideration in the curriculum. Indeed, a major determinant of curriculum quality is the extent to which knowledge of child (i.e., cognitive, psychomotor, social, emotional, and spiritual) and music development are applied to instructional practice. Beginning attempts at such application is evident in the early Pestalozzian music education practices of Nageli and Pfeifer (1810). Here educators organized their curriculum content into a simple-to-complex teaching order. In addition, it was recommended that each step or musical exercise be completed before moving on to the next. So much so, in fact, that teachers were trained not to move on to a new task until at least 70% of the children had mastered the previous one (Keene, 1982). We can only guess at the potential dullness of such regulated repetition. However, Pestalozzi and his colleagues must be remembered as important pioneers of the sequencing of music instruction for children.

The evolution of sequencing in Canadian elementary music education can often be traced to promoting curriculum objectives rather than to an attempt to meet children's developmental needs. The predominance of music reading goals in curricula at the turn of the 20th century, for example, prompted educators to sequence content in an order that facilitated growth in appropriate psychomotor skills. Whatever the method applied (e.g., tonic solfa, note names, etc.), content was sequenced according to easy-to-complex rhythmic and melodic patterns as these contributed to the development of reading music. Little thought was given to selecting or sequencing music in relation to children's cognitive or socioemotional needs. Even when the writings of Hall (1906) (child study movement) and Dewey (1934) (progressive education), began to affect content by influencing teachers to replace singing exercises with children's rote songs (the song method), sequencing continued to be related mostly to psychomotor development. Although some attempts were made to select and sequence repertoire that would be of interest to children, most repertoire was contrived and musically repetitious (Green & Vogan, 1991). Few of these songs could really be called "children's songs" as they bore little relation to the natural chants and singing games of early childhood. The result, of course, was that content selection and sequencing continued to be less than successful at meeting children's cognitive and socioemotional developmental needs.

The importance of the Kodály and Orff approaches for directing Canadian elementary music teachers' consciousness toward the need to meet children's complete developmental needs in music learning cannot be underestimated. Curricula developed from these instructional practices have most often utilized materials that were developmentally appropriate both from a psychomotor (e.g., vocal range, rhythmic structure, etc.) and socioemotional perspective. The use of repertoire such as chants, rhymes, singing games, and so on, truly reflected an attempt to involve children with learning materials that were child-centered. Further, sequences for movement activities were based on knowledge of children's physical development. Although musical concepts were sequenced to reflect individual goals for musical achievement (i.e., Kodály: music reading and writing; Orff: music improvisation and creativity) each approach should be viewed as excellent examples of elementary music curriculum involving sequencing that attempts to meet the cognitive, psychomotor, and socioemotional needs of children (Montgomery, 1993).

Today, any number of teaching sequences exist to guide instruction. Provincial curriculum guides, published series texts, and elementary music method books all contribute to our knowledge about developmentally appropriate sequencing. Inevitably many elementary music teachers have taken the route of simply leaving their curriculum planning to these external forces. Teachers have adopted prescribed sequencing intact with little modification according to individual classroom situations. Although the complexity of current classrooms makes planning time harder to come by (King & Peart, 1992), according to Eisner (1985) "the role of the teacher in curriculum decision making is important because the teacher serves as the interpreter of educational policy and because the teacher is the major mediator of what shall be taught — if not learned — in the classroom" (p. 129). It seems likely that external sources such as curriculum guides or series texts should be viewed only as starting points for curricular decisions since teachers need to modify, stretch, and redirect prescribed content/sequencing in order to make it more appropriate for the unique population of children they teach. Indeed, elementary music teachers need to be reminded that they should *teach children music*, not teach music to children. Thus, successful learning in the elementary music class is dependent on teachers playing an active role in the curricular decision-making process of their individual classrooms.

So how do we make all this learning happen in the 21st century? Well, I believe one of the major answers is staring us squarely in the face. As a profession we must renew with great vigor the 150-year-old fight to place music specialists in *every* elementary school in Canada. We can't let ourselves get discouraged or even sidetracked by the financial setbacks of the last decade. If we truly believe that elementary music education should provide students with a curriculum that heightens their personal sense of musical meaning, then we must utilize trained music specialists who have the expertise to create and implement viable curriculum.

Experiences in the 20th century have only reinforced our understanding that classroom teachers simply don't have the time, energy, or musical and pedagogical knowledge to design and ensure a quality elementary music program. Why is it that after several generations of children in this country we still have a population of adults with little musical knowledge? We seem to be in a vicious circle that allows unqualified classroom teachers to continue to pass on their illegitimate musical knowledge to the next generation. What with the increasing complexity of the 21st century classroom, it is very clear that music specialists have the best chance at bringing our educational goals of a musically literate society into concrete reality.

Unfortunately, the job ahead will involve more than just renewal of our various advocacy attempts with the local, regional, and provincial powers that be. We can't expect our campaign to lobby for specialists in every school to produce results quickly, as the battle for music specialists has already been waged for many years. Parallel to our continuing the fight, then, we must not forget the lives of the children who will be greatly affected by the preservice classroom teachers currently in teacher education programs across the country. We must somehow ensure that these teachers receive the best music education possible in order to help children move towards the goal of positive musical growth.

Given the limited time-frame of most classroom teachers' music method courses, it seems imperative to determine what can and cannot be done during this compact amount of time. The practice in the past has been for universities to provide these preservice students with simplified versions of specialist methods courses. Curriculum usually consisted of time spent partly on the fundamentals of music notation plus various pedagogical advice on teaching music.

I believe it makes more sense for universities to design curricula that heighten the classroom teacher's beginning musical sense. Since research indicates that musical learning with children proceeds most effectively in a sound before symbol environment, why not concentrate on this aural stage of musical learning in the classroom teacher's university music method class. At least if we can prepare classroom teachers to deliver a viable aural curriculum in music, children will be better prepared for encountering musical symbols at a later stage in their musical development. This argument does not imply that symbolic interaction is not important for elementary school children, only that it would be better for the classroom teacher to teach some part of music education well rather than all parts badly.

This solution must of course only be temporary, as the goal should always be to move towards a point in Canadian history when classroom teachers will no longer be in a position to muddy the waters. Certainly the partnership possibilities that could be forged between specialists and generalists in nurturing the musical lives of children could be exciting. We just need to find the most positive way to keep going until we reach that moment.

Certainly the teacher education of music specialists must also be examined. The current practice of offering Kodály and Orff courses as separate methodological components in university preservice training could continue to promote the divisiveness that exists between proponents of these approaches. As both share the belief in the sound before symbol learning process, the importance of centering instruction around musical structure, and the need to sequence content, skills, and activities according to children's developmental needs, it might make more sense to offer a combined university method course that teaches how to include Kodály and Orff teaching strategies into a broader sound before symbol elementary music curriculum. Certainly musical experience with reading and writing music (Kodály) and creative performance with percussion instruments (Orff) are part of musical knowing. However, preservice teachers need to be encouraged to develop sound before symbol pedagogies that provide children with multiple perspectives of music. In addition, the musical sounds in 21$^{st}$ century children's lives most likely will be quite diverse. Thus, music content as well as experiential practice should be reflective of this reality.

All in all, the future is hopeful. If we can stand firm in our belief that elementary music education can, and should have a strong impact on children's musical development then our goal is clear. Our road to accomplishing this task may take several unexpected twists and turns, but our focus need never dim. All parts of the elementary music teaching process — the curriculum, teacher education, and music specialists — need to work together for success. I am confident we are up for the challenge because our commitment to Canadian children will require nothing less.

## References

Amen, B. (1982). *The effect of selected factors on the time spent teaching music by elementary classroom teachers.* Unpublished doctoral dissertation, Indiana University, Bloomington.

Barry, N. H. (1992). Music and education in the elementary music method class. *Journal of Research in Music Education, 39,* 248–61.

Bresler, L. (1993). Music in a double-bind. Instruction by non-specialists in elementary schools. *Bulletin of the Council for Research in Music Education, 115,* 1–13.

Brown, E. 1993). *Elementary music education curricula in public schools in Canada.* Unpublished doctoral dissertation, Northwestern University, Chicago.

Davidson, L., & Scripp, L. (1992). Surveying the coordinates of cognitive skills in music. In R. Colwell (Ed.), *Handbook of research on music teaching and learning* (pp. 392–413). New York: Schirmer Books.

Dewey, J. (1934). *Art as experience.* New York: Minton, Balch, & Company.

Eisner, E. (1985). *The educational imagination: On the design and evaluation of school programs.* New York: Macmillan.

Green, P., & Vogan, N. (1991). *Music education in Canada: A historical account.* Toronto: University of Toronto Press.

Hall, S. (1906). *Youth.* New York: Appleton.

Keene, J. (1982). *A history of music education in the United States.* London: University Press of New England.

King, A., & Peart, M. (1992). *Teachers in Canada: Their work and quality of life.* Ottawa, ON: Canadian Teachers Federation.

Krehbiel, H. (1990). *Illinois fine arts: Elementary classroom teachers perceptions of music instruction.* Unpublished doctoral dissertation, University of Illinois, Urbana-Champaign, Indiana.

Montgomery, A. (1990). The effect of selected factors on the use of instructional time by elementary music specialists in Atlantic Canada. *Canadian Journal of Research in Music Education, 32* ( 3), 48–61.

Montgomery, A. (1993). Professional development: Is it closer than you think? *Ostinato: National Journal of Orff Canada, 20* (1), 20–22.

Montgomery, A. (1994). Competencies in music teaching for the elementary grades. *Canadian Journal of Research in Music Education, 35* (4), 25-35.

Montgomery, A. (1995a). The importance of music teaching competencies as rated by elementary classroom teachers & university methods instructors. *Canadian Journal of Research in Music Education, 36* (7), 19–26.

Montgomery, A. (1995b). Training Canadian Kodály educators for the year 2000. *Alla Breve: National Journal of the Kodály Society of Canada, 25* (3), 3–8.

Montgomery, A. (1997). Orff or Kodály: What's all the fuss? *Canadian Music Educator, 39* (1), 11–13.

Moore, R. (1981). Comparative use of teaching time by American and British music specialists. *Bulletin of the Council for Research in Music Education, 66,* 62–68.

Nageli, H., & Pfeifer, M. (1810). *Method of teaching singing according to Pestalozzian Principles.* London, UK: Sonnesheim.

Pestalozzi, J. (1898). *How Gertrude teaches her children* (E. Cooke, Ed.). London: Sonnenshein. (Original work published 1800)

Ratliff, N. (1991). *Selected factors and their influence on the Kodály elementary general music teachers allocation of instructional time.* Unpublished doctoral dissertation, Indiana University, Bloomington, Indiana.

Ryerson, E. (1853). *The Common School Acts of Upper Canada and the forms and regulations for executing their provisions.* Toronto: Lovell & Gibson.

Shand, P. (1982). Part I: The status of music education in Canada. *Canadian Music Educator, 23* (3), 18–30.

Smith, A. (1985). *An evaluation of music teacher competencies identified by the Florida Music Educators Association and teacher assessment of undergraduate preparation to demonstrate those competencies.* Unpublished doctoral dissertation, Florida State University, Tallahassee.

Vandenberg, G. C. (1993). *Northern California classroom teachers perceptions of their preparation to teach music in grades 2–5.* Unpublished doctoral dissertation, University of San Francisco, San Francisco, California.

Verrastro, R. & Leglar, M. (1992). Music teacher education. In R. Colwell (Ed.), *Handbook of research on music teaching and learning* (pp. 676–696). New York: Schirmer Books.

Walter, A. (1969). The growth of music education in Canada. In A. Walter (Ed.), *Aspects of Music in Canada* (pp. 300–326). Toronto: University of Toronto Press.

Zimmerman, M. (1991). Psychological theory and music learning. In R. Colwell (Ed.), *Basic Concepts in Music Education II* (pp. 175–174 ). Niwot, CO: University Press.

Zimmerman, M. (1993). An overview of developmental research in music. *Bulletin of the Council for Research in Music Education, 116,* 1–17.

# Chapter Seven

# Music for *All* Canadians
## Dream or Reality at the High School Level

*Mary Kennedy*

## Prologue: Setting the Scene

To say that educational curricula and specifically music education curricula in Canada are in a state of flux would be a gross understatement. Province after province, in a seemingly never-ending stream of activity, is revising and reworking music and fine arts curricular documents. Some recent examples of high school music courses will help clarify the scene.[1] British Columbia has recently completed its *Music 8–10* (British Columbia Ministry of Education, 1995), *Fine Arts 11* (British Columbia Ministry of Education, 1995), and *Music 11–12: Composition and Technology* (British Columbia Ministry of Education, 1996) integrated resource packages. The remaining grade 11 and 12 music courses have yet to be revised. Alberta has a new general music 10, 20, 30 program of studies (Alberta Education, 1993). Saskatchewan recently introduced a revised *Band 10, 20, 30* (Saskatchewan Education, 1993*), Choral 10, 20, 30,* (Saskatchewan Education, 1997), and an *Integrated Arts Education 10, 20, 30* curriculum (Saskatchewan Education, 1996). Ontario has just released its new music 1 to 8 (Ontario Ministry of Education and Training, 1998) and 9–10 curriculum documents (Ontario Ministry of Education and Training, 1999). The 11 and 12 music documents are in progress. Nova Scotia presented its *Foundation for Arts Education Validation Document* at the 2nd National Symposium of Arts Education held in Victoria in August, 1998. Newfoundland and Labrador produced both *Intermediate*

*Curriculum* and *Ensemble Performance 10, 11, and 12* documents (Newfoundland & Labrador Department of Education, 1993). Still, the work continues as arts educators, curriculum writers, and education ministry personnel attempt to keep pace with current educational trends, demands from public and professional lobby groups, and the visions of students, teachers, and parents.

Recent initiatives generated by the National Symposium for Arts Education have helped raise the profile of music and arts education in Canadian schools. First, the three symposia have increased communication among fine arts educators and ministry personnel from a number of provinces. The mere fact that Anne Hill, Fine Arts Coordinator for British Columbia Ministry of Education, could make available to me the names of fine arts coordinators in other provinces is evidence of this increased communication. Second, the symposium steering committee has as one of its goals the development of a shared vision for arts education document which will be distributed nationally. Such a document will most certainly help arts advocacy groups at both provincial and local levels. Third, the cross-pollination of curriculum documents evident, for example, in the new Nova Scotia *Dance Curriculum* (Nova Scotia Department of Education and Culture, 1999) which credits both British Columbia and Saskatchewan dance curriculum writers for content, can only serve to enhance and strengthen the cause of arts education across the country as shared wisdom percolates through present and future curriculum documents. The recent coming together of arts educators at the national symposia has helped foster this cross pollination and shared wisdom.

Given the foregoing account of contemporary curricular renewal in arts education, it might be tempting to conclude that the arts, and, in particular, music have made significant inroads into Canadian public school programs at the high school level. Sadly, this is not the case. While gains have been made through the implementation of a fine arts graduation requirement in British Columbia, Saskatchewan, and Nova Scotia,[2] arts education courses remain largely elective at the secondary level. Thus it is altogether possible for a student to travel through grades 7–12 with no exposure to the fine arts at all. A poignant portrait is presented by Thompson (1999) who reports on the current situation in Ontario:

> At this point I must mention the sad fact that the York Region Separate School Board has had to cut most music programs in the schools due to

lack of funds. Only two or three Separate High Schools have band programs at the present time; elementary schools only provide music classes if and when someone of the staff or even senior students have a special interest in music which they try to pass on in their own time. (p. 39)

As Thompson reports, lack of funds can eliminate programs, but so can lack of interest. Elective courses are subject to the minimum numbers game; thus a course in which fewer than the minimum number of students are enroled (often this number is 10) will be cancelled. Music teachers are forever needing to attract students through enticing course outlines, engaging activities, and exotic field trips.

## Problem: The Missing Music Students

So the present situation in Canada is that only a small percentage of high school students is involved in arts education.[3] Of that small number, an even smaller percentage is enrolled in music education courses. Why? As has already been noted, music courses at the secondary level are largely elective. Students enroll on the basis of interest and/or advice of parents and guidance counsellors. The advice of these adults is subject to influences from institutions for higher learning that often do not use marks in non-examinable subjects to calculate the entrance grade point average (GPA)[4] and also from society itself and the value it places on music and the arts. Exploring this avenue of inquiry yields some useful insights.

It is a well-known fact that many scholars have professed a belief in the universality of musical behavior. Blacking (1973) writes: "There is so much music in the world that it is reasonable to suppose that music, like language and possibly religion, is a species-specific trait of man" (p. 7). Blacking developed his theory after living with and studying the Venda people of South Africa for a period of two years during the 1950s. He observed that all Venda citizens participate in musical activities from an early age. Some are considered more skilled than others, but all are involved musically. Aiello (1994) agrees that "music and language are universal, innate expressions of human cognition and communication. Their universality is evident in the fact that all cultures express themselves verbally and musically" (p. 41). Campbell (1998) makes reference to the musical potential of young people. She writes: "All children, to a greater and lesser degree, are musical. In fact, I would venture to say that children probably have much more music inside them than we tend to credit them with" (p. 169). However, Campbell's statement and the views of Blacking, Aiello, and many others, run counter to a pervasive belief operative in society today — namely that the populus is divided between the musical "haves" and "have-nots." There are those who are perceived to be musically talented or gifted, and they are thought to be a special breed, set apart from the rest. One is either born with musical talent or one is not. According to Hanley (1989), some secondary music courses exacerbate this misconception.

> Often described as elitist, performance programs contribute to the belief that music can only be practised by the talented and that music is a mystery to be fully enjoyed only by the chosen few, thereby questioning whether music should be taught in the schools at all or should be left to the conservatories who specialize in producing performers. (p. 59)

Hanley proposes to rectify this situation by advocating the adoption of a general music model — or inclusive music courses designed for all students. She contends this is the best course of action to both challenge the beliefs and practice of music education and to address the needs of all secondary music students.[5] Hanley's call for secondary general music courses a decade ago has been realized in the crafting of revised Canadian music curriculum documents. Recent junior high music curricula in British Columbia and Ontario have favored a general music model while Alberta has designed a grade 10, 11, and 12 general music course.

But do curriculum documents really influence teacher practice and pupil enrolment? Just what is the status of secondary fine arts enrolment in Canada? How does music enrolment fare when compared with that of other fine arts subjects? I was able to secure enrolment statistics from four provinces: British Columbia, Alberta, Saskatchewan, and Nova Scotia. I was interested in determining the numbers of students enrolled in the various fine arts subjects at the secondary level. As the reports from each province varied in details, I decided to compare total head-count numbers in the three (or four) fine arts disciplines for the academic year 1996–97. Some surprising information emerged (see Table 1).

As you can see, in three of the four provinces, enrolment in visual arts exceeds that in music. In British Columbia, drama is slightly ahead of music as well. Tsisserev (1997) examined the British Columbia secondary fine arts enrolment figures over the ten-year period (1982-1993) and concluded that:

among the arts subjects in the school curriculum, the most popular subject in the last decade was the visual arts.... In 1982, music was in second place...and drama was in third place.... A decade later, however, enrolment choices had changed dramatically. Drama increased...while music decreased..., thereby becoming the least popular arts course. (p. 12)

**Table 1. Number of students enroled in the fine arts in four provinces in 1996–97**

| Province | Grades | Discipline | No. of Students |
|---|---|---|---|
| British Columbia | 8-12 | Dance | 400 |
| | | Drama | 28, 168 |
| | | Music | 28, 130 |
| | | Visual Arts | 48, 695 |
| Alberta | 10–12 | Drama | 12, 223 |
| | | Music | 12, 752 |
| | | Visual Arts | 20, 523 |
| Saskatchewan | 10-12 | Drama | 4, 031 |
| | | Music | 7, 322 |
| | | Visual Arts | 9, 147 |
| Nova Scotia | 7-12 | Drama | 2, 393 |
| | | Music | 20, 774 |
| | | Visual Arts | 9, 416 |

While we must be cautious about forming conclusions based upon evidence from fewer than half of the country's provinces, still the numbers presented cause us to ponder the reasons for visual arts' seeming ascendancy in three of four provinces considered. Could it be that visual art courses, by their very nature, encourage a student's creative impulse thus providing an appealing outlet for adolescent individualism and egocentrism? Tsisserev (1997) suggests this possibility and advocates for the institution of more secondary music composition courses to meet the creative needs not addressed in music performance courses. Could it be that, in British Columbia at least, students are most often fulfilling the fine arts/applied skills 11 course requirement by taking 2 credits of visual arts and 2 credits of computers? Anne Hill thinks that this is largely the case. In a conversation with me, she explained that at present it is rare for teachers to construct a locally developed course that would address the stated outcomes of both music and applied skills. More teachers can see ways of melding visual arts and computers into a neat 4-

credit course that is easy to timetable than can envision other possibilities and combinations. She worries, however, that such a course does not always fulfill the learning outcomes of the *Fine Arts 11* document (British Columbia Ministry of Education, 1995). In response to my query about the viability of combining computer music with applied skills, she stated that this combination would work well — the composition and technology course (British Columbia Ministry of Education, 1996) is available for use as the fine arts component — but that music educators have often been reticent about this approach, adopting a "don't pollute or dilute" attitude towards their courses. This attitude has discouraged cooperation between disciplines (personal communication, December 13, 1999). Whatever the reasons, the result is clear: precious few students are enrolled in secondary fine arts courses country wide, and fewer students are enrolled in music than in the visual arts in British Columbia, Alberta, and Saskatchewan. What can we do to increase secondary fine arts enrolment in general and, more specifically, what can we do about the problem of the missing music students?

## Proposal: Creative Music Education

To increase secondary fine arts enrolment in general will necessitate a continuing effort on the part of arts educators to inform, reform, and transform attitudes of administrators, parents, university personnel, ministry of education officials, and society as a whole to the point where the arts are deemed essential to education *at every level of schooling*. The National Symposium for Arts Education and the Canadian Conference of the Arts are two organizations committed to this task.

To address the problem of the missing music students, I propose to attract some of them through a two-fold strategy: (1) through the institution of composition courses at the secondary level and (2) by the incorporation of opportunities for composing into existing secondary performance courses. Surely, this is not a new idea, you may retort! Certainly you are right, I would respond. R. Murray Schafer championed the creative approach to music education in Canada nearly three decades ago. In *Creative Music Education* (1976), Schafer compiled into one volume five booklets which documented "nearly fifteen years of teaching in Canadian and American schools, universities, and summer music camps" (p. ix).

Schafer's practical and unorthodox (certainly in 1976) ways of engaging children with music making blew the windows of existing ideologies of music education wide open as teachers began to see the value of creative activities for their young charges. Soundscape pieces became a common occurrence in elementary music classrooms. I showed the National Film Board's *Bing, Bang, Boom* (National Film Board, 1969), which was based on Schafer's work with grade seven students in a Scarborough music classroom, to my grade seven and eight students for many years as an introduction to a unit on creative music making. But did this creative activity infiltrate the mainstream of junior and senior secondary music education? Is it a common occurrence today to find students creating soundscape pieces or producing individual compositions in secondary music classrooms? It is my contention that it is not. Of the four provinces whose enrolment statistics I consulted, only British Columbia listed specific courses in music composition (and this only at the grade 11 and 12 levels.)[6]

I am not saying that there is no composition taking place at the secondary level. There are examples of instrumental/choral teachers who have devised electronic music courses which attract students with a wide variety of backgrounds. These courses most easily fit into junior secondary school elective time slots. There are, moreover, examples of music teachers who are running successful composition classes at the senior secondary level. Again it is a numbers game. Administrators insist on a minimum class size for a course to be scheduled, and often, senior secondary students are squeezed out of elective courses they would like to take due to pressure from the academic side of the curriculum. There are also instrumental/choral teachers who encourage music students who seem to have a "bent" for composition by giving them opportunities to showcase their creative efforts at school concerts. These examples notwithstanding, the fact remains that present secondary music courses are largely performance-based and reach a relatively small percentage of the total student population.

I propose to widen the parameters of existing secondary music programs by (1) instituting music composition courses as part of the fine arts elective package[7] and (2) incorporating opportunities for composing into existing performance-oriented courses. It is my belief that in making space for students' individual creative expression, we will both enrich existing performance courses and attract nonperformance-oriented students to the music room.

### Support for creative music-making

The composer, Paul Creston (1971) lent support to the creative approach nearly 30 years ago:

> [I]t has always been my belief that musical composition is not for the chosen few but for every normal person; that it should be as much a part of academic studies as literary composition — not necessarily to make professional composers of everyone, as we do not intend to make authors of every student of literature, but for the joy of individual creation. There is no more effective way to learn the evaluation and enjoyment of music than through creative participation. (p. 36)

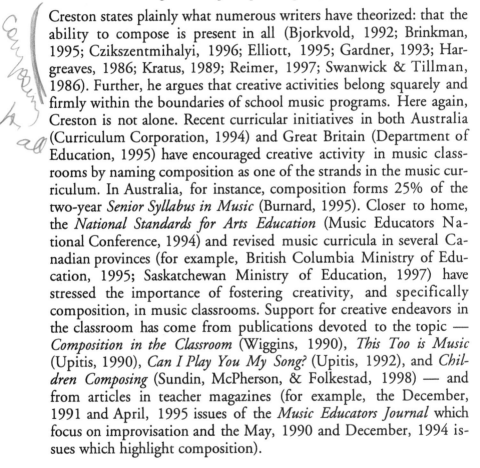

Creston states plainly what numerous writers have theorized: that the ability to compose is present in all (Bjorkvold, 1992; Brinkman, 1995; Czikszentmihalyi, 1996; Elliott, 1995; Gardner, 1993; Hargreaves, 1986; Kratus, 1989; Reimer, 1997; Swanwick & Tillman, 1986). Further, he argues that creative activities belong squarely and firmly within the boundaries of school music programs. Here again, Creston is not alone. Recent curricular initiatives in both Australia (Curriculum Corporation, 1994) and Great Britain (Department of Education, 1995) have encouraged creative activity in music classrooms by naming composition as one of the strands in the music curriculum. In Australia, for instance, composition forms 25% of the two-year *Senior Syllabus in Music* (Burnard, 1995). Closer to home, the *National Standards for Arts Education* (Music Educators National Conference, 1994) and revised music curricula in several Canadian provinces (for example, British Columbia Ministry of Education, 1995; Saskatchewan Ministry of Education, 1997) have stressed the importance of fostering creativity, and specifically composition, in music classrooms. Support for creative endeavors in the classroom has come from publications devoted to the topic — *Composition in the Classroom* (Wiggins, 1990), *This Too is Music* (Upitis, 1990), *Can I Play You My Song?* (Upitis, 1992), and *Children Composing* (Sundin, McPherson, & Folkestad, 1998) — and from articles in teacher magazines (for example, the December, 1991 and April, 1995 issues of the *Music Educators Journal* which focus on improvisation and the May, 1990 and December, 1994 issues which highlight composition).

### Instituting music composition at the secondary level

A perusal of recent Canadian secondary music curriculum documents shows the inclusion of the terms "creating," "creation," or "composition" as organizers in most courses. Whether the course is called *Music 8–10* (British Columbia), *Music 9–10* (Ontario) or *General Music, Instrumental Music, Choral Music 10, 20, 30* (Alberta), creative activities are stipulated as part of the overall curriculum. Therefore, proposing the institution of secondary music composition activities should be congruent with current Canadian educational thinking.

Music composition can form the content of an entire music course, it can be incorporated as a module within a general music syllabus, or it can be embedded within a performance-based course. Some examples and strategies follow.

*Music composition courses/modules.* Tsisserev (1997) reports that "in the 1990s, three Greater Vancouver secondary schools began to implement music composition as part of the curriculum for students in grades 10–12" (p. 20). Also in British Columbia, several Victoria area secondary schools have implemented music composition courses.[8] These British Columbia schools have used an approach to composition using MIDI technology, an approach advocated by Folkestad, Hargreaves, and Lindstrom (1998), Ladanyi (1995), and Reese (1995). Folkestad, Hargreaves, and Lindstrom and Ladanyi report on research studies conducted outside regular music classrooms. Reese describes a teacher-designed MIDI course for junior high school music students. In computer music courses, students are typically introduced to the medium, given some simple exploratory exercises to build both familiarity and confidence with the particular software being used, and then directed to complete a series of composition tasks. Students work in pairs or alone, depending on available equipment. A thoughtful teacher can tailor assignments to students' abilities and interests. Despite the fact that computers have infiltrated schools in wide numbers in recent years, a relatively small number of schools have been able to set up full-scale MIDI labs due to the forbidding cost of the equipment.[9] Therefore it is important to consider alternative avenues and media for composing.

Composition using acoustic media is documented by Bunting (1987), Burnard (1995), Dunn (1992), and Hogg (1994). In each of these examples, composition forms one element of a holistic music course. Bunting describes his work with secondary students in Britain, focussing on the compositional efforts of two fifteen-year-old boys during a period of two terms. The two boys were enrolled in a secondary music course involving performing, composing, and listening. Neither boy had any experience of music-making outside school. During the early part of the course, the boys acquired some playing skill — one chose keyboard and the other, bass guitar. Their first composition effort was, understandably, an adaptation of a bass and chord "riff" from a familiar popular song. Bunting documents the progress of the two boys over the course of the two school terms, noting both his own interventions (providing sound stimuli, specific direction at times, and feedback and suggestions for improvement) and the compositional development of the two boys.

Burnard (1995) reports on her work with eleven Year 11 (15–16 year old) students at an independent girls' school in Australia. As noted earlier, composition forms 25% of the two-year senior syllabus in music. Burnard describes four composition projects undertaken by her students over four terms of classwork. Burnard's students were privileged in that "all students could read and write musical notation and were actively involved in instrumental or vocal tuition" (p. 33). Burnard was interested in the relationship of task structure to composition effort. Consequently, the four composition tasks contained varying degrees of choice. Students were given first a prescriptive task, followed by two types of choice tasks, and finally, a freedom task. The prescriptive task was to

> write a waltz for keyboard. Your waltz should demonstrate and display a variety of nineteenth century romantic keyboard characteristics and stylistic features. It should be a minimum of 24 bars, in ternary form, and demonstrate the use of modulations. (p. 36)

In contrast, the freedom task was to "write a piece for voice(s)" (p. 36). Burnard found that her students experienced task constraints and freedom differently depending on their individual working styles, backgrounds, and self-concepts as composers. She recommends that teachers offer students different types of composition activities, incorporating both structured and nonstructured tasks.

Dunn (1992) devised a secondary music course in Britain in which she aims "to enable students to express themselves through music, just as they are expected to use the tools of language for creative writing and art materials for original work" (p. 49). Dunn begins in year 7 by sorting students for class music into three groups based on musical background alone. She justifies her approach as follows: "Pupils thus work in a group which suits the level of musical attainment they have reached, and with this possibly controversial arrangement we cope well with the different needs of the groups" (p. 50). Dunn begins work with the least experienced using strategies reminiscent of Schafer. Students work in pairs or small groups creating sound pieces without notation. Notation is introduced to these students gradually, as they learn aspects of music through improvised composition. Dunn has developed her course up to the GCSE[10] level.

Hogg (1994) conducted an ethnographic study of 43 secondary music classrooms in Australia and Britain. She was interested in determining strategies that facilitate student composition. Her observations led her to the following general conclusions: (1) composition tasks must be musical and suit student(s)' abilities; (2) there should be provision for both small group and individual composition projects; (3) teachers should strive for a balance between student self-direction and teacher intervention; (4) sufficient time should be allowed for completion of the tasks.

Although the majority of the foregoing examples are drawn from countries outside Canada, I believe they can apply equally well to current Canadian classrooms. The examples are meant to serve as pointers on how to incorporate composition activities into music courses rather than as a prescribed course of study. It is my own personal philosophy that there is no one *right* way to teach composition or, for that matter, music. What I do know, from my own experience in working through a composition unit with my grade 10 general music students[11], is that students can be both excited by the activity of composition and encouraged by appropriate feedback. In my course I made a point of inviting a local composer to hear and comment on my students' composition efforts. The students hung on his every word! One of the comments which he reserved for me alone was so telling that it is etched in my memory. Reflecting on the students' first efforts, an assignment where they had been asked to create a short piece using four timbres from the KORG M1 sound-bank, he remarked: "It's fascinating to see what the students with no musical training create. They haven't learned any rules of melody and harmony and consequently their pieces are freer — they know no bounds!" This comment alone convinces me of the necessity and viability of integrating composition activities into music courses.

From music composition courses and general music courses where a composition module is included, we turn to the second strategy: that of the introduction of composition opportunities into

performance-based courses. Since most secondary school music programs are performance-based, this option is likely to be viewed by
the reader as the most realistic one to adopt.

*Incorporating composition opportunities into performance-based
courses.* The discussion of this strategy will centre around two distinct approaches: one that involves the class as a whole and a second
that creates opportunities for individuals to compose. Examples
will be drawn from the literature and from my own research.

Kaschub (1997) describes an intriguing project in which professional composers were brought into music classes and directed to
guide group composition efforts. One of those experiments is pertinent to the discussion here. A professional composer worked with an
85 member high school choir to write both the lyrics and music for
an SATB piece. Due to limited rehearsal space and the desire to
accommodate students who wished to participate in instrumental
music as well, the choir rehearsed in two halves. Choir A rehearsed
on Monday and Wednesday, choir B on Tuesday and Thursday, and
choirs A and B met on alternate Fridays. The composer worked
with the choir each Friday. Kaschub explains:

> The project was undertaken with limited technology. Musical ideas
> were sketched and revised on a chalk board, copied down, and made into
> transparencies for the next class meeting. Students were also provided
> with photocopied handouts of the musical ideas generated in each work
> session. As ideas were posted on the board, time would be spent singing
> each idea and manipulating the musical material melodically, har-
> monically, rhythmically, and texturally. These brief explorations were
> designed to help the students understand how composers manipulate mu-
> sical ideas into larger musical units. A total of fifteen work sessions
> took place throughout the fall and winter of the year and two dress re-
> hearsals and the concert premieres of the piece in the late spring. (p. 16)

A project of this type demands both a large time commitment on
the part of the teacher and the students and the financial resources
necessary to engage the services of a professional composer. However, the benefits of such an endeavour far outweigh the drawbacks.
Students involved in such a project learn about the processes of
composition from the hand of a master; assisting music teachers are
shown how to introduce composition into their classrooms;[12] students incorporate new music into their choral repertoire; and students improve in their ability to work as a team.

A second approach involves facilitating individual student composition efforts within a performance-based secondary music course. With the exception of jazz ensembles where students are trained in improvisation techniques and are expected to improvise solos in concerts, school performance groups do not traditionally incorporate composition into their courses. My proposal would change that situation. The suggestions are based on results from a recent study in which I compared the compositional processes of a high school and a collegiate composer (Kennedy, 1999). Donna was a high school senior and Laura, a graduate composition major. Both had started composing at a young age. The following excerpt details useful strategies:

> Both Donna and Laura feel that anyone can compose music, but that, according to Donna, "you have to try!" Donna also felt that exposure and support were helpful, while Laura claimed that a "necessary interest" and "hard work" were requirements for the endeavour. Both demonstrated the process of composing as a solitary affair, practised in a state of quiet repose.... As music educators interested in cultivating the art of composition in adolescents, we can learn much from the stories of Donna and Laura.... Many modern high schools are constructed with a large music room surrounded by several smaller practice rooms, often containing pianos and/or keyboards. This would seem to be an ideal environment for nurturing high school composers. Students could work alone in the various practice rooms, taping their composing sessions if notational skills are not well developed, while the teacher circulated to assist or offer suggestions where needed. I would even venture to suggest that students without keyboard skills be encouraged to hum their melodies into a microphone so as not to interrupt the flow of musical material. Notation can be taught and the ear developed. What is most important is to keep the creative spark alight. (p. 162)

One further lesson can be drawn from the stories of Donna and Laura. Both composers referred to the therapeutic quality of composing music. "Donna suggested that it created meaning for her, helping her to 'put emotions in perspective.' Laura agreed and stated that 'making music was a way to deal with my wide emotional spectrum constructively without going crazy'" (Kennedy 1999, p. 163). I do not mean to imply that composing music is the only route to psychological wholeness. However, the example does provide evidence for the claim that creative activities can have a beneficial effect on adolescents. All the more reason then, to incorporate these activities into all secondary music courses.

## Prognosis: Rhetoric vs. Reality

Having surveyed the current situation in Canada with regard to secondary music curriculum reform, arts advocacy, and secondary arts enrolment, and having proposed a way out of the current dilemma of the small percentage of the student population enroled in secondary school music courses through the implementation of music composition courses and opportunities for composing music at the secondary level, it is time to "get real," as they say, and offer a realistic prognosis for the future.

Although I am a strong believer in the value and benefits of fine arts and specifically music education for all Canadians at all levels of schooling, I am acutely aware of the constraints placed on administrators and time-tabling experts today. I am also aware of the information gap between arts educators and the public-at-large who do not realize the tangible and intangible benefits to students and, by extension society, of an education rich in fine arts subjects. I feel a little like Winston Churchill when he said to the British House of Commons in the midst of World War II "I have nothing to offer you but blood, toil, sweat, and tears " (Bartlett, 1956, p. 75). Arts advocacy must continue at all levels in all jurisdictions of this country. Administrators need to be provided with creative ways of time-tabling fine arts subjects at the secondary level so that students can enrol in music without jeopardizing other academic courses; parents and guidance counsellors need to be made aware of the value of arts education so that they encourage young people to continue to enrol in music courses at the secondary level; universities need to be convinced to include scores in arts subjects in the calculation of entrance GPAs; and most importantly, *all* provincial ministries of education need to institute a fine arts graduation requirement. Everyone needs to know what arts educators know: that, as a popular bumper sticker proudly proclaims, *music makes a difference.*

At the beginning of this new millennium, I urge all arts educators to keep the faith and to hold the torch of music high. The words of twelfth grader, Nathaniel Davis (*Kids Voices*, 1996), give us courage for the journey and provide an appropriate place to close: "To me, music is life. Everything good about life is expressed through music. It is part of everyone's life. Whether it's a song on the radio, or a piece of historical culture, music surrounds us" (p. 18).

# References

Aiello, R. (Ed.) with Sloboda, J. (1994). *Musical perception*. New York: Oxford University Press.

Alberta Education. (1993). *General music: 10, 20, 30 program of studies*. Edmonton, AB: Author.

Bartlett, J. (1956). *The shorter Bartlett's familiar quotations*. New York: Permabooks.

Bjorkvold, J. R. (1992). *The muse within: Creativity and communication, song, play from childhood through maturity* (W. H. Halverson, Trans.). New York: Harper Collins. (Original work published 1989)

Blacking, J. (1973). *How musical is man?* Seattle, WA: University of Washington Press.

Brinkman, D. J. (1995). *The effect of problem-finding and creativity style on the musical compositions of high school students*. Unpublished doctoral dissertation, University of Nebraska, Lincoln, Nebraska.

British Columbia Ministry of Education. (1995). *Fine arts 11: Integrated resource package*. Victoria, BC: Author.

British Columbia Ministry of Education. (1996). *Music 11–12: Composition and technology: Integrated resource package*. Victoria, BC: Author.

British Columbia Ministry of Education. (1995). *Music 8–10: Integrated resource package*. Victoria, BC: Author.

Bunting, R. (1987). Composing music: Case studies in the teaching and learning process. *British Journal of Music Education, 5*, 32–46.

Burnard, P. (1995). Task design and experience in composition. *Research Studies in Music Education, 5*, 32–46.

Campbell, P. S. (1998). *Songs in their heads*. New York: Oxford University Press.

Creston, P. (1971). A composer's creed. *Music Educators Journal, 47* (7), 36–39, 91–93.

Curriculum Corporation. (1994). *A statement on the arts for Australian schools*. Carleton, Victoria: Author.

Czikszentmihalyi, M. (1996). *Creativity: Flow and the psychology of discovery and invention*. New York: HarperCollins.

Department of Education. (1995). *Music in the national curriculum*. London, UK: HMSO.

Dunn, R. (1992). Teaching music through individual composition: A music course for pupils aged eleven to eighteen. *British Journal of Music Education, 9*, 49–60.

Elliott, D. J. (1995). *Music matters*. New York: Oxford University Press.

Folkestad, G., Hargreaves, D. J., & Lindstrom, B. (1998). Compositional strategies in computer-based music-making. *British Journal of Music Education, 15* (1), 83–97.

Gardner, H. (1993). *Creating minds*. New York: HarperCollins.

Hanley, B. (1989). General music: music education for all students. In B. Hanley & G. King (Eds.), *Re-thinking music education in British Columbia* (pp. 58-67). Victoria, BC. University of Victoria.

Hargreaves, D. J. (1986). *The developmental psychology of music*. Cambridge, UK: Cambridge University Press.

Hogg, N. (1994). Strategies to facilitate student composing. *Research Studies in Music Education, 2,* 15–24.

Kaschub, M. (1997). A comparison of two composer-guided large group composition projects. *Research Studies in Music Education, 8,* 15–28.

Kennedy, M. A. (1999). Where does the music come from? A comparison case study of the compositional processes of a high school and a collegiate composer. *British Journal of Music Education, 16* (2), 155–175.

*Kids voices: Young people talk about music.* (1996). Reston, VA: Music Educators National Conference.

Kratus, J. (1989). A time study of the compositional processes used by children ages 7–11. *Journal of Research in Music Education, 37* (1), 5–20.

Ladanyi, K. S. (1995). *Processes of musical composition facilitated by digital music equipment.* Unpublished doctoral dissertation, University of Illinois, Urbana-Champaign, Illinois.

Lehman, P. (1988). A music program for 2001. In T. Gerber & W. Hughes (Eds.), *Music in the high school: Current approaches to secondary general music instruction* (pp. 3–12). Reston, VA: Music Educators National Conference.

Music Educators National Conference. (1994). *National standards for arts education.* Reston, VA: MENC.

National Film Board. (Producer). (1969). *Bing, bang, boom* [Film]. (Available from the National Film Board, P. O. Box 6100, Station A, Montréal, PQ, H3C 3H5)

Newfoundland & Labrador Department of Education. (1993). *Ensemble performance 10, 11, & 12.* St. John's, NF: Author.

Newfoundland & Labrador Department of Education. (1993). *Intermediate curriculum.* St. John's NF: Author.

Nova Scotia Department of Education and Culture. (1999). *Dance 11.* Halifax, NS: Author.

Nova Scotia Department of Education and Culture. (1999). *Foundations for arts education.* Halifax, NS: Author.

Ontario Ministry of Education and Training. (1998). *The Ontario curriculum grades 1–8: The arts.* Toronto, ON: Author.

Ontario Ministry of Education and Training. (1998). *The Ontario curriculum grades 9 & 10: The arts.* Toronto, ON: Author.

Regelski, T. (1981). *Teaching general music: Action learning for middle and secondary schools.* New York: Schirmer Books.

Reese, S. (1995). MIDI-assisted composing in your classroom. *Music Educators Journal, 81* (4), 37–40.

Reimer, B. (1989). *A philosophy of music education* (2nd ed.), Englewood-Cliffs, NJ: Prentice-Hall.

Reimer, B. (1997). Music education and the twenty-first century. *Music Educators Journal, 84* (3), 33–38.

Saskatchewan Education. (1996). *Arts education 10, 20, 30.* Regina, SK: Author.

Saskatchewan Education. (1993). *Band 10, 20, 30.* Regina, SK: Author.

Saskatchewan Education. (1997). *Choral 10, 20, 30.* Regina, SK: Author.

Schafer, R. M. (1976). *Creative music education.* New York: Schirmer Books.

Sundin, B., McPherson, G. E., & Folkestad, G. (Eds.). (1998*). Children composing.* Malmo, FL: Lund University.

Swanwick, K., & Tillman, J. (1986). The sequence of musical development: A study of children's composition. *British Journal of Music Education, 3,* 305–339.

Thompson, I. M. (1999). Whither Ontario music education into the new millennium? *Canadian Music Educator, 41* (1), 35-39.

Tsisserev, A. (1997). *An ethnography of secondary school student composition in music: A study of personal involvement within the compositional process.* Unpublished doctoral dissertation, University of British Columbia, Vancouver, British Columbia, Canada.

Upitis, R. (1990). *This too is music.* Portsmouth, NH: Heinemann Educational Books.

Upitis, R. (1992). *Can I play you my song?* Portsmouth, NH: Heinemann Educational Books.

Wiggins, J. H. (1990). *Composition in the classroom.* Reston, VA: Music Educators National Conference.

---

[1] The terms "high school" and "secondary school" are used interchangeably throughout this paper to refer to students in grades beyond what is normally considered to be elementary school. The coversion of school grades into school types (elementary, middle, junior secondary/high, senior secondary/high) varies throughout North America, between Canadian provinces, and even within Canadian provinces. There is no standard pattern.

[2] Other provinces may have instituted a fine arts graduation requirement. I obtained information on only these three.

[3] I was not able to secure statistics on this matter, but a conservative estimate would be between 5–10%.

[4] The three main British Columbia universities calculate their GPA on English 12 and three other provincially examinable subjects.

[5] U.S. scholars Lehman (1988), Reimer (1989), and Regelski (1981) also support general music education.

[6] British Columbia revised its grade 11–12 composition course in 1996.

[7] I advocate music composition be included at all levels of schooling — not just grades 11 and 12.

[8] As stated earlier, the grade 11–12 composition and technology course was completed in 1996. Prior to that time there had been a *Music Composition 11–12* course on the books. What is being pointed out here is the difference between a ministry-approved course and actual practice. What is actually being taught?

[9] In my small Catholic independent school, we had two work stations in the music classroom.

[10] General Cambridge Secondary Exam — one of the high school leaving exams used in Britain. Dunn's report was written prior to the new British National Curriculum. Presumably, her course is now adapted to fit current guidelines.

[11] I devised this course prior to the writing of the new British Columbia music curriculum.

[12] The music teachers in Kaschub's study felt confident about continuing composition activities with their classes after the project ended.

# Chapter Eight

# Sounds Surround Us

## *Barbara Graham*

Recently at a small gathering at a friend's home, I felt suffocated by noise and sound. With effort I was able to simultaneously focus on the threads of the conversation as well as on the melodic lines and rhythmic structures of the ubiquitous background music. I was also, however, trying to block out the mechanical household sounds of the heating, lighting, and air filtration systems. Others at the gathering were nodding and smiling, seemingly content, imprisoned in their concentric bubbles of sound. I longed, not for silence, but for a listener's guide, something that would help me decode the numerous sound stimuli that assaulted my senses and filled my consciousness.

This gathering was a relatively quiet event. The music was played as backdrop to the event. The crowd was small, and the several conversations were subdued. There was no shouting, no barking dogs, no television voices, or computer-generated sounds. Nevertheless, I was mentally drained. My ear was pulling me to the music; my responsibility as guest pulled me to the voices. During the drive home, I remembered several previous occasions when the sonic environment penetrated my consciousness to the extent that it invaded and disrupted my ability to enjoy what I was doing. I wondered about the implications of this changing "sound surround" for the music education of our young people.

More than 30 years ago, R. Murray Schafer (1988) wrote passionately, convincingly, and eloquently about the pollution of our sonic environment. His concern and the strategies he suggested for re-opening our ears continue to provide inspiration to music educators, musicians, and interested citizens. Nonetheless, our ears are still being assaulted. The environment is even more polluted than it was 30 years ago. The humming of fluorescent lights, the droning of household appliances, the clattering of keyboards, and the roaring and jangling of motors, while not new to our ears, still compete for our attention. Human voices, sounds of instruments, bird songs, and animal cries are juxtaposed to these mechanical sounds. The electronic sounds of radios, boom boxes, computers, video games, as well as the sound tracks of television and movies all invade our environments.

Music educators work with children and adolescents whose ears have been stopped by this surfeit of sound. Most of us, including children, have learned to ignore sounds as we adapt to the "sound surround" of our lives. One of the continuing challenges facing music educators is to engage in what Schafer called "ear cleaning" (1988, p. 46) with our students. In order for us to address this challenge, we need to renew our commitment to the universe of sound. By this remark, I mean that we must experiment with both naturally produced and electronically generated sound while exploring and assimilating a variety of music practices from many cultures. We must celebrate the fact that making music is a universal human practice and recognize that it is practised differently in different cultures. We must renew our passion for the processes as well as the products of music practices. We music educators will need to reconfigure and reframe the role of music and of music educators in classrooms and schools.

Before I explore these ideas more deeply, I want to situate them within the confluence of forces that have exerted pressure on music educators, music education, and on music programs during the past decade. These phenomena are significant in and of themselves. Taken together, they have transformed our educational context.

Local boards of education, in their attempts to fulfil their political, financial, and educational responsibilities and to be accountable to their public, have examined their priorities and reviewed their existing policies and programs. Many music educators have been asked to articulate a rationale for music programs to help local boards in their review process and to justify the teaching of music as a subject in public schools. We were asked to leave our classrooms, rehearsals, our communities and explain our work — the magic and challenges of creating, performing, and listening to music — to policymakers. Many of us collaborated with the music industry and with members of other arts organizations. We advocated successfully and were able to maintain existing music programs in Canadian schools.

At the same time, provincial departments of education began the lengthy process of curriculum revision. For the most part, the new curricula are grounded in a constructivist approach to learning (Brooks & Brooks, 1999) in which inquiry, exploration, and the personal expression of knowledge and creativity are stressed. Paradoxically, governments also introduced performance standards which specified expectations for student achievement.[1] They mandated testing of all students at strategic points along the learning continuum. Although provincial curricula and performance outcomes are developed and put into policy documents by governments, it is teachers who must understand, implement, and help students meet the new requirements. Teachers have been inundated with new directives and curricula but not with the necessary support to implement and use them effectively.

During the process of curricular revision, many provincial governments subsumed music education within the heuristic of "arts education." Institutions responsible for preservice teacher education and for implementing arts education curricula can only introduce preservice teachers to the practices of making and responding to music. An introduction to the rich traditions of Western music and to the music practices of other cultures, however, is an insufficient foundation on which to build a practical and effective music pedagogy. During their preservice years many novice teachers explore multiple art forms. Few study either music education or the successful integration and infusion of musical elements into the curriculum. Most elementary teachers are not graduates of music programs; they have not enjoyed multiple opportunities to explore music making or to understand the musical development of children.

Unfortunately, music specialists in elementary schools are an endangered species. What is of equal concern to me is the absence of music teachers and guided music programs in day-care facilities and in after-school and community organizations that offer learning experiences for children. Who will initiate and guide Canadian children into the joy, excitement, and challenges of making music if there continues to be a dearth of music educators in day-care facilities, elementary schools, and youth groups?

Our transformed educational context, the current emphasis on science and technology, the increasing numbers of preschool children in day-care facilities, the ease with which we can hear music from around the world, the ubiquitous sonic environment of our society, and the variety of music being produced for popular consumption, present new challenges and exciting possibilities for instruction in and through music for Canadian children and youth. Music educators need to step back from the routine of their professional lives and re-examine the structures and routines of  school. We need to reconsider the role of music in the lives of Canadian children and adults. We need to articulate several possibilities for an enriched role for music. Four important questions lead us to some significant issues that music educators need to address. I have used them to frame what follows:

1. What are the expressive potentials in music that each age group of students can develop?
2. What knowledge, skills, attitudes, and understandings do teachers need in order to help children and youth realize these expressive potentials?
3. What are the basic elements of music?
4. What music must be taught?

My purpose in this chapter is neither to provide definite answers to these questions nor to promote particular methods or approaches for music instruction. I am challenging the profession to explore a more "dialogic" (Bakhtin, 1981), developmental, reflective, and inclusive approach to music education. At the same time, I am encouraging music educators to demand that all children receive opportunities to grow into a rich musical life. A dialogic approach to music practices builds on the responsive capacities of children and teachers and on current knowledge about human development (Vygotsky, 1987; Gromko & Poorman, 1998). It is grounded in a view of music as a responsive and universal social practice.

Human beings are compelled to respond to sensory stimuli. Our response is to put form on the never-ending swirl of events and sensations that surround us (Bakhtin, 1981). Babies actively seek to make sense of these events as they attempt to understand how their worlds function. We know that infants confer special significance on species-specific vocalizations. We also know that they prefer the voices of their mothers over all others. By the age of six months, babies are capable of detecting changes in two dimensions of sound that are foundational to making music. They are able to detect changes in the pitch contours of melodic lines as well as in rhythmic patterns (Werner & Marean, 1996, p. 137). There is a growing body of evidence demonstrating that babies prefer melodies with certain tonal contours, such as descending intervals and sustained vowels

(Dowling, 1994, p. 184). Both these elements are characteristic features of "motherspeak" and the lullabies of many cultures.

These and other findings, verified through clinical experiments, corroborate what many musicians and interested parents have observed and recorded about their children's development. Babies are able to discriminate among sounds and do respond to various aspects of the sound surround. Over time, particular sounds, melodies, and rhythms become associated with particular activities. When these particular sounds are heard, they lead to expectations of other sounds and events. Initially, these associations are not limited to the sounds of the activities but rather encompass the entire activity. Playing games, eating, watching television, reading stories all become associated with their accompanied sound, sight, and tactile stimuli. In this way, sounds become imbued with meaning (Meyers, 1994).

Toddlers spontaneously play with vocal sounds, sounds from their stories, nursery rhymes, as well as from familiar melodies (Dowling, 1994, p. 185). Their play is characterized by repetition of the elements they find significant and appealing. These elements are usually single words, short phrases, or variations of pitch and rhythm. In their early efforts to imitate songs and musical figures, children can only approximate the contours of phrases. They bind the rhythmic patterns very closely to the words of the song. During this spontaneous play, toddlers work with the gestalt (p. 186). They experiment with the whole activity, with melody, rhythmic patterns, and movement.

When babies and toddlers engage in this spontaneous play, they are attempting to use their emerging musical and linguistic knowledge. They create idiosyncratic and new phrases and patterns as they gain control over the musical and linguistic structures that have significance in their lives. Gradually they develop the ability to accurately recall the echoic images stored in their brains. During the early period of development, between the ages of one to six years, children become more accurate in reproducing songs and isolating constituent musical elements (Davidson, 1994, p. 113). With guided experiences in listening, they develop the ability to distinguish figure and ground. At this point, they become able to separate melodic elements from rhythmic ones in order to examine each element as a discrete entity.

We know that hearing is a complicated process involving mental representation, decision making, inference, and interpretation (McAdams & Bigand, 1993, p. 1). When listening to music we engage in "instant perceptual problem solving" (Bamberger, 1994, p. 131). When we hear music and other sounds, we organize them into patterns and assign them to categories based on our associations, previous experiences, and knowledge. We adjust these internally constructed categories, our understanding of how the sonic world functions, by incorporating, assimilating, and appropriating new information into our perceptual frameworks (Bakhtin, 1981). When we notice and consciously select new sound patterns and use them for our own purposes, we gain control over them and add them to our existing repertoires of organized sounds. The meanings we attribute to these sounds evolve as our understanding of the abstract generalizations embodied in the sound systems develops.

What we expect to hear influences (perhaps even determines) what we are able to hear (Sloboda, in Bigand, 1993, p. 232). Early exposure to music helps children create a repertoire of musical schema and prototypical forms that are stored in their memories (Bharucha, 1994, p. 215; Sloboda, in McAdams & Bigand, 1993). Since the organization of sound in music is highly determined by cultural rules and conventions, children store recurring musical schema that are significant to them. All musical listening involves listeners' active efforts to relate music to their broader experiences. Individual composers, listeners, and performers make sense of particular pieces of music at a personal level and construct shared meanings within their social groups. Music then becomes associated with the group, the values, and affective relations within the group. Each act of listening and performing is a shared experience between the performer and the listener and among listeners. The quality of the shared experience is dependent on the musical understanding each member brings to it

Canadian children live in a world of music. Music lulls them to sleep, provides the background for many activities, accompanies their play, and punctuates their television viewing. Music has been incorporated into video games and computer programs to enhance children's enjoyment of the activities. The sounds become associated with these activities. By participating in the activities of their homes and communities, children accumulate sound associations and expectations. They learn to ignore sounds that have no meaning or significance for them. Gradually children construct their personal knowledge of the system of relationships between various musical elements, such as pitch, duration, dynamics, and timbre. This knowledge, while extensive, will quite probably remain tacit. Few early and middle childhood educators and not many parents have the necessary background experiences and knowledge to help children learn to discuss their personal musical knowledge systems. I am claiming that one goal of music education is to enable children and youth to make their musical knowledge explicit. This goal can only be realized when people with extensive knowledge and understanding of music, of human development, and of pedagogical principles initiate our young people into a variety of musical practices.

Despite the numerous opportunities for children to listen to music in their homes and as accompaniment to leisure activities, their musical knowledge remains bounded by and limited to the musical experiences of their homes and communities. Canadian families do not necessarily listen to a variety of musical styles or to music from cultures other than their own. For the most part, children's musical knowledge will be saturated with the sounds, pitches, motives, figures, rhythms, and timbres found in Western music and featured in television, in movies, and in popular music for children. Early experiences with music and organized sound play a role in children's ability to learn culture-specific rules for melody creation and rhythmic improvisation. If these early experiences are guided by music educators committed to providing authentic and culturally varied music-making experiences, children will learn the music practices and sound systems of many cultures.

We have learned that children grow into the intellectual life of those around them (Vygotsky, 1978). Teachers in elementary schools and day-care facilities structure their classroom activities to help children grow into a literate and numerate life, into the intellectual life of society. I am suggesting that children will also grow into the musical life of those around them. Teachers of young children recognize the importance of music and the other arts for healthy human development. They create opportunities for children to listen and respond to music. In many early years classes, children are encouraged to draw, paint, and use their bodies to express and respond to the feelings evoked by music. These experiences, while enjoyable, are not sufficient to ensure the development of musical knowledge and understanding. It is most unfortunate that very few early and middle childhood educators are able to help children represent their musical knowledge or to challenge and nurture the development of musical understanding. What might day-care facilities, early childhood music classes, and public school classrooms look like if they were structured to help children grow into a musical life? What kinds of knowledge, skills, and habits of mind are required if teachers are to nurture communities of music performers and responders in their classrooms?

In classrooms in which literacy and numeracy are valued, children and teachers "see themselves as" authors and mathematicians. Everyone's efforts to write and to do math are celebrated, discussed, and explored. Similarly, in classrooms where music is valued, children and teachers "see themselves as" musicians. In these classrooms, teachers have realigned their relationships both to their students and to creating, listening, and performing music. In these classrooms, the previous knowledge and experiences of all members of the classroom are valued and respected. In these classrooms, all members see themselves as learners of music, willing to learn about and participate in a variety of music practices and conventions.

I have worked with teachers who structure instruction in and through music as invitations to enter multiple musical practices. These teachers help children search for personal relevance in music. They build on the previous musical knowledge and background experiences of their students to thoughtfully guide children's exploration of various systems to organize sound into music. These teachers listen to their pupils to learn what is sonically meaningful to them. These meaningful sound patterns become the material to build bridges between the pupils' stored echoic images from their homes and communities and the music practices of the Western canon and other cultures. Such transcultural bridges involve communication between the various cultures, each one affecting the other. These classrooms and schools are alive with purposeful music making centred around listening, evaluating, creating, and performing.

In these classrooms, students experiment with combinations of sounds and instruments to capture their sonic impressions for others. They engage in perceptual problem-solving activities (Bamberger, 1994). They develop systems of notation to represent their compositions and to record their ideas for the future. They learn to honour the conventions and systems of Western music while exploring their personal interests and questions about music. They are encouraged to pursue inquiry into musical practices that are meaningful and evocative to them. They conduct research by listening to musical practices from other cultures. In these classrooms, teachers help students acquire the tools necessary for them to participate in the music practices of their several cultures.

Although musical understanding originates within the "sound surround" and musical practices of home and community, it need not be limited to these communities. To broaden and deepen our knowledge and understanding we need opportunities to engage in transcultural musical experiences. Transcultural experiences bring musical practices from a variety of cultures and traditions together. The diverse practices and cultures reciprocally influence and interanimate each other (Wertsch, 1991).

Students could begin to deepen and broaden their musical understanding by bringing and exploring music that speaks to them. They would be encouraged to play this music for the class and discuss why the music is important to them. The variety of music introduced into the classroom in this way would then serve as resources for examining musical practices, styles, and elements. Students would be encouraged to expand their sonic perceptual horizons through multiple listenings of music brought by their peers as well as music from a variety of time periods and cultures. Throughout these transcultural experiences, students would reflect on their idiosyncratic reactions. How did they respond to the rhythmic patterns? What effect did the melodic patterns have? Were the melodies and rhythms equally important in creating the musical impression? What skills and techniques did the performer/composer use to create the musical impression? Individual reflections would be discussed and analyzed within their classroom learning community. All members would then enter into a dialogue with a variety of music. Students could also be encouraged to think about how multiple interpretations of the same music and different expressions of the universal themes of our humanity open new possibilities for hearing the world.

The approach sketched in the preceding paragraphs begins with active listening. We need to help students view active listening as a suspension from life rather than as an accompaniment to life (Blum, 1996, p. 119). Listening, however, is only the beginning. Students also need opportunities to experiment with various musical genres and practices by participating as performers and composers, striving to acquire technical and interpretive skill and knowledge. Such active participation presents new challenges and opportunities for discussion and increases students' awareness of the multiple ways that people engage with each other and with the world.

Students move from their personal musical knowledge schema to those of the larger group, guided by the knowledge of the members of the group. They would seek to understand the knowledge of other members of the group by sharing in the backgrounds and experiences that have helped the others construct their ideas and understanding of music. Teachers in these classrooms need to be able to foster the impulse to listen to learn in their students and in themselves. Teachers in classrooms where the development of a rich musical understanding is the goal need to be articulate and accomplished music performers and educators. They must believe that a "musical and intellectual life" is important for participation in the global community.

Musical knowledge and understanding change as students develop and mature (Davidson, 1994, p. 102). Students become able to make more complex musical decisions as more options become available. The acquisition of skills and concepts is more than the simple accumulation of skills into our toolkits. Rather, the relationships within our previous skills undergo a transformation. For example, when I learn several new fingering patterns or when I master a particular bowing technique, more possibilities and nuances of interpretation are available to me. I understand the relationship between my body and my instrument in a new way. I also understand the relationship between pitch and sounds differently. I am able to experiment with tonal quality by listening to differences when I play a note on one string or on a different string. I evaluate the qualities of tone in order to make more informed interpretive and musical decisions.

When some members of the community acquire new skills or obtain more sophisticated technical equipment, the skills and dispositions of all members are influenced. For example, the widespread use of computers has dramatically changed how we communicate with others and how we conduct research. The use of laser as a surgical tool has transformed not only the practice of medicine but also society's attitudes towards healing. In music, the development of synthesizers, electronic instruments, and recorded music has transformed the lives of performers, listeners, and composers. The possibilities afforded by and through these new technologies are limitless. How can music educators best exploit these technologies to enhance their work and to help students develop richer understanding and appreciation of music?

One ramification of the new technologies is the availability of music from diverse cultures and the choice of interpretations of particular works made accessible by recording technology. We are able to hear exquisite interpretations and recordings of our favourite pieces of music whenever we wish. In addition, the proliferation of musical "texts" through a variety of media now available has blurred the boundaries that exist between music and other arts as well as between musical styles and genres. Computer technology allows students to borrow sound files to create their own compact disks. Folk idioms permeate rock music. Hip hop, gospel, country and western, and jazz music all interanimate (Wertsch, 1991) each other. Videos are superimposed on recordings of popular songs. Sound tracks for television and movies use excerpts from symphonic works and concerti to heighten the emotional response of audiences. All of this music is part of the sound surround of our students. We need to create opportunities for students to discuss their listening activities and experiences knowledgeably. More students need to be involved in collaborative projects between symphony musicians, music educators, and music students. These collaborative partnerships create bridges of understanding. Events, such as Winnipeg's New Music Festival, bring the audience onto the stage to experience the performance differently. Such initiatives successfully introduce a variety of cultural practices and musical traditions to audiences and create excitement in the community.

If we are serious as a profession about providing musical experiences and an education in music for our youth, we need to exploit the possibilities of our current "sound surround." Advances in technology present music educators with both challenges and possibilities. Our response to our changing contexts, as individuals and as members of the professional community of music educators, must be guided by knowledge and understanding about music and about the benefits of participating in a rich musical life. Each of us must consider our particular contexts and communities when we define participation in a musical life. We can begin by building on the strengths of our students and their families to link the rich history and traditions of Western music to their musical practices. From this beginning we can collaborate with our colleagues in music to increase our music understanding and knowledge. Sounds surround us. What will be our response to them?

## References

Aiello, R., & Sloboda, J. A. (1994). *Musical perceptions.* New York: Oxford University Press.

Bakhtin, M. M. (1981). *The dialogic imagination: Four essays by M. M. Bakhtin* (M. Holquist, Ed.; C. Emerson & M. Holquist, Trans.). Austin, TX: University of Texas Press.

Bamberger, J. (1994). Coming to hear in a new way. In R. Aiello & J. Sloboda (Eds.), *Musical perceptions,* (pp. 131-151). New York: Oxford University Press.

Bharucha, J. J. (1994). Tonality and expectation. In R. Aiello & J. Sloboda (Eds.), *Musical perceptions* (pp. 214–239). New York: Oxford University Press.

Bigand, E. (1993). Contributions of music to research on human auditory cognition. In S. McAdams & E. Bigand (Eds). *Thinking in sound: The cognitive psychology of human audition* (pp. 231–272). Oxford, UK: Oxford University Press.

Blum, P. C. (1996). Typification, transcendence, and critique: On the social construction of new age music. In F. B. Dasilva & D. L. Brunsma (Eds.), *All music: Essays on the hermeneutics of music* (pp. 117–132). Aldershot, UK: Avebury.

Brooks, M. G., & Brooks, J. G. (1999). The courage to be a constructivist. *Educational Leadership, 57* (3), 18–24.

Dasilva, F. B., & Brunsma, D. L. (Eds.). (1996). *All music: Essays on the hermeneutics of music.* Aldershot, UK: Avebury.

Davidson, L. (1994). Songsinging by young and old: A developmental approach to music. In R. Aiello & J. Sloboda (Eds.), *Musical perceptions,* (pp. 99–130). New York: Oxford University Press.

DeNardo, G. F., & Kantorski, V. J. (1998). A comparison of listeners' musical cognition using continuous response assessment. *Journal of Research in Music Education, 46* (2), 320–331.

Dowling, W. J. (1994). Melodic contour in hearing and remembering melodies. In R. Aiello & J. Sloboda (Eds.), *Musical Perceptions* (pp. 173–191). New York: Oxford University Press.

Gromko, J. E., & Poorman, A. S. (1998). Developmental trends and relationships in children's aural perception and symbol use. *Journal of Research in Music Education, 46* (1), 16–23.

McAdams, S., & Bigand, E. (1993). Introduction to auditory cognition. In S. McAdams & E. Bigand (Eds.), *Thinking in sound: The cognitive psychology of human audition* (pp. 1–9). Oxford, UK: Oxford University Press.

Meyer, L. B. (1994). Emotion and meaning in music. In R. Aiello & J. Sloboda (Eds.), *Musical perceptions,* (pp. 3–39). New York: Oxford University Press.

Robinson, J. (Ed.). (1997). *Music and meaning.* Ithaca, NY: Cornell University Press.

Schafer, R. M. (1988). *The thinking ear.* Toronto: Arcana Editions.

Sloboda, J. (1994). Music performance. In R. Aiello & J. Sloboda (Eds.), *Musical perceptions* (pp. 153–169). New York: Oxford University Press.

Vygotsky, L. S. (1978). *Mind in society: The development of higher psychological processes.* (M. Cole, V. J. Steiner, S. Scribner, & E. Souberman, Eds.). Cambridge, MA: Harvard University Press.

Werner, L. A., & Marean, G. C. (1996). *Human auditory development.* Boulder, CO: Westview Press.

Wertsch, J. V. (1991). *Voices of the mind: A sociological approach to mediated action.* Cambridge, MA: Harvard University Press.

---

[1] For examples of performance standards, consult provincial policy documents and curriculum guides.

# Chapter Nine

# The Role of Musical Thinking in Selected Canadian Elementary Music Curricula
## Evidence of Success and Ideas for Consideration

*Betty Anne Younker*

## Introduction

We have been told that music cognition is unique to human brains (Fiske, 1990); that experiencing music is a way of knowing (Reimer, 1999); that music is an intelligence (Gardner, 1983). Accepting these premises, we need to understand how thinking in sound can be enhanced and nurtured. Enhancement of musical thinking may contribute to enlightened and knowledgeable consumers who are actively engaged while experiencing music. Promoting musical thinking should be a goal of our music programs as suggested by many music educators including Richards and Milligan (1998) who questioned:

> Do you want students who can play the clarinet part in *Night on Bald Mountain* in the band or to develop a lifelong relationship [to] great music? Do you want students who can memorize lines in a play, or those who have an understanding of the complexity of human emotions and motivation? (p. 79)

Boardman (1989) argued that the profession has been successful in defining what should be taught (content) and how students will show, through various musical behaviours, their understanding of the

169

content. The profession has been less successful, however, in developing independent musical thinkers. Specifically, we are successful at teaching the elements of music and asking students to do such things as recognize, identify, demonstrate, read, play, and reproduce but we are less successful at asking questions that enable students to generate possibilities, to critically (musically) examine those possibilities, to decide on solutions that are meaningful, and to further explore and evaluate alternative possibilities. The importance of including such opportunities has been recognized by many in the field. As Webster and Richardson (1994) stated:

> If there is one thing that emerges from the new theoretical and empirical work in music psychology, it is the fact that music teachers must encourage children to think more deeply and more imaginatively about music and to engage students in a wider variety of music experiences i f real music learning is to occur. (p. 8)

The question that begs to be answered is whether or not real music learning has occurred and is occurring in the classroom.

The purpose of this paper is to define musical thinking and assess the status of potential musical learning as a result of examining curricula content found in selected Canadian elementary music curricula. Guiding this inquiry will be the following questions:

(1) What is musical thinking?
(2) What kind of classroom environment is necessary for musical thinking to flourish?
(3) Do the selected curricula provide for musical learning to occur?
(4) What activities would be included in the selected curricula if musical thinking were expected?

To help answer the first question, I will refer to Dewey's (1933/1991) writings on thinking, specifically, his definition of thinking, explanation of inductive and deductive reasoning, and thoughts about the educational implications of expecting students to think. The second question will be addressed by describing the kind of classroom environment, including the interaction between educator and students, that would be conducive to thinking. The last two questions will be investigated by examining three elementary music curriculum guides:

(1) the *British Columbia Integrated Resource package: Fine Arts K to 7* (IRP, British Columbia Ministry of Education, 1998),

(2) the *Ontario Curriculum Grades 1–8: The Arts* (Ontario Ministry if Education and Training, 1998), and

(3) the *Prince Edward Island Elementary Music Curriculum Guide: Grades 1 to 6* (Prince Edward Island Department of Education, 1997).

The reason for the different grade span in each curriculum is the varying school structures across provinces. In this chapter, I will examine only grades one to six in the three documents.

## Dewey's Thoughts on Thinking

### Definition of thinking

I will use the term musical thinking to refer to thinking reflectively about and within music. To construct my definition of musical thinking, I used the writings of Dewey (1933/1991) as a basis for the definition and the discussion in this section. Dewey was a philosopher who wrote extensively about various, and yet related, disciplines including philosophy, politics, and education. He endorsed the pragmatic views of William James and supported free inquiry and the scientific method. His interest in how we think resulted in many publications that have had an impact on education and the arts. Dewey wrote extensively about reflective thinking, what it meant and involved, and how it should permeate all aspects of education.

Dewey stressed the importance of thought because of the independence we can gain from thinking. He suggested that "thought affords the sole method of escape from purely impulsive or purely routine action" (p. 14). It shapes independencies in that we can go beyond responding to instincts and appetites which are shaped by outward circumstances and our inner state. It moves beyond stimulus and response kinds of behaviours to ones that involve reflection and thought. It goes beyond developing habits formed from social influences which can lead to inadequate and mistaken beliefs.

According to Dewey, "Thinking…is defined accordingly as that operation in which present facts suggest other facts (or truths) in such a way as to induce belief in the latter upon the ground or warrant of the former" (pp. 8–9). Dewey discussed specific thinking characteristics as opposed to specific-subject thinking characteristics. Every subject requires intellectual inquiry, and we should strive to generate thinking that can be used in all areas of study. The steps that are involved in reflective thinking include:

(1) a felt difficulty,
(2) its location and definition,
(3) suggestion of possible solution,
(4) development by reasoning of the bearings of the suggestion, and
(5) further observation and experiment leading to its acceptance or rejection, that is, the conclusion of belief or disbelief. (p. 72)

The trained mind is able to determine how far each step needs to be explored, as the process of each is case-specific and is sensitive to each problem, and is expert (well practised) in methods of attack and solution. Dewey's definition of thinking and outline of steps involved in reflective thinking provide a standard against which to judge the inclusion in specific curriculum guides of activities and instructions that can empower students to think reflectively in music.

## Inductive and deductive reasoning

An interaction occurs in all reflection and involves inductive and deductive reasoning that is

a movement from the given partial and confused data to a suggested comprehensive (or inclusive) entire situation, and back from this suggested whole — which as suggested is a meaning, an idea — to the particular facts, so as to connect these with one another and with additional facts to which the suggestion has directed attention. (Dewey, 1933/1991, p. 79)

The inductive part includes the building of an idea whereas the deductive part includes developing, applying, and testing the idea. During these processes, isolated facts are organized, connections are made, and relationships established. It is crucial to remember that all conclusions are still open to further observation and testing. This interaction, then, constitutes a complete act of thought and occurs in a dynamic and recursive fashion.

## Educational implications

In most cases, students are asked to gather isolated segments, pieces of material, and information in a disparate form through means of memory work, observation, and/or authority. As a result, the students cannot see the relevance of each fact because of the out-of-context and uninvolved manner in which these facts are presented. Quite often, students are immersed in the processes of manipulation and lose sight of the bigger picture, the context, and reason for doing the activity. They are involved, then, with the inductive process that is limited to "inhaling"' facts. The absence of the deductive process means that they do not experience connecting and organizing relationships and learning as a coherent and meaningful whole. These students do not gain the necessary further understanding about the inter- and intra-relationships of the elements of music within a meaningful context.

When opportunities are given for the students to make connections, quite often the intellectual pursuit ends once they are made. Students understand how the parts are related, in a general way, and make an inductive inference. If they are correct, the response is accepted; if it is incorrect, however, then in most cases, the teacher assumes a leadership role and helps students find the reasoning behind the incorrectness of the inference. If a complete thought were to be carried out by students, they would reason about the why and how and apply the solutions in new situations.

If the deductive phase is to be complete and effective, there should be no introduction of definitions, rules, general principles, or classifications. Deductive considerations should not be introduced until the students have become acquainted with the facts about which they will think. In addition, the results of the general reasoning processes need to be tested by applying them to new concrete cases. It is only in the transfer and application of results to new situations that mastery over the general principle occurs, that full understanding is achieved. If the new situations are new, then they will "differ in manifestations from the cases used in reaching the generalization" (Dewey 1933/1991, p. 99), providing further evidence of ownership over and understanding of the general principle. Furthermore, observation and experimentation are necessary if effective and integral thinking are to be developed. Students must engage in activities that modify physical conditions, in which they manipulate the information in a concrete fashion.

### The environment

Quite often, in a traditional music class, the educator communicates information to students who sit in rows and respond when called upon, instead of "setting up opportunities for discovery learning" (Pautz, 1989, p. 67). Pautz suggested that lecturing students is favored because lectures allow, in a limited period of time, copious amounts of information to be delivered from teacher to student, therefore, accomplishing as much as possible in the shortest amount of time. Downloading quantities of information from teacher to student and back to teacher should not be the intent, but rather the provision of a haven where students are given time to explore, discover, reflect, and respond. Students need time to reflect and respond while thinking musically — that is, they need time to explore, shape, edit, refine, and evaluate musical possibilities. Music educators need to realize, as Pautz (1989) suggested "that thinking takes time, that creating takes time, and that enabling students to become independent learners takes time" (p. 67). Despite the many reforms in which discovering and facilitating have been encouraged and lecturing discouraged, the setting of the classroom, particularly at the secondary and postsecondary level, has not changed since formal schooling began (see Gardner, 1991; Sizer, 1992).

Richardson (1998) discussed various factors that could interfere with encouraging thinking in the classroom. One is related to the roles of the educator and student. As noted in the previous paragraph, traditionally, educators view students as empty vessels waiting to be filled. "Filling vessels" promotes a safe environment (for the teacher) and attributes power to the teacher. In an environment in which thinking is encouraged, the power shifts from teacher-based knowledge and teacher-formulated problems to a sharing of knowledge and student-formulated problems. This power shift requires different roles for students and educator. One crucial change in the various roles is one that requires educators to move from a master/apprentice relationship to one of listener and respondent in a more equal relationship.

Thus far, using Dewey (1933/1991) as a basis, I have developed a definition for musical thinking and identified specific steps involved in reflective thinking. In addition, the characteristics of an environment that is conducive to music thinking have been suggested. In the following sections I will examine the three selected curricula to identify opportunities for musical thinking to occur and the concrete ways such thinking is promoted in the curricula, and tosuggest further activities through which musical thinking might be encouraged and enhanced.

## British Columbia Curriculum: The Fine Arts

### Introductory sections

The introduction contains philosophical statements about the unique and essential aspects of musical experiences and about the role music can play in students' development as educated citizens. As well, an overall goal and list of objectives are given. Next, an overall explanation about how the content is organized for the different grade levels is followed by suggestions for promoting a music classroom that is conducive to learning.

The next section contains information organized around three approaches: creating music, presenting and performing music, and responding to music. The content in this section is adapted, with permission, from content found in Saskatchewan's *Arts Education: A Curriculum Guide for Grades 1–5* (1991). This lengthy and informative section offers key words and suggestions that can guide music educators to empower musical thinking. The following segment will examine the specifics included for each approach.

*Creating music.* Under "creating music," exploration, selection, combination, refinement, and reflection are included as parts of the creative process. During this process students are to experience, gain knowledge, experiment, and facilitate simultaneously and in a recursive fashion. In addition, students are to be provided opportunities in which they can take creative risks without the constraints of predetermined, quality standards. It could be inferred that after risks are taken, ideas presented, and some knowledge acquired, the students would be involved in establishing criteria. Statements articulating this involvement, however, would strengthen this opening section.

The inclusion of words like "exploration," "reflection," "experiment," and "facilitate" suggests the authors' intent that musical thinking will be promoted. The writers steer teachers along this path by giving directions for facilitating students' creative development. It is suggested that beginning activities be structured and teacher-directed and become less structured and teacher-directed as the students acquire skills and confidence. Throughout all parts of the creative process, the teacher's role should involve coaching, guiding, and discussing.

When giving examples for inspiring and assisting the creative process, the authors offer suggestions that can encourage exploration. The suggestions and directions for guiding composing activities could generate student-formulated problems with student-directed activities. In this section, the wording indicates that the teacher's role is that of facilitator, and students are to be encouraged to think musically. Examples given include the student deciding, interpreting, creating, exploring, transforming, collecting, developing (that which is meaningful and personally relevant), refining, and evaluating. Other suggestions for engaging the students in "creating music" that mirror the terminology used by writers who discuss musical thinking include discussing, reflecting, assessing, evaluating peers' work, rehearsing, applying, expanding, and redirecting.

The terminology is rich with words that are associated with, and examples that are reflective of, thinking, reflective thinking (Dewey, 1933/1991), and musical thinking (Richardson, 1998). This terminology plus the emphasis placed on how to promote student-formulated problems and student-directed activities guides the educator in terms of the "how to" when facilitating musical thinking. What is not present are examples of effective questioning techniques. Effective questions can ignite students to reason beyond the acceptance of initial answers to why and how the solutions work or could be improved upon. These processes are important aspects of evaluating and refining.

*Presenting and performing music.* The authors suggested that presenting and performing established as well as their own works allow students to shape and refine musical ideas while integrating acquired knowledge and attitudes and employing acquired skills. Suggested opportunities for developing, and applying knowledge and skills in preparation for the presentation and performance include, among other behaviours, interpreting, organizing and implementing, applying and designing, and directing. These suggestions provide evidence that many aspects of musical thinking would be promoted in the classroom. According to Dewey, part of the investigative process includes the roles of inquiry and reasoning during which facts and experiences are accumulated. During the processes of inquiring and reasoning, the investigator suggests, develops, applies, decides, and evaluates. What is missing in this section are suggestions that would involve the students in re-evaluating and modifying ideas after a presentation or performance. This next step is crucial, according to Dewey, in reflective thinking processes.

*Responding to music.* In this section, the authors support an environment that is conducive to feeling comfortable when expressing personal opinions. The students need to be reassured that their ideas will be represented and reminded that their ideas could augment their peers' response experiences. The suggestions represent an interactive and open environment in which the students' input is considered and can influence the work of their peers. If we are attempting to empower musical thinking then we must recognize the importance of, and embrace, student input. Not only is it crucial to understand what we do with their input but also to respect their input. This suggestion can have tremendous potential in developing a democratic classroom, one that includes characteristics of learning and schooling as espoused by Dewey (1933/1991, 1938) and other pertinent writers (see Gardner, 1991; Sizer, 1992).

The authors suggested that educators should encourage a variety of aesthetic responses that involve feelings evoked by the music; references associated with personal, social, and cultural experiences; and analysis and interpretation of the music. Dewey discussed the involvement of emotions and experiences in the reflective process. Richardson (1988) pinpointed this aspect of Dewey's thinking when explaining how reflective thinking has as its origin experiences of the individual and that "it entails the process by which the individual derives his own meanings and significance from the experience" (p. 30). Recognizing the significance of past experiences is crucial as we invite and respond to students' responses and realize that this process is part of their development as musical thinkers. In this section of the document, it is suggested that we accept these intuitive responses that are initially void of analysis. These responses, or suggestions, are fueled by curiosity which, at first, is not intellectual but is necessary for the beginnings of intellectual activity (Dewey, 1933/1991).

Other evidence of encouraging musical thinking is found in the instructions for realizing listening activities. Suggested steps in which to involve students when listening include:

1. preparation,
2. first impression,
3. description,
4. analysis of content and effect,
5. interpretation, and
6. informed judgment.

Many similarities can be found between these steps and the five steps that occur in reflection as outlined by Dewey. Preparation for the listening activity includes the music teacher establishing a focus for listening and the students responding with first impressions. While this step does not constitute a "felt difficulty," they are similar in that there is a reaction to a stimulus, a reaction that could contain felt difficulties. Through own and peers' simultaneous responses, the students begin to locate and define what was heard, structuring the aural event into multiple possibilities. Through description, some of the possibilities become solidified, while others are rejected. As the students analyze the content and effect, they are asked to examine the inter- and intra-relationships of the elements in an attempt to determine how the music evokes responses. It is also suggested that students be asked to identify evidence of particular cultures, eras, and styles. This analysis can enhance or cause rejection of initial responses and descriptions. The next step, interpreting, involves students in reflecting and discussing what is meaningful about the music to each of them and considering the influence of their experiences and perceptions of the world. This influence was discussed in the previous paragraph, and again reflects Dewey's thinking about the relationships between past and present experiences (also see Dewey, 1934, 1938). The final step for listening activities as outlined in this section of the curriculum document is called "informed judgement." The students are asked to discern whether or not there are differences between their initial responses and present judgements as a result of discussions, research, and reflection. This description does not involve further observation and experimentation (Dewey's fifth step) but does allow the students to discern differences between initial responses based on reactions and informed judgements that involve musical thinking. It also allows the students to understand the relationship between reflective thinking about music and the musical experience, an experience that, hopefully, will be deeper and wider as a result of their reflective thinking about the music.

### The main body

In the main body, prescribed learning outcomes, suggested instructional strategies, suggested assessment strategies, and recommended learning resources are described for specific grades. In the prescribed learning outcomes, expectations are listed and organized around behaviours and specific concepts without any indications about how the music teacher is to engage the students in the behaviours. These indications are found in the next section, "Suggested Instructional Strategies," in which a small number of suggestions are given in the form of activities. Indicated are ways in which the students should be involved, that is, the "how" from the student's perspective. The behaviours cover a wide range of active involvement and levels of thinking as shown in the following representative list: perform, compare and contrast, compose, describe, identify, justify, act as a leader, categorize, classify, experiment, analyze, discuss, explore, and practise. What is absent are instructional strategies like those that were included in the opening sections. If educators make the connection between the "how" discussed in the previous sections and the "what" and "how" from the students' perspective as discussed in this section, then there could be many opportunities for the students to think musically.

The following section, "Suggested Assessment Strategies," contains instructions that include the how and what when distinguishing accuracy of knowledge and skills and range of students' assessment skills and provides specific examples of open-ended questions and sentence stems when involving students in reflection-based activities. When distinguishing the range of students' assessment skills, it is suggested that students compare their notation systems with standard notation and then assess another student's work. During this process, they are to compare and contrast, evaluate, and identify. These activities could involve the students at another level of thinking if:

1. when asked to compare one notation system with another, they were also asked to describe why and how one notation system is more or less effective than the other and what changes need to be made for one to be more effective;

2. when asked to discern one thing another student did well, they were also asked to describe why it was done well;

3. when asked to describe aspects of the design of the melody, they were also asked to include other possibilities that would enhance or change the melody; and

4. when asked to describe an additional thing that requires more knowledge, they were also asked to include why they need to learn more about what was targeted and how they could acquire additional information.

The suggested open-ended questions and sentence stems involve the students in identifying, exploring, applying, comparing and contrasting, evaluating, and concluding. Some of the suggestions represent many aspects of Dewey's (1933/1991) definition of reflective thinking. The students are asked why and how, to apply acquired knowledge and skills, to explore possibilities, and to draw conclusions and defend choices. There is the potential for asking students to further experiment by applying conclusions in new situations, however, this step is implicit and not explicit. For example, the students are asked to complete various sentence stems such as, "We can improve by...." To ensure further experimentation, there needs to be the following suggestion: After asking students to finish the sentence stem "We can improve by....," ask them to apply the suggestion in the next related activity and assess the effectiveness of that suggestion.

### Summary

The British Columbia Curriculum Guide has much potential to guide educators when facilitating musical thinking. When comparing the various sections, the introductory sections contain, to a greater degree, suggestions and instructions that can guide music teachers when attempting to provide opportunities for musical thinking to be nurtured than do the sections in the main body. In terms of the sections in the main body, the "Suggested Assessment Strategies" section dispenses the most complete ideas for how to nurture musical thinking. There can be, then, opportunities for students in music classrooms to engage in developing ideas and applying and testing those ideas. What is missing, however, are suggestions about how to engage students in that last step of reflective thinking as outlined by Dewey. While it could be inferred that you would engage the students in further application and testing of products and seek their reasoning for why solutions work or do not work, the step would be explicit if the authors had added effective how and why questions that could generate that next step of thinking.

## The Ontario Curriculum: The Arts

In the introductory sections, the authors include how involvement with music and other subjects can develop the ability to think critically. As well, it is suggested that teachers should encourage students to use critical-thinking skills, among other skills, when planning, producing, and assessing works of art. These statements reflect an acceptance that these skills can and should be involved when learning music.

The role of the teacher and student is also addressed in the introductory part of the curriculum. In terms of the teacher's role, it is suggested, among other things, that hands-on activities be implemented thereby ensuring that acquisition of knowledge and skills occurs through concrete experiences that include manipulatives. As well, it is emphasized that the teacher provide an environment in which students are encouraged to discover and develop their artistic ability. The former point reflects Dewey's (1933/1991) thoughts about the relevance of concrete experiences to active learning that involves reflection while the inclusion of "discover" in the latter point reflects Dewey's suggestion that active learning includes, among other things, discovery.

Activities that involve acquiring information ("knowledge of elements"), composing ("creative work"), and critically thinking about music ("critical thinking") are outlined for each grade in this curriculum. This triadic approach appears to be consonant with Dewey's (1933/1991) thinking when he suggested that to ensure reflective thinking, both induction and deduction need to be part of the thinking process. With the inclusion of both types of thinking, it appears that the student would acquire knowledge about and manipulate the elements, connect and organize relationships, and test by applying the results to new concrete cases. As well, the student would gain an understanding of the relationships between and within the elements and of the parts to the whole.

### Knowledge of elements

When examining the specific expectations that are outlined for each grade, it is apparent that much thought was given to what the students should accomplish. Under "Knowledge of Elements" it is specified that students are to show knowledge about specific musical elements through identifying, distinguishing, reproducing, describing, demonstrating, recognizing, reading, interpreting, explaining, singing, playing, and classifying. These behaviours represent different implied levels of thinking across a somewhat narrow spectrum.

### Creative work

Under "Creative Work," the spectrum of implied thinking broadens to include expressing, manipulating, producing, creating, accompanying, changing, reading, conducting, and performing. Many of the expectations include involving known content which indicates transferring and applying; manipulating specific musical elements which indicates exploring alternative possibilities; and creating original material which indicates exploring, evaluating, testing, and concluding. These behaviours are often found in descriptions of creative behaviours and indicate the presence of musical involvement and learning. This presence is only implied, however, because of the absence of instructions or suggestions about how to involve the students. Students could create a composition without reflecting, refining, testing alternative possibilities, exploring many options, and reasoning about why choices were made. Without these processes, musical thinking is not being nurtured. Without descriptions of student-formulated and teacher-formulated problems, (Richardson, 1998), we cannot be assured that students will indeed be given opportunities to find, as well as solve, problems. Without examples of questions like, "What do you think about the way the section sounded?" to which students would respond by formulating musical problems, articulating those problems, discussing possible solutions, evaluating possible solutions, converging on a solution, and exploring alternative solutions (Dewey, 1933), we cannot be assured that the kind of thinking outlined by Dewey is occurring.

### *Critical thinking*

In this section, it is suggested that students will communicate thoughts and feelings, identify, listen, describe responses, express responses, recognize mood, recognize that mood can be created, explain preferences, recognize and explain the effects of musical choices, describe how a composer manipulates the elements, and describe interrelationships. Since no definition for critical thinking is given or suggestions for instructional strategies, it is difficult to ascertain if the authors conclude that each of identifying, listening, communicating, describing, expressing, recognizing involves critical thinking or whether they conclude that critical thinking involves each of these as part of a larger process. Nevertheless, all of these activities could be realized without involving critical (reflective/musical) thinking, as defined in this chapter. Activities that suggest musical thinking include explaining preferences, recognizing and explaining the effects of musical choices, describing how a composer manipulates the elements, and describing interrelationships. Again, as with the activities listed under "Creative Work," without the provision of specific instructional strategies, it cannot be assumed that teachers will know how to involve students in all aspects of musical thinking.

### *Summary*

While it appears that students' musical thinking would be nurtured as a result of the wide range of suggested thinking skills, it is less apparent how this thinking is to be nurtured. What is missing from this guide but included in the British Columbia and Prince Edward Island guides are suggested instructional strategies which would provide guidance for the music teacher about how to involve students in reflective thinking as outlined by Dewey (1933/1991). For example, when an incorrect answer is given about acquired knowledge or an insufficient solution is provided when composing or thinking about music, how do you engage the students in reasoning about why and how? What questions are asked and by whom? What is needed are activities that include articulating why and how a work was produced and applying solutions to new situations for further experimentation and evaluation. This aspect of thinking is crucial to reflective thinking as outlined by Dewey or for our purposes, to musical thinking.

## Prince Edward Island Elementary Music Curriculum Guide

The first goal of the elementary music program is as follows: "to develop competency in problem solving, critical thinking and decision-making through experiences with music" (p. 10). The desire, then, to nurture students' critical thinking while engaged in musical learning has been recognized and stated publicly. The curriculum guide is organized around four areas, each of which contains experiences relevant to that area: musical participation (experiences in creating, listening, and performing), musical understanding (experiences in understanding musical concepts), musical appreciation (experiences in valuing the contribution of musicians in the past and present in various cultures), and musical technology (experiences in using and applying technologies). I will give a brief description of the content for each area and then examine in more detail the suggested instructional strategies given for outcomes in each area and for listening activities.

### Musical participation

In the overall section of musical participation, singing in unison is highlighted as "the core activity of the music classroom" (p. 11). In addition it is suggested that traditional school instruments be used to explore sounds and stylistic differences and generate discussions about how composers produce variety in compositions.

Creating sounds, listening, and performance are treated as subcategories and discussed separately. Creating sounds involves personal exploration and creativity and the opportunity to develop and use critical and divergent thinking skills. It is also suggested that composers and musicians be encouraged to come and speak to the students about musical experiences in an attempt to fuel discussion about feelings, ideas, images, characteristics of style, and personal reactions to music. Through performance, students can share their compositions as well as, music learned in the classroom. The importance of a positive experience within casual to formal settings is stressed; there is, however, no mention of reflection. As well, there is no definition for critical or divergent thinking skills, nor are there reasons given for why these skills should be used and developed.

### Musical understanding

In this section, the authors stress that students need to understand the inter- and intrarelationships between and within the elements of music. The elements should be experienced in a meaningful context to ensure that the students can understand and transfer what is understood to other listening, creating, and performing activities.

### Musical appreciation

This section is divided into aesthetic awareness and community awareness. For the former, it is suggested that students gain an understanding about experiences that are unique to music and those that are functional in nature within societies and cultures. Common and different roles of music within societies and cultures should be explored in an attempt to provide the students with a broader view of how music has been, and is, a significant part of our lives. Outreach to resources such as local composers, musical groups, and cultural organizations could provide rich information about the cultural happenings of the community.

### Historical and cultural awareness

Music from a variety of cultures, eras, and genres should be integrated into the music program. In addition, study of the social, cultural, and historical characteristics relevant to the selection of music will provide a context when attempting to gain further insight into the meaning, role, and function of the music.

## Music technology

Technology should be investigated and utilized as a means for furthering and expanding musical experiences. Understanding how technology is used in the music profession from a performer, listener, and composer's perspective can heighten students' awareness about how music is transmitted and manipulated.

## Suggested instructional strategies

Instructional strategies are suggested for the realization of each listed outcome. These strategies consist of descriptions of activities for student engagement. The activities are to be a means through which the students can experience and become knowledgeable about each outcome as well as provide an opportunity for the educator to assess the extent of the experience and knowledge.

*Musical participation — Suggested instructional strategies.* Students are asked to engage in behaviours such as discover, explore, lead, brainstorm, evaluate, and share, behaviours that involve active participation. Based on the suggestions, educators would involve students in various activities during which students would seek out possible solutions, converge on the most appropriate one, and, in some activities give reasons why choices were made and defend those reasons. Defending reasons resembles the fourth step of Dewey's (1933/1991) reflective thinking and, therefore, involves the students in extensive musical thinking. What they are not asked to do, however, is to apply the choices in another, and yet similar, activity. This step would allow for further observation and experimentation in which the students would construct additional reasons for accepting their choices or adopting alternative solutions.

When the students are asked to evaluate and reflect, they are asked to describe how they felt about their performances in various venues and how they might improve future performances. These activities offer opportunities to seek alternative solutions (see Dewey's fifth step). Students need to complete this kind of thinking by explaining why certain solutions would be more effective than others, performing the repertoire with the accepted suggestions, and reflecting on and evaluating the new performance. This type of involvement will, hopefully, contribute to a greater understanding of the music they are performing which, in turn, will enhance the musical performance.

The students are asked to "defend their choices" in various activities such as selecting "classroom repertoire that could be used to accompany" a compiled list of "sounds made in a natural and constructed environment" (Prince Edward Island Department of Education, 1997, p. 25). This step provides opportunities for students to articulate the reasoning process that occurred while choices were being made as well as guarantees that reasoning was part of the process. The next step, to ensure reflective thinking as supported by Dewey, would be to ask students to repeat the same activities with choices made, explore other possibilities, accept new possibilities or retain original choices and provide reasons for decisions made.

In certain performance activities, the students are to determine through discussion, how to constructively critique student and professional performances; determine appropriate language and criteria; and apply the established criteria while writing reviews of a given performance. In these activities, students would, from an evaluative perspective, apply terminology and knowledge about skills and understanding of expression. As with the above examples, the next step would embrace a discussion about what criteria were most effective and why, and what were not as effective and why. This step would lead the students back to the "brainstorming" table to generate other suggestions. One can envision a debate that would generate multiple possibilities, require a defense for each suggestion given, and spark the process of reasoning. Applying what was created to a real situation extends musical thinking and allows for opportunities to see what was effective and what was less effective.

*Musical understanding — Suggested instructional strategies.* To show understanding of the various elements, students are given opportunities to do various activities, some in which they create, create and defend, discuss, apply, and discern and reason. In the activities in which the students create with known elements, they are manipulating known material to compose new products. This outcome provides concrete evidence of understanding and allows the students to master the particular concept. Dewey (1933/1991) discussed the importance of students manipulating information in a concrete fashion to increase ownership over and understanding of the concepts. In other situations, the students are asked to create new material that is suitable as an accompaniment to a known song based on its form. Here students are asked to explore opportunities and decide on a solution that is compatible with the song. In some of these activities students are asked to defend their decisions — a crucial part of the reflective process. To strengthen this process, the students need to explore additional possibilities and accept or reject first choices, entertain alternatives, and defend decisions.

When asked to discuss how specific sounds or a piece of music could be used to "illustrate stories, create images, and evoke particular emotions" (Prince Edward Island Department of Education, 1997, p. 33), the students are given an opportunity to conjure up stories, images, and emotions without any restrictions or parameters. The next step is to ask why and how each story or image could be represented by a sound. During this exercise, it is imperative to enforce that there are no right or wrong answers but that the defense involves reasoning.

In a number of activities, the students are to apply their understanding of the relationships between parts and whole of a particular product. For example in one activity, the students are given the opportunity to create visual images that represent music and then asked to view peers' images and decide what, if any, characteristic viewed in their peers' works could be incorporated into their own work. To do this activity, the students would need to understand the relationships between what was chosen and the specifics of their work, in addition to the whole of their work. Dewey discussed the importance of understanding, organizing, and connecting meaningful relationships between the parts in relation to the whole. What is missing are examples of questions to ask in case the reasons for the choice do not show evidence of this understanding, questions that are framed around why and how. It is imperative that the music educator ask questions that will guide the students' thinking in this direction to enhance their understanding of the relationships between the parts and the whole.

When asked to discern the level of difficulty to complete a task, students are also asked to give reasons for the level of difficulty. Not only must they discern the level of difficulty but they must also understand what aspect of the task contributes to the difficulty, a reflection of musical thinking. A question that could further the students' musical thinking would include, "How could the task be made easier? harder?"

*Musical awareness — Suggested instructional strategies.* The suggestions given in this section that require some aspects of musical thinking include asking students to make connections between music and another art form and between music and the various functions music serves. When asking students to discern relationships between visual and aural stimuli in a commercial, one activity involves them deciding on the type of music that would be compatible with what they see and the product being sold. Their thinking is extended when they compare and contrast their answers with the music that has been written. The final step involves them writing music for the commercial. Here the students are exploring possibilities and deciding; comparing and contrasting; and manipulating the elements, evaluating, refining, and deciding. Further steps would include asking the students what and how their answers reflect and represent what is being sold, how the experience would differ if opposite musical characteristics were used, for what other kind of commercial could the music be used, for what contrasting kind of product could the music represent? For each answer, the follow up questions would include how and why. These questions would allow the students to develop, apply, explore alternative suggestions, reason, and defend, all necessary aspects of thinking as outlined by Dewey (1933/1991).

Other activities include the students making connections between music and culture and between composers and their contributions to society. How music represents culture and culture represents music is investigated. What is the cause and effect relationship? Is it an interactive relationship? The students are asked to investigate the purpose of music that has a specific function, to explain the cultural context of the music, and to decide to what degree the music represents a specific culture. These engagements require the students to move from looking for right and wrong answers to thinking logically with reason and purpose. A suggestion that deserves special note is to have students "invent cultures, including music and explanations of the cultural contexts of the music" (p. 46). The possibilities of thinking in this exercise are endless.

*Music technology — Suggested instructional strategies.* The inclusion of technology allows students to manipulate the elements in a concrete fashion, an essential activity if learning is to occur. While varying the elements, students are involved in exploring, making choices, evaluating, refining, and deciding. They are able to determine how different arrangements of elements can affect style or performance. The suggestions given in this section would open the world of technology to the students and involve them in many concrete problem-finding and problem-solving activities.

## Listening

The section that is devoted to listening in this document is similar to the Responding Section in the British Columbia IRP (British Columbia Ministry of Education, 1998) in terms of general suggestions (e.g., encouraging students to offer opinions and be aware of how their answer may enhance a peer's listening experience), and steps taken when listening (preparation, first impressions, description, analysis, interpretation, gathering background information, and informed judgement). The comments made in reference to the British Columbia guide would also apply here. The difference between the two presentations is that included in the Prince Edward Island guide are detailed suggestions that can be helpful to the music teacher when nurturing students' musical thinking.

## Summary

The Prince Edward Island *Elementary Music Curriculum Guide* for grades one to six provides abundant guidance for music educators in that province. In addition, the range of activities in which the students can experience music and gain knowledge about music within a larger context is admirable. Artistic, cultural, historical, functional, gender, social, technological, and career-related topics are covered. The guide, plus the tradition of hiring music specialists in Prince Edward Island to realize a curriculum, can fortify the strong music programs that have been in place over the years. An addition that would strengthen an already strong guide would be to include instructional strategies that give examples of activities and effective questioning techniques exemplifying Dewey's (1933/1991) fifth step to a larger degree, and his fourth step to a smaller degree. This addition would intensify the students' musical thinking.

# Conclusions

Of the three documents, British Columbia's and Prince Edward Island's curricula devote sections in which instructional and assessment strategies are given. This kind of information can provide guidance about how to empower musical thinking and can define the roles required of teachers and students if thinking is going to be promoted. The Ontario guide devotes a section to the role of the student and the role of the parent. In addition, it outlines what is required for four achievement levels; there is, however, no guidance for the music teacher about how to engage students in activities that involve musical thinking.

In all of the curricula guides, descriptions of activities and expectations include words that are characteristic of reflective thinking. It is important to remember, however, that it is often the way those activities are realized in the classroom that marginalizes students' musical thinking. When activities are included in the curriculum, they reflect a certain vision held by the author. The interpretation of those activities, and hence the realization, are nevertheless largely dependent on the experiences, knowledge, understandings, teaching style, and beliefs of the educators who implement them in the classroom. Interpretation and realization of the listed activities could be enhanced if effective questioning that would guide the students to think musically were included. Interpretation and realization could also, however, result in activities that are controlled and contrived.

Activities in which students acquire information but do not have experiences transferring, making decisions, exploring possibilities with the acquired information, and applying solutions to new situations can inhibit students' musical thinking. Once experiences of transferring, etc., are included, it is essential that an autocratic teaching style be abandoned (Richardson, 1998). Students' involvement at all stages of exploring, evaluating, refining, deciding, and defending is fundamental. When students do arrive at an incorrect or less than meaningful answer, the role of the educator is not to explain the reasoning behind the incorrect or insufficient solution but to ask questions that guide the student through this next step, one that includes reasoning about why the how and why, and provides opportunities for applying solutions to similar cases. This reasoning phase is a vital part of thinking.

If we are to make changes at the elementary level in terms of what it means to think musically and how that looks in a music classroom, then change needs to begin in music education classes at the university level. If we, as music educators of future music educators, do not know what it means to think musically then we need to involve ourselves in activities that require us to locate and define, suggest possibilities, develop by reasoning of the bearings of the suggestion, and observe and experiment to provide support for accepting or rejecting beliefs. As Richardson (1998) stated:

> Those of us in music teacher education need clear examples of critical thinking to show our students if we ever hope to see them nurturing the critical thinking of their own pupils. Those of us working in the music

classroom, studio, or rehearsal need specific strategies to lead students to think critically within the discipline of music. (p. 108)

It is our job to know our facts and be able to distinguish facts from opinions. To accomplish this discrimination requires us to know what is going on in our field, which can be accomplished by reading professional journals and attending conferences and workshops. In this way we can identify standards against which we can evaluate possibilities and solutions. This can be done by reading current professional journals and attending conferences and workshops. In other words, music teacher educators and music teachers need to be independent, knowledgeable, musical thinkers. We need to accept that there are not always answers, and when there are, we do not have to be the ones to supply them (Richardson, 1998). We need to "let go of" some of the power that can be felt in a classroom and welcome further inquiry, debate, and reflection. We need to be more comfortable with "chaos in the container" and realize that chaos can be productive and constructive.

## References

Boardman, E. (1989). The relationship of music study to thinking. In E. Boardman (Ed.), *Dimensions of musical thinking* (pp. 1–7). Reston, VA: Music Educators National Conference.

British Columbia Ministry of Education. (1998). *Integrated resource package — Fine arts K to 7*. Victoria, BC: Author.

Dewey, J. (1991). *How we think*. Buffalo, NY: Prometheus Books. (Original work published 1933)

Dewey, J. (1934). *Art as experience*. New York: Perigee Books.

Dewey, J. (1938). *Experience and education*. New York: Collier Books, Macmillan.

Fiske, H. (1990). *Music and mind: Philosophical essays on the cognition and meaning of music*. Queenston, ON: Mellen Press.

Gardner, H. (1983). *Frames of mind: The theory of multiple intelligences*. New York: Basic Books.

Gardner, H. (1991). *The unschooled mind*. New York: Basic Books.

Ontario Ministry of Education and Training. (1998). *The Ontario curriculum, grades 1-8: The arts*. Toronto: Author.

Pautz, M. (1989). Musical thinking in the teacher education classroom. In E. Boardman (Ed.), *Dimensions of musical thinking* (pp. 101–109). Reston, VA: Music Educators National Conference.

Prince Edward Island Department of Education. (1997). *Elementary music curriculum guide: Grades 1 to 6*. Charlottetown, PE: Author.

Reimer, B. (1999). Facing the risks of the "Mozart Effect." *Music Educators Journal, 86*, (1), 37–43.

Richards, P., & Milligan, D. (1998). The case for a multidisciplinary arts education curriculum. In B. A. Roberts, (Ed.) *Connect, combine, communicate: Revitalizing the arts in Canadian schools* (pp. 75-88). Sydney, NS: University College of Cape Breton Press.

Richardson, C. P. (1998). The roles of the critical thinker in the music classroom. *Studies in music from The University of Western Ontario, 17,* 107–120.

Saskatchewan Education. (1991). *Arts education: A curriculum guide for Grades 1-5.* Regina, SK: Author.

Sizer, T. (1992). *Horace's compromise: The dilemma of the American high school.* New York: Houghton Mifflin.

Webster, P. R., & Richardson, C. P. (1994). Asking children to think about music. *Research Studies in Music Education, 2,* 8–14.

# Chapter Ten

# Assessing for Success in Music Education

## Rodger Beatty

The assessment and evaluation of students' achievements in music education remains central for the teacher in determining the knowledge and skills that students have learned. The current movement towards global competitiveness and calls for restructuring and accountability from various levels of government have recently provided the climate for music educators in Canadian schools to focus on high standards or expectations for school students. These standards require excellence and clear evidence of achievement.

Traditionally, music educators have been extremely involved with the process but mainly measured the final product of performance. Authentic assessment, as in real life situations, stresses the importance of the processes of learning as well as the final products.

This chapter will discuss how Canadian music educators have traditionally gathered information to meet a variety of assessment and evaluation needs. Next, an overview of practices in assessment in contemporary Canadian music education will be presented. Finally, challenges facing music educators for the future will be suggested.

## The Context of Assessment in Schools

Assessment has many purposes. Dietel, Herman, and Knuth (1991) suggest that assessment may be utilized by policy makers, school administrators, teachers, parents, and students. Policymakers use assessment to set standards, focus on goals, or monitor the quality of education. They may also utilize assessment to reward/sanction various practices, formulate new policies, direct resources including personnel and money, or determine the effects of tests. School administrators may use assessment to identify program strengths and weaknesses, delineate program priorities, or to assess alternatives and/or program improvements. Teachers use assessment to diagnose individual learning challenges and determine further learning direction, monitor student progress, undertake curriculum evaluation and refinement, provide constructive feedback to students, motivate students, and determine student grades. Parents and students use assessment to assess student strengths and weaknesses, determine school accountability, or make informed educational and career decisions.

There is a difference between assessment and evaluation. Assessment of student achievement involves the process of gathering of information or data about student progress — what they know and what they are able to do. The main function of assessment is to provide benefit directly to students in the form of accurate, constructive feedback about the quality of their growing musicianship. Evaluation involves grading, ranking, or other summary value judgments or decisions regarding the level or quality of a music behaviour or other endeavour (Boyle, 1992; Elliott, 1995). Evaluation may include both quantitative and qualitative descriptions of characteristics in addition to the value judgments of the behaviour described (Abeles, Hoffer, & Klotman, 1995).

## Characteristics of Effective Assessment

Effective assessment of student achievement provides accurate data on student performance and enables teachers and other decision makers to make appropriate decisions. Assessments which show both validity and reliability are considered effective. A good assessment actually measures what it is intended to measure. This concept is known as validity. In general, the results of a good assessment or test represent something beyond how students perform on a certain task or a set of items; they represent how a student performs on the objective which those items were intended to assess. Test validity is tied to the purposes for which an assessment is used. Thus, a test might be appropriate for one purpose but inappropriate for other purposes (Abeles, Hoffer, & Klotman, 1995; Boyle, 1992; Dietel, Herman, & Knuth, 1991).

The concept of reliability refers to the consistency and stability of a test or scale. Will the results of the assessment for this person or class be similar if they are gathered at some other time or under different circumstances or if they are scored by different raters? When measurements are consistent over several data collections they are said to have high reliability. The high degree of agreement among a group of judges is that of interjudge reliability (Abeles, Hoffer, & Klotman, 1995; Dietel, Herman, & Knuth, 1991).

## Assessment and Evaluation in Music Education in Canadian Schools

Traditionally, assessment in music education in Canadian schools has been product-oriented or test driven. As well, excessive emphasis has been placed upon the acquisition of psychomotor skills and factual knowledge. For many music educators, assessment and evaluation in music education have been synonymous with testing, and the testing has been linked to giving grades. Bates (1984) suggested that pressure from outside sources that advocated extensive music performance and the relative ease with which this type of learning can be evaluated by teachers were key reasons for this outcome. The results reported by Roberts (1994), in a major study of assessment in music education in Canada, suggested that teachers prioritized performance or practical tests as the most important of all assessment tools. Group and individual projects were also designated as very important. In addition, written in-class tests and examinations were identified as important areas of assessment.

To consider carefully the topic of evaluation in music education in a national context, the Queen's University Symposium on Evaluation in Music Education was convened in February 1990. The results of the symposium suggested that widely divergent practices in assessment and evaluation existed in music education in Canada (Bates, 1992a; Bates, 1992b; Beatty, 1992; Hanley, 1992a; Hanley, 1992b; Knight, 1992; Porter, 1992; Willingham, 1992). In 1991, The Canadian Music Educators Association/L'Association Canadienne des Éducateurs de Musique created a National Task Force on Evaluation in Music Education to develop projects in evaluation and to suggest standards for music education in Canada. Hanley (1994a; 1994b; 1994c) reported on developments for devising and testing new alternative approaches to assessment where the students would become more involved in their own learning.

## From Product- to Process- and Product-Oriented Assessment

In music education, the work of Gardner (1983) and his colleagues in his theory of multiple intelligences (MI) has spurred great interest in investigating alternative ways of assessment. Gardner posited that there are seven forms of human competence that are relatively independent: linguistic, logical-mathematical, spatial, bodily-kinesthetic, musical, interpersonal, and intrapersonal intelligences. He argued that since each intelligence displays a unique characteristic set of psychological processes, it is vitally important that these processes be assessed in an intelligence-fair manner. Intelligence-fair measures seek to respect the unique modes of thinking and performance that distinguish each intelligence. Standardized tests, which almost exclusively stress linguistic and logical-mathematical skills, are limited. Educators need to take a broader view of human achievement and performance as they appear in each domain of accomplishment. Standardized testing or the formal testing model illustrates an objective, product-oriented, decontextualized form of assessment.

In contrast to the formal testing model, Gardner and Hatch (1989), using the MI theory, suggested that intelligences are always contextualized and should be assessed in term of their cultural manifestation in specific domains of endeavour and with reference to particular adult "end states." This "apprenticeship" model involves a form of process-oriented assessment which occurs entirely within the context of the learning material, surrounded with the particulars of the craft or skill (Willingham, 1993a).

Elliott (1995) built on this notion of the "apprentice" in his praxial philosophy of music education. In the praxial philosophy, the teacher assumes the role of expert while the student acts as apprentice. Music making is a matter of musical knowledge-in-action or musicianship. The student is actively engaged in authentic music making projects replicating those of a musician (performing, creating, listening, conducting, composing, or arranging). Ongoing reflective questioning guides the learner to a deeper and more informed level of musicianship.

Authentic assessment can be referred to as alternative assessment or performance-based assessment. It is a valid assessment system which provides information about the particular tasks on which students succeed or fail, but more importantly, it also presents tasks that are worthwhile, significant and meaningful (Archbald & Newmann, 1988). Furthermore, authentic assessment provides a powerful qualitative view of students' abilities to formulate new questions, to reflect critically and develop self-knowledge, to pursue work over time, and to arrive at performance standards of excellence (Wolf, 1987, 1989).

## Arts PROPEL: Authentic Assessment in the Arts

In 1985, Harvard Project Zero, Educational Testing Service, and the Pittsburgh Public Schools joined in a multiyear project, entitled Arts PROPEL to develop powerful version of the qualitative modes of assessment (Brandt, 1987; Wolf, 1987; Wolf, 1989). The Arts PROPEL project assessed growth and learning in music, visual art, and imaginative writing at middle school and high school levels. It had two basic aims: (1) to design ways of evaluating student learning that provide information to teachers and school systems while modeling personal responsibility in questioning and reflecting on their own work and (2) to find ways of capturing growth over time so that students could become informed and thoughtful assessors of their own growth as learners (Wolf, 1989). The project was based on the premise that the most desirable method of assessing learning is to assess it in context. In assessing artistic growth, the competencies of artistic production, artistic perception, and artistic reflection were therefore monitored (Beatty, 1996; Willingham, 1993b).

The authentic assessment within Arts PROPEL involved three components: domain projects, process-folios or portfolios, and reflective interviews. Domain projects involved independent problem solving in the arts. In music education this work includes performance in solo or group setting, literature analysis, conducting, music composition/ arranging, etc. The artist-teachers or experts monitor short- and long-term student musicianship growth in technical mastery and interpretive skill (Gardner, 1989; Walters & Gardner, 1990; Willingham, 1993b).

Process-folios or portfolios record and track a student's involvement over time in various works of art. In music education, portfolios should contain a diverse range of representative works in process. Portfolios provide a vision of the processes that underlie the long-term development and evolution of artistic thinking. The teacher can observe and examine the particular profile of skills and how they change or improve over time (Dirth, 1994; Wolf, 1987).

Reflective interviews involve students in critical reflection on their own body of work. During these interviews the full scope of student work is assessed: the self-awareness level of students, personal strengths/weaknesses, and personal styles (Wolf, 1987).

## Assessing for Success in Music Education

In order to assess for success in music education, teachers must embrace various form of authentic assessment. Authentic assessment accentuates the significance of the process of learning as well as the product. When teachers employ a variety of authentic assessments, students are guided to advance beyond the "one correct answer" type of thinking to explore the open-ended problems that encourage higher order thinking skills. They are inspired to make their own connections and draw inferences (Farrell, 1997). Teachers who employ these types of assessments clearly plan authentic and meaningful learning tasks so students will engage in learning opportunities. They systematically gather evidence that guides their teaching.

**Examples of Authentic Process Assessments**

- student conference or interviews
- documented observations
- student journals
- student self-assessments: directed critiques and open-ended critiques (oral and written)
- reflective interviews
- behavioural checklists

**Examples of Authentic Product Assessments**

- solo and ensemble performance
- essays with prompts
- scoring criteria which students have access to prior to the assessment occurring
- projects with rating criteria
- student demonstrations or investigation in expository or interdisciplinary formats
- paintings, dramas, concerts, dances, stories or essays with rating criteria
- attitude inventories
- surveys
- response journals
- enhanced standardized or multiple choice questions with a section for explanation by the student
- open-ended problems. (Farrell, 1997, pp. 4–5)

Authentic assessment may be grouped into five categories: self-assessments, peer assessments, group assessments, portfolio assessments and teacher created assessments.

## Self-assessments

Self-assessments illuminate students' perception of how they are performing. Through self-assessment, students are guided to take ownership for their own learning. Students judge their own work repeatedly as it is in progress, finally completed and/or compare it to earlier or later works. As a result of being involved in this self-assessment enterprise, students develop a greater understanding of assessment and evaluation, and the venture provides them with a means for assessing their own growth and setting learning goals for the future.

Self-assessment tools may include: attitude inventories, surveys, and reflective response journals. Students' self-assessments aid the teacher in determining what students have learned and provide a meaningful indication for improving instruction in the classroom and assigning of grades in the evaluation stage.

Wells (1998) suggests that student self-assessment tasks could be directed critiques or open-ended critiques. In directed critiques, students are presented with clearly defined performance dimensions for their self-assessments. For example, ninth-grade instrumental music students may be asked to view a videotape of their rehearsal and assess their performance based upon the following dimensions: balance, dynamics, intonation, articulation, tempo, and posture. For open-ended critiques, students choose to select their own performance dimensions. In this case, the aim is to reflect on the most important aspects for improving the performance.

One effective way to assess direct or open-ended critiques is through the use of rubrics. A rubric is an established set of analytical criteria for scoring or rating a student's performance on tasks that requires the rater to select from different descriptions of levels to assess actual achievement. It is characterized by a series of statements describing the criteria for a range of levels of achievement (1–4) of a process, a product, or a performance (Draper, 1998; Hickey, 1999; Whitcomb, 1999).

To develop scoring criteria, first decide if the focus will be on the process, the product, or both the process and product. Gathering various samples of rubrics from other areas of the curriculum (e.g., language, visual Arts, etc.) will be beneficial. Write descriptors for the important characteristics of the task. Gather samples of students' work; field test the rubric by pilot testing the criteria to investigate whether the rubric helps make accurate judgments about students' work. Involve students in providing input into the draft criteria. Then review the criteria and try them again until the rubric scores deeply portrays the quality of work desired. Table 1 presents an example of a rubric for a directed critique.

**Table 1. Assessment rubric for a directed critique**

| Level 1 *Emerging* | Level 2 *Developing* | Level 3 *Competent* | Level 4 *Powerful* |
|---|---|---|---|
| The student • minimally describes and analyzes the specific strengths and weaknesses of his/her performance • gives limited or vague suggestions for the improvement of weaknesses • makes limited reference to musical events • shows limited use of music terminology • demonstrates limited understanding of the elements of music | The student • generally describes and analyzes the specific strengths and weaknesses of his/her performance • gives some suggestions for the improvement of weaknesses • makes some reference to musical events • shows fair use of music terminology • demonstrates partial understanding of the elements of music | The student • substantially describes and analyzes the specific strengths and weaknesses of his/her performance • gives most of the suggestions for the improvement of weaknesses • makes specific reference to musical events • shows good use of music terminology • demonstrates substantial understanding of the elements of music | The student • accurately describes and analyzes the specific strengths and weaknesses of his/her performance • gives effective suggestions for the improvement of weaknesses • makes strong reference to musical events • shows excellent use of music terminology • demonstrates thorough understanding of the elements of music |

*Peer assessments*

Peer assessments allow students to collaborate and converse with others through discussion, sharing, and learning from the perceptions of others. With guidance from the teacher, students assess other students' work either individually, with a partner, or in groups. Students acquire valuable insights in their response to and assessment of the works of their peers. By engaging in the critique of works in progress as well as completed products, students learn to value the creative process. As they learn from one another, students learn to value the viewpoint and contributions of others.

### Group assessments

Group assessments focus on how a group as a whole has progressed. Through critical reflection, students gain insight into working with others; they learn from one another. Group assessments can help to improve social and communication skills amongst members of the musical group whether they are a class, choir, band, orchestra, or other music ensemble.

### Portfolio assessments

Portfolio assessments involve a purposeful collection of student work over a period of time that tells the story of the student's efforts, progress, or achievement in a given area (Arter & Spandel, 1992). The artifacts in a presentation/product portfolio may be collected by teacher, by student, or by teacher and student in consultation. The content of the portfolio must be multisourced. It must include a rich array of student work examples, domain projects, student participation in the selection of portfolio content, the guidelines for selection, the criteria for judging selection, and evidence of student self-reflection. In music, the student portfolio may include: audio cassette or videotapes, compositions, critiques and comparisons of musical works including the student's own, error detection exercises, journal entries, written quizzes or tests, reflective interviews, and "biographies of work" (e.g. drafts, notes, or false stArts).

Portfolios depict the artistic thinking processes of the students and give meaning to their long-term development. Domain projects provide students with real life or authentic contexts. Students leave school and follow years of long-term projects that require moment-to-moment monitoring and many judgments of errors and worth. These projects over time allow students and teacher to see the accumulation of process work; students experience reflective musical practice through active music-making in real life contexts.

Utilizing portfolio assessment has benefits for both teacher and students. The teacher can observe and examine the particular profile of skills and see how it changes or improves over time. For the students, portfolios provide an avenue for collecting and documenting their work over time. Portfolios encourage ownership by both students and teachers. Students take ownership of their work and their thoughts. Teachers act as owners of curriculum development and much of the learning sequence. Jointly teachers and students share ownership of assessment (Beatty, 1996).

Fitzsimmins (1996) shared students' responses about their perceived value of the process: "I found it very valuable because you could look back at a paper or something and remember how good it felt to get that mark or comment," (p. 34) and "It keeps things from being lost. The portfolio is a confidence builder" (p. 34).

Portfolio usage has benefits in our very transient school populations. When used across different school boards or districts, portfolios help teachers get a deeper sense of what newly transferred students have already learned. Domain projects, portfolios, and reflective interviews promote the development of higher order thinking skills. Through their reflective practice and critical evaluation of others and self, students become informed musicians thinking in action.

There are potential benefits for establishing clear criteria for judging merit of portfolios; portfolios can be assessed using a checklist or rubric in terms of production, perception, and reflection. Production concerns the performance or composition of music, perception refers to listening to one's own playing, and reflection is describing or judging what one hears. Using the Arts PROPEL model, Dirth (1994) reported the usefulness of portfolio reviews which incorporated checklists for major components of inclusion, a section for comments along with an overall rating scale for each category (production, perception, and reflection).

### Teacher-created assessments

Teacher-created assessments embody those assessments developed by the teacher and applied by the student. These may include open-ended problem-solving tasks, individual/group performances, projects/exhibitions, culminating exhibitions, concept maps, and enhanced multiple-choice questions. It is imperative that criteria be clearly stated for these types of performance-based assessments.

*Open-ended problem-solving tasks.* Open-ended problem-solving tasks challenge students to respond in writing or through musical expression (e.g., composition, performance, movement to music, dramatic interpretation to music, critique, etc.). These tasks may be either individual- or group-oriented. The problem must be clearly defined and embody the opportunity for more than one correct answer. If the problem solving is to be group-oriented, individual accountability must be built into the learning challenge. Open-ended problem-solving tasks develop students' higher-order thinking skills; they learn to think, solve, and communicate. Assessment tools may include rubrics, checklists, anecdotal records, numerical or qualitative rating scales, and peer and self-assessments.

*Individual or group performances/presentations.* Individual or group performances/presentations can encompass a wide variety of forms (e.g., musical performances, compositions, listening logs, written reports, panel discussions, visual displays, etc.) In individual performances/presentations, students work independently with or without teacher assistance to create a project from start to finish. In group performances/presentations, students collaboratively work together to formulate, develop, and implement a project that may include a diverse scope of student learning expectations.

Whenever a student participates in a music ensemble as part of a music festival that is judged or sings/plays a solo at an audition, the student is engaged in a type of performance-based assessment (Robinson, 1995). Usually the assessment involves the traditional rating scale. This type of assessment includes a number of categories (such as accuracy, tone, enunciation, technique, intonation, phrasing, interpretation) where the performance of student is assessed according to a number (5–4–3–2–1) or letter (A–B–C–D–F) rating based on a scale. The disadvantage of this type of assessment is that the distance between units is often unequal; when judgments are made, they may be based on subjective opinions of "goodness" for a given category.

Criteria-specific rating scales provide more objective evaluation of performance-based tasks. Two types of criteria-specific scales are continuous rating scales and additive rating scales. Continuous rating scales outline a sequence of increasingly difficult musical or technical criteria. Attainment of a certain rating is conditional upon the successful completion of all previous criteria. In additive rating scales, the criteria descriptors are not organized sequentially, and attainment of a certain rating is not dependent upon the successful achievement of all previous criteria levels. Teachers should use precise language in describing the assessment criteria (Robinson, 1995).

Other assessment tools most often used for musical performance tasks are rubrics, anecdotal records, checklists, individual performance self-assessments, critiques, error detection exercises, and peer assessments.

*Projects/exhibitions.* Projects or exhibitions are authentic forms of assessment that provide creative and imaginative learning opportunities for the students to demonstrate over time (either several hours to several weeks) their capability to define a problem, develop a plan, carry out the procedure, produce a final product and communicate the end results. In this form of teacher-created assessment, students need to show the application of their learning in an imaginative way that challenges them through task endurance and time management. As in many other performance-based or authentic assessments, there will be a variety of "correct answers" or solutions.

Ratings scales, rubrics, checklists and peer and self-assessments are viable tools of assessment for use with projects or exhibitions. Criteria need to be lucidly stated and linked to the learning expectations for this assessment task.

*Culminating exhibitions.* Culminating exhibitions provide an imaginative way for students to demonstrate a performance or final product is a result of work accomplished over a more extended period than projects/exhibitions. Often, this type of teacher-created assessment is used as a graduating exhibition highlighting the students' growth over time. The resulting exposition usually encompasses both oral and written forms in a public demonstration. A committee of teachers, students (peers) and adults from the school community may assess the enterprise. In the exhibition, students must interpret their learning and defend their creative work. Usually in this kind of assessment, students must include a critical self-reflection delineating the learning journey they have undertaken. As in projects and exhibitions, rating scales, rubrics, checklists, and peer and self-assessments comprise appropriate ways for assessing these types of authentic tasks.

*Writing reports.* Writing reports are valuable ways to determine acquired knowledge in order to plan for subsequent learning or to compare understanding of a particular content area in a pre to post relationship. These reports or essays may be assessed according to a set of criteria. Analytical criteria-type rubrics or checklists provide efficient ways for assessing these types of writing tasks.

*Research papers.* In these assessments, students are mainly asked to research and to write on an assigned topic. Research papers provide viable avenues to ascertain the level of student comprehension and application of learning in the concepts and elements of music. Often assignments of this type are designed to help demonstrate the students' understanding of musical styles, theoretical analysis, and/or historical context; linking their understanding with required musical performance provides an inclusive way to effectively develop student learning. The establishment of clear expectations and assessment criteria is critical. The development of lucid outlines for research papers will assist students in accomplishing this type of teacher-created assessment. Tools such as checklists, analytical criteria rubrics, and peer and self-assessments present effective ways for assessing research papers.

*Concept maps.* Concept maps or web chArts are assessment tasks designed to depict visually a learner's understanding of the interrelationship among the concepts and one major idea. Through the use of lines and ovals, learners graphically show the connections from the main idea to the other concepts. In assessing concept maps, Farrell (1997) suggests awarding 1 point for each musical element and I point for each linking word or phrase.

*Enhanced multiple-choice questions.* Enhanced multiple-choice questions are generally tasks which assess whether students know musical concepts or skills and the ways in which they may apply them in various situations. In this teacher-created assessment, students must use more than one strategy in solving the question by forging connections among the concepts. In order to select the correct answer, students must compare and contrast various choices in deducing the right response. Questions may take two or three minutes to solve. Rubrics or checklists are optimal choices for assessing success in this type or authentic task.

## How Can Teachers Assess for Success?

Creative teachers will reply that they can assess for success and they certainly want to do it, but this kind of assessment does require work and time. Ensuring that assessment is strongly linked to instruction is key to teachers having successful assessment in music education. In preparing for effective assessment in the classroom, teachers must plan for a variety of instructional strategies which enable students with different backgrounds, abilities, learning styles, and interests to learn effectively. Teachers must provide students with appropriate learning resources for them to reach their full potential. They must ensure that the learning resources are relevant to the interest of the students and free of bias. Effective teachers must check that learning activities are accurately planned to reflect the needs and interests of students in their classes; important aspects they need to consider are gender, ethno-cultural variety, religions, ages and background of students. In addition, they should recognize and make appropriate modifications for students with special needs.

By monitoring and assessing student progress throughout the unit or learning encounter and by adjusting instructional methods where needed in order to respond to individual student needs such as styles and rates of learning, teachers can develop effective programs of authentic assessment in music education. It is important that teachers incorporate a wide variety of authentic process and product assessment strategies to provide students with a range of opportunities to demonstrate their learning growth. The assessment and evaluation practices that teachers select need to be appropriate for the ages and levels of maturity of students in the classroom.

## The Challenges of Authentic Assessment in Music Education

As we embark on this next century, certain issues present challenges for Canadian music educators in their pursuit of assessment for success. Currently, portfolios can be assessed in a variety of dimensions. If portfolios (containing a wide variety of process and product authentic assessments) are to be used at the school district, provincial, or national levels, a common reliable means of assessing students of varying abilities will need to be investigated and created.

Music educators who have embraced the alternative or performance-based assessment movement have found that, in order for authentic assessment to be effectively implemented in their classroom, they need to find different ways for storage of the various aspects of students' work. Fitzsimmins (1996) documented the great challenge of keeping large portfolio storage boxes in her music room. With the advancement of new technologies for scanning and electronic storage of creative materials on computer disks, music educators will need to embrace these innovative technologies to assist with storage challenges.

Active music educators are very busy individuals usually involved in many extra-curricular or co-curricular music ensembles. The time factor required to read, watch, listen to, and assess whole works, journals, compositions, audiotapes, videotapes, reflective interviews, etc. in relation to each student's profile of growth may appear overwhelming for many music teachers. Finding creative strategies to build authentic assessments directly into the student learning process is critical if music teachers are to manage their time and meet the demands of daily classroom life. Using technology and computer-based assessment tracking devices may help music educators meet the challenge of making assessment a natural outgrowth of classroom learning.

The training of teachers in authentic assessment strategies will continue to be a growing challenge for both preservice and inservice teacher education. Teachers need to become aware of the assumptions behind their assessment practice and reform past perceptions and practice when warranted. School boards/districts and provincial ministries/departments of education must devote time, energy and finances to ensure effective staff development to promote the use of authentic assessment of student learning.

As students assume a greater role in assessing their own learning and the work of others in an authentic assessment framework, the dynamics of the teacher-student relationship change. Students are asked to assess their own performance and that of others within their group; teachers then must learn to give up control of this area. Teachers must learn that self-assessments and peer assessments are most meaningful and can capture significant interpretations; the eventual goal of such involvement is the development of independent learners.

In the future when authentic assessment becomes more commonplace in secondary schools, college and university entrance requirements will need to be reconsidered. It will be necessary for innovative admission requirements to be developed to reflect that student learning is much more than product-oriented final marks.

Through performance-based assessments, students experience reflective musical practice because they are engaged in active music-making in real life contexts. Authentic assessment tools provide a powerful enhancement of teachers' understanding of students' music learning, inform further instruction, and promote students' self-knowledge and their attainment of performance standards of excellence. As Canadian music educators embrace further the compelling model of authentic assessment, they will experience greater success in assessment and the joy of learning music will be more deeply shared and enjoyed by all.

## References

Abeles, H. F., Hoffer, C. R., & Klotman, R. H. (1995). *Foundations of music education* (2nd ed.). New York, NY: Schirmer.

Archbald, D. A., & Newmann, F. M. (1988). *Beyond standardized testing: Assessing authentic academic achievement in the secondary school.* Madison, WI: University of Wisconsin, National Association of Secondary School Principals.

Arter, J. A., & Spandel, V. (1992). Using portfolios of student work in instruction and assessment. *Educational Measurement: Issues and Practice, 11,* 36 & 44.

Bates, D. (1984). Evaluation of students in music classes. *Canadian Music Educator, 26* (2), 7–16.

Bates, D. (1992). Editorial: The Queen's symposium on evaluation in music education. *Canadian Music Educator, 33* (5), 3–4.

Bates, D. (1992). Opinions on the status of evaluation in music education in Canada. *Canadian Music Educator, 33* (5), 15–18.

Beatty, R. J. (1992). Evaluation in music education: An Ontario perspective. *Canadian Music Educator, 33* (5), 35–36.

Beatty, R. J. (1996). Opening up assessment in music education. *The Recorder, 38* (2), 43–46.

Boyle, J. D. (1992). Evaluation of music ability. In R. Colwell (Ed.), *Handbook of research on music teaching and learning* (pp. 247–285). New York, NY: Schirmer.

Brant, R. (1987). On assessment in the Arts: A conversation with Howard Gardner. *Educational Leadership, 45* (4), 30–34.

Dietel, R. J., Herman, J. L., & Knuth, R. A. (1991). *What Does Research Say About Assessment?* Oak Brook, IL: North Central Regional Educational Laboratory. Available: http://www.ncrel.org/sdrs/areas/stw_esys/4assess.htm

Dirth, K. (1994, April). *Portfolio assessment for performing groups.* A paper presented at the Music Educators National Conference, Cincinnati, Ohio.

Draper, A. (1998). Making the grade: Authentic assessment in music, K-8. *Teaching Music, 6* (2), 34–35, 48.

Elliott, D. J. (1995). *Music matters: A new philosophy of music education.* New York, NY: Oxford University Press.

Farrell, S. R. (1997). *Tools for powerful student evaluation.* Fort Lauderdale, FL: Meredith Music Publications.

Fitzsimmins, S. (1996). The music duotang and portfolio. *The Recorder, 39* (1), 33–34.

Gardner, H. (1983). *Frames of mind.* New York, NY: Basic.

Gardner, H. (1989). Zero-based Arts education: An introduction to Arts PROPEL. *Studies in Art Education, 30* (2), 71–83.

Gardner, H., & Hatch, T. (1989). Multiple intelligences go to school: Educational implications of the theory of multiple intelligences. *Educational Researcher, 18* (8), 4–9.

Hanley, B. (1992a). Assessment and evaluation in music education. *Canadian Music Educator, 33* (5), 7–13.

Hanley, B. (1992b). Student assessment in music education. *Canadian Music Educator, 33* (5), 19–24.

Hanley, B. (1994a). Sample for assessment exchange: Students as judges. *Canadian Music Educator, 35* (3), 44.

Hanley, B. (1994b). Assessment exchange: Student self evaluation. *Canadian Music Educator, 35* (5), 7–10.

Hanley, B. (1994c). Assessment exchange: An idea bank for music educators. *British Columbia Music Educator, 37* (1), 20–25.

Hickey, M. (1999). Assessment rubrics for music compositions. *Music Educators Journal, 85* (4), 26–33.

Knight, S. (1992). Evaluation & alpha and omega. *Canadian Music Educator, 33* (5), 25–32.

Niebur, L. (1994). Assessment as a class activity. *Music Educators Journal, 80* (5), 23–25, 47.

Porter, B. (1992). Report from the Halifax County-Bedford District School Board, Nova Scotia. *Canadian Music Educator, 33* (5), 37–39.

Roberts, B. (1994). Assessment in music education: A cross-Canada study. *Canadian Music Educator, 35* (5), 3–6.

Robinson, M. (1995). Alternative assessment techniques for teachers. *The Recorder, 37* (3/4), 105–110.

Walters, J., & Gardner, H. (1990). *Domain projects as assessment vehicles in a computer-rich environment.* (Technical Report NO. 5). New York, NY: Center for Technology in Education. (ERIC Document Reproduction Service NO. ED 324 367)

Wells, R. (1998). The student's role in the assessment process. *Teaching Music, 6* (2), 32–33.

Whitcomb, R. (1999). Writing rubrics for the music classroom. *Music Educators Journal, 85* (6), 26–32.

Willingham, L. (1992). Musical growth: Need we evaluate it? *Canadian Music Educator, 33* (5), 41–43.

Willingham, L. (1993a). Evaluating musical growth in an authentic context. *The Recorder, 35* (4), 153–158.

Willingham, L. (1993b). *Classroom assessment and evaluation in the Arts.* Scarborough, ON: Scarborough Board of Education.

Wolf, D. P. (1987). Opening up assessment. *Educational Leadership, 45* (4), 24–29.

Wolf, D. P. (1989). Portfolio assessment: Sampling student work. *Educational Leadership, 46* (7), 35–39.

# Chapter Eleven

# Paradox and Possibility
## Arts Assessment in the Elementary Grades

*Katharine Smithrim*

## Introduction

Assessment in the arts is rife with paradox.[1] Walter Pitman, former MP, MPP, and university president, is one of Canada's wisest and most knowledgeable advocates for the arts. In a recent book he makes the following observation:

> [The] belief in the lack of standards in arts instruction has a long history emerging from many decades of trivialization of the arts in North American society. Yet there is surely no fragment of our lives in which we expect such obeisance to the gods of quality as in our experience with the arts. We accept incompetence on our shopping trips, mediocrity in any number of services we request at the gas pump or bank counter, but we demand excellence when we attend a theatre, a concert hall and dance studio or an art gallery.... The local newspaper may provide nothing but flattery and hyperbole in its coverage of sports, business and professional activities, but even small-town symphonies and theatres receive the critical assessment and intense evaluation normally accorded to a doctoral dissertation. (p. 116)

Therein lies a first paradox: the arts may be regarded as trivial and yet, in the real world of arts in performance and exhibition, the arts are assessed according to the highest standards. Within education, at the secondary school level, the same paradox exists. It is acknowledged by students and teachers that high school arts studies can be some of the most demanding and rigourous courses, and yet universities in Canada routinely disregard grades in secondary

school arts courses even for entrance into their own fine arts programs. Some of the questions this paradox raises are "What are these
*highest standards* in the public realm of the arts, and in arts education?" "Who decides what *highest standards* are?" "How do people
make judgements about arts performance and exhibitions in society
and in schools?" and "What is the relationship between how arts are
evaluated in the real world and in schools?"

Another paradox lies in the apparent incompatibility between
evaluation/assessment and the arts. While evaluation and assessment
are embedded in a tradition that values correct answers, logical
processes, and substantiated theories, the arts involve multiple solutions, flights of imagination, and open-ended processes. In the form
of testing, evaluation most often stresses knowledge learned or acquired from others, while work in the arts is frequently generated
from one's own experience. Many approaches to assessment, such as
portfolios and observation which seem more appropriate in the arts,
have resurfaced or been developed, but do any assessment strategies
exist which actually illuminate the impact of the *aesthetic* process?

A third paradox is inherent in the time in which we live — the
transition from the modern to the postmodern era, and how this
transition affects education. One postmodernist claims that "[t]o
think of evaluation in post-modern terms is virtually impossible"
(Doll, 1993, p. 172). His statement is based on his view that, in the
past, evaluation has been based on two assumptions which no longer
hold. The first is that "our purpose as teachers is to have students
acquire a particular, set body of knowledge in a particular way."
The second is that "evaluation in terms of grades is the assessment
of how much of this canon and its method the student has acquired"
(p. 172). Doll argues that in a postmodern, transformative curriculum, there is no ideally set norm, no canon.[2]

I call each of these issues in arts education a paradox rather than
a problem. When we face a problem, we expect to find a solution. A
paradox generally has no solution. In a paradox, when both sides are
honoured, it may be possible to maintain a tenuous balance. A new
solution *might* emerge, but it is important to be able to live in the
tensions of the paradox. Working within paradox requires caring for
both or all sides of an issue, humility towards the ideas and the
players, and imagination. In a society which favours polarization —
win/lose, either/or, right/wrong, rich/poor, and pro/con — the ability to live with ambiguity, holding in balance two or more oppos-
ing ideas or forces is a new skill required of teachers. I will address
each paradox in turn, beginning with the third. In this chapter I have

used the words assessment, evaluation, and grading to mean the following:

- Assessment is the process of gathering information to *plan for* meaningful instruction for students.
- Evaluation involves placing a value judgement on work.
- Grading involves attaching a symbol to the results of evaluation.

## Signs of Our Times

Teachers of the arts often end a disagreement by saying "Well our methods may be different, but our goals are the same." However, we are living in a time of such transition that arts teachers' goals are not the same, in fact they can be fundamentally different. Without entering into a lengthy explanation of this time of transition from modern to postmodern thought, some sign posts are helpful. This list in Table 1 is simplistic, but it can point to how this transition is affecting schools, teaching and education.

The roots of postmodernism are the scientific discoveries which shook humankind's belief that the universe was stable and predictable — some of these discoveries lie within quantum physics and chaos mathematics. We are moving beyond a time in which predictability and control were the prizes of the scientific method, to a time when science is finding ambiguity, unpredictability, and instability at the very core of things.

How we make sense of the world is changing. "[W]e live between the no longer and the not yet, a time when formerly comfortable holds on making sense of the world no longer suffice" (Lather & Ellsworth, 1996, p. 70). A frequent and hasty judgement of the effects of postmodernism on education is that it means that all standards are gone, and "anything goes." For me, the two most important influences are our changing view of knowledge and of the way people learn. The view that knowledge is constructed by individuals and groups rather than absorbed or transferred is now generally accepted. What is not so easily accepted is the postmodern view of the changing roles of teacher and student. Particularly in music education, where the teacher is often the *conductor*, challenges to teacher knowledge and authority may be perceived as threatening at a fundamental level.

Rasberry suggests that

> living well within the postmodern moment becomes learning to live well with the contradictory and competing expectations and demands placed upon us from within the classroom and from outside forces. It is a time for us, as teachers, to look closely at our own practice and learn to trust what comes out of the particulars, letting go of more generalized calls for one kind of classroom practice or another (because they no longer work). We construct our own sense of things, we trust that certain things can be true to our practice while knowing that these things are not necessarily the Truth. (G. Rasberry, personal communication, December 12, 1999)

## Table 1. From modern to postmodern thought

| Modern Thought | Postmodern Thought |
| --- | --- |
| Students and teachers value: certainty, scientifically proven knowledge, security, information. | Students and teachers value: living with paradox and practical knowledge, ambiguity, imagination, flexibility. |
| Teachers own the knowledge. | Students and teachers own knowledge, and this knowledge is unique to the particulars of their own classroom dilemmas and complexities. |
| Students get knowledge from teachers. | Students and teachers learn from their interactions with each other, from resources, and from their environment |
| The curriculum is set. | Students and teacher develop curriculum. |
| Teachers "cover" curriculum. | Students and teachers learn how to learn. |
| Challenges to the teacher are threatening. | Challenges to teachers are required for teachers to perform their role in the interactive process. |

One of the key principles in Gordon's (1984) learning sequence theory, that you should be able to measure what you expect your students to learn, represents a modernist view of assessment. Doll's (1993) suggestion that "evaluation would be a negotiary process within a communal setting for the purpose of transformation" (p.

174) represents a postmodern view. The roles that teachers and students assume determine the role of assessment. No matter where individual teachers or provincial ministries of education are along this transition continuum, the writing on the wall is clear: "The focus of assessment today is shifting to the student; teachers are expected to use observational skills to a greater degree than previously in this century; furthermore, assessments should be appropriate, be an integral part of the curriculum, be ongoing and involve students" (Hanley, 1992).

One possible way to find a balance in this paradox is to regard students as co-creators of curriculum and assessment strategies. Two powerful and revealing questions for music teachers to ask at any level are "What do *you* really want to learn in music" and "How will you choose to demonstrate what you have learned?" For those who would find this practice risky and irresponsible, incorporating the students' curriculum and assessment ideas for a quarter of the programme, or even a tenth of it, is one way to "try on" a more balanced role relationship between teacher and student.

## Once a Frog, Always a Frog

The second paradox is the apparent incompatibility between evaluation and the arts. When I was in grade one in 1956 in a small Ontario town, our teacher seated us in rows according to our singing ability. I was a good little singer and was therefore in the "Bluebird" row beside the blackboard wall. In the next row were the sparrows, then there was a big drop to a row of blue jays, a row of crows, and finally, in the row closest to the window, the children who for many reasons were not yet "singers" at all by our teacher's standards — the "frogs." I am still haunted by the notion that not one of those frogs, or even crows or blue jays has every enjoyed singing since. Inappropriate evaluation killed the singer in over half the children in that grade one classroom.

In elementary schools, a wide discrepancy exists between provinces and between school jurisdictions in arts curriculum and assessment policies. The thoughtful teacher in the elementary classroom has always had questions and concerns about assessment in the arts. Those questions and concerns reveal the teacher's regard for the artistic sensibilities in each child and for appropriate ways to encourage development without killing the artistic spirit of the child. We all know someone who stopped singing as a young child after a music teacher told him or her to mouth the words. We all know people who decided they couldn't "do art" after a whole year in which the teacher never once selected their art work to "put up" in the classroom. How then are we to address the challenge of assessment in the arts in ways that encourage development without doing injury to the artistic self in each child? How can we keep the aesthetic nature of the arts paramount in both curriculum and assessment?

I suggest two principles of arts assessment which have helped me address those questions:

1.  Regard every child as an artist. Picasso once said "Every child is an artist. The problem is how he [sic] remains an artist once he grows up." Each child's artistic and aesthetic development is the most important consideration for assessment in the arts at the elementary level. In order to ensure that each child's artistic growth remains the prime consideration, teachers can first ask of every arts activity and assessment practice: "Will this activity enhance the artistic life of this student?" or "Does this activity have the potential to damage the artistic life of this student?" and then choose only the enhancing activities.

2.  In order to enrich artistic development, assessment must be rich in context, respect diversity, encourage different ways of exhibiting different strengths, and develop the abilities of self-assessment. Assessment strategies are rich in context when they take place *over time* in the student's *daily environment* (e.g., observations of the same child involved in classroom musical activity at four different times over a two-month period). Ways to respect diversity include offering choice of activity and considering students' own  cultural arts experiences and knowledge. Examples of ways in which students can exhibit different strengths include: portfolios, audio- and videotapes of out-of-school arts activity, and chosen modes of performance. Self-assessment is a skill which students develop through experience. Beginning in kindergarten, it is important that arts assessment has a large self-assessment component.

Some of the best descriptions and examples of assessment strategies appropriate for arts assessment in these times which I've encountered are to be found in Saskatchewan's Education's excellent resource documents, *Grade 6 Arts Education Curriculum Guide* (Saskatchewan Education, 1994). The following is a summary of one section in the guide.

Although there are several types of endeavours in arts education, they are placed in the two following categories for the
purpose of establishing appropriate assessment strategies:
process and product. When assessing each student's learning
*processes* in the arts, teachers can observe (a) all arts activities
and projects in progress, (b) the actual process of creative
problem solving, (c) individual, pair, and group work in
progress, (d) portfolios, including rough drafts and notes, (e)
notebooks and sketchbooks, (f) ongoing visual and written
journal entries, (g) use of computers and other technology,
(h) video and audio cassettes of student work in progress,
and (i) student reflection. Assessment techniques to use include: anecdotal records, observation checklists, portfolios,
conferences, analysis of audio and video records, and self assessment.

When assessing each student's *products* or *presentations* in
the arts, teachers can observe (a) collective and individual
arts projects and presentations, (b) portfolios, (c) audio and
video tapes, (d) contract criteria, (e) the student's previous
products or presentation, and (f) students' reflections. Possible assessment techniques include: anecdotal records, observation checklists, tests, portfolios, conferences, self-assessment, analysis of audio and video records. (pp. 31–32)

Although most of us are familiar with these strategies and techniques, and many of us support their use at least in theory, if not in
practice, two problems inherent in these techniques limit their effectiveness: the time and money required for documentation and the
making of aesthetic value judgements.

### Documentation

Documentation is a key element in supporting the assessment strategies suggested above. Documentation takes attention, time, and
some money. The Reggio Emilia schools in Italy offer some of the
best models of appropriate and effective arts-based education.
Young children are encouraged to express themselves through many
"languages" or modes of expression, including words, movement,
drawing, painting, sculpture, shadow play, collage, and music. A
central concept in these schools is that of the *atelier* — a studio space
designated for arts activity containing the best materials possible to

promote artistic expression. Each school also has an *atelierist*, an artist-teacher who supports teachers in curriculum development and documentation. Documentation of the children's work is considered of such importance that teachers have a half day a week devoted to assessing documentation. One recommendation in Reggio Emilia schools is that all schools find ways to provide "Documentarions" for classroom teachers. The only practical way to have help with documentation in Canadian schools is through classroom volunteers. We can advertise for parent and grandparent volunteers: for photographers, for people to videotape and audiotape children. Educational assistants and student teachers can also fulfill this role.

No elementary teacher has time to do rich assessment of every aspect of every child's development in the arts. Teachers, no matter what is mandated, can exercise their ability to adapt and choose assessment programs appropriate to their own class, curriculum, and philosophy. Like Whitehead's (1929/1967) advice to teachers not to teach too many subjects but to teach thoroughly those they choose to teach, teachers in the midst of this paradox might be well advised not to evaluate too much, but to evaluate thoroughly what they do choose. Specific and detailed reporting is most helpful to parents and students. Effective documentation provides those specific details. The will to invest the necessary time and attention to documentation is a necessary partner to those assessment strategies which are rich in context, respect diversity, encourage different ways of exhibiting different strengths, and develop the abilities of self assessment.

### Making aesthetic value judgements

Making aesthetic value judgements is the other problem inherent in assessing arts processes and products. Portfolios, for instance, are gaining widespread acceptance as an assessment technique. We may know why they are valuable and what to include in them, but do we know how to assess and evaluate them? Standards of excellence will vary from person to person, depending on the person's experience and knowledge. These thoughts lead us directly back to the first paradox presented at the opening: the arts are judged by the highest standards even though they may be regarded as trivial.

Who is in a position to set these standards and make these aesthetic judgements, and at what stage in a child's artistic development do any kinds of judgement become appropriate? In the public realm, anyone is entitled to make value judgements of performances and works of art. Those who call themselves critics and who publish or broadcast their critiques are expected to have sufficient knowledge and experience to support their value judgements. In schools, widening the circle of assessment to include peers, self, other teachers, parents, guest artists, the school secretary, the principal, and the custodian would reflect arts assessment in the real world. Teachers, however, if they are to publish their critiques must, likewise, have sufficient knowledge and experience to support their value judgements.

How we assess performance and creative work has been a subject of much thought in the field of aesthetic philosophy. Beardsley (1950) carefully examined many kinds of criteria for assessing performance and creative work. Only three criteria emerged from Beardsley's critical examination as defensible and appropriate: intensity, complexity, and unity. Too much of any of these attributes is as undesirable as too little. For each person there is an optimal amount, but probably everyone requires some element of each of the three. Let's look at each one in terms of a theatre performance.

**Intensity**     Was there substance, energy, vigour,
            power, profundity? To what degree?

**Complexity** Was there conflict, were there several layers of
            meaning, surprises, ambiguity? To what degree?

**Unity**      Did it make sense? Was there progression,
            a relationship or development that made
            all the parts ultimately hang together?

The questions to support the three criteria would change if you were evaluating a grade 6 student's performance of his or her own music composition, a grade 4 student's recorder playing, or a school performance by a touring opera company. Nonetheless, Beardsley's three criteria can form a solid foundation for teachers' value judgements of student work, and for students' assessment of their own and others' performances and works of art.

For children in kindergarten and the primary grades, appropriate arts experiences involve play, exploration, and communication. The arts are one of the voices or languages of childhood. Observation, documentation, and anecdotal reporting can be appropriate. Grading using numbers, letters or words (e.g. E for excellent, S for satisfactory ) is not generally appropriate at the primary level in the arts. Young children do not have the capacity to understand that a low grade in any of the arts means that the child did not meet grade level expectations. The child only hears that he or she cannot sing, dance, do art, or drama. Children's artistic selves can sustain life-long damage through the practice of grading in the arts at the primary level. Here, as in all decisions regarding assessment, the goals of arts education should determine assessment practices. The danger, in some jurisdictions, is that assessment and grading expectations will determine goals and curriculum. It is easy to test whether children can write rhythm notation, or draw musical symbols, or write key signatures. If teachers are required to give grades, they teach things that can be graded. If students know that their creative work is to be graded, they will produce work which they think the teacher will value. They are not likely to take risks or allow their imagination to push the boundaries of the assignment. Students can be limited, rather than enriched, by their teachers' standards.

Some will argue that even though grading may not be appropriate for creative work in the early grades, it is appropriate for skills and knowledge in the arts. In that case, it is the responsibility of the teacher to be clear about what the grade represents (e.g., colour theory: A, *not* Art: A, music notation: B, *not* Music: B). If I were required to grade children at the primary level, I would give every child the highest possible grade, acknowledging that it makes a travesty of the inappropriate mandate to grade and at the same time knowing that a good grade sends an important message to every child that he or she is capable in the arts. Helping children feel that they are good in the arts may well be the most important goal and outcome in arts education for young children.

For students in the junior and intermediate grades, and indeed at the secondary level as well, it makes sense to ponder Pitman's observations about assessment of the arts in the public domain. Wiggins (1989), special consultant on assessment for the Coalition of Essential Schools in the United States, in an article about striving for more authentic and equitable assessment, holds up real life performance by athletes and musicians as a model for good evaluation. After criticizing the testing culture in schools for breaking subject matter up into bits for testing purposes he says: "Coaches of musicians, actors, debaters, and athletes know better. They know that what one learns in drill is never adequate to produce mastery" ( p. 706). After saying that what is so harmful about some current evaluation practices is that they frequently reinforce the belief that "mere" right answers are adequate demonstrations of ability, Wiggins proclaims: "Again, this is a mistake rarely made by coaches, who know that their hardest and most important job is to raise the standards and expectations of their students" ( p. 706). Enriching student's standards and expectations is a worthy outcome of curriculum and evaluation.

One way to align the arts in schools more with the arts in the real world is to adopt assessment practices from that public arts world: performances, exhibitions, critiques, and reviews. Many arts educators have been doing just that for years, and now other disciplines are learning ways to adopt and adapt those strategies in other subject areas. But are we using these strategies with enough depth? Are we willing and able as teachers to accept the students' visions, approaches, or understandings? The public is often not ready to accept what the artist does. Audiences yelled and hissed and walked out of the first performances of Beethoven's Fifth Symphony. They walked out in silent disgust from the first performance of Cage's *4'33."* Students as artists sometimes surpass their teacher's knowledge, ability, and imagination. I will offer one personal teaching anecdote as illustration. A graduate level "Arts-Based Education" course I taught a few years ago was arts-based itself. We created and performed a puppet presentation of Shakespeare's *A Midsummer Night's Dream* as the basis for our reading, discussion, and writing. One student in the class had worked in the design division at Stratford Festival. Her puppet of Titania exceeded everyone else's creation in every way, including Beardsley's intensity, complexity, and unity. In the midst of all our effusive and complementary appreciation of her Titania, I noticed the look of frustration and dissatisfaction on the creator's face. When I asked her about her response, she explained how she was unhappy with various aspects of her creation. As we all began to refute her concerns with even more compliments, the look on her face changed to pain, and I realized that her work was "out of our league" so to speak and that if we really listened to her critique of her own work, there was much provocative potential for new learning available to us. My critique of her work was not nearly as valid or informative as her own. The paradox of the humble expert is one worth contemplating for teachers of the arts at all levels.

## Into the Future

The most important outcomes I hold for arts education cannot be assessed, evaluated, or graded because they reveal themselves long after children have left elementary school, for example in the development of a life-long disposition towards making music and making art; in an attitude of curiosity and acceptance of unfamiliar dance, drama, music, and visual arts; and in the ability to imagine the "as if" worlds of others' environments and cultures (Greene, 1995).

There are benefits of effective assessment however: the ability to clearly judge our own performance with courage and compassion and the ability to base decisions on personal standards. The ultimate assessment of teachers' and students' development in the arts may well be our ability to use the arts for our personal well-being and for the well-being of all life on this planet. If we keep these long-term benefits in mind when we create our curriculum and assessment models, we will not go wrong.

**Acknowledgements.** Thanks to Martin Schiralli and Gary Rasberry at the Faculty of Education, Queen's University for their contributions to this chapter.

## References

Beardsley, M C. (1950). *Practical logic.* New York: Prentice Hall.

Doll, W. (1993). *A post-modern perspective on curriculum.* New York: Teachers College Press.

Edwards, C., Gandini, L., & Forman, G. (1993). *The hundred languages of childhood: The Reggio Emilia approach to early childhood education.* Norwood, NJ: Ablex.

Gordon, E. (1984). *Learning sequences in music.* Chicago, IL: GIA Publications.

Greene, M. (1995). *Releasing the imagination: Essays on education, the arts, and social change.* San Francisco, CA: Jossey-Bass.

Hanley, B. (1992). Student assessment in music education: Report on a research project for the British Columbia Ministry of Education. *Canadian Music Educator, 33* (5), 19–24.

Lather, P., & Ellsworth, E. (1996). This issue: Situated pedagogies — Classroom practices in postmodern time. *Theory into Practice, 35* (2), 70–71.

Lund, P. (1994). Idea keepers: Young children's drawings and writing. *Visual Arts Research, 20* (1), 20–34.

Pitman, W. (1998). *Learning the arts in an age of uncertainty.* North York, ON: Arts Education Council of Ontario.

Saskatchewan Education. (1991). *Arts Education: A Curriculum Guide for Grade 2.* Regina, SK: Author.

Saskatchewan Education. (1994). *Grade 6 arts education curriculum guide.* Regina: Author.

Whitehead, A. N. (1967). *The aims of education.* New York: Free Press. (Original work published 1927)

Wiggins, G. (1989). A true test: Toward more authentic and equitable assessment. *Phi Delta Kappan, 70* (3), 703–713.

Wolf, D., Bixby, J., Glenn, J., & Gardner, H. (1991). To use their minds well: New forms of student assessment. In G. Grand (Ed.), *Review of research in education* (pp. 31–74). Washington, DC: American Educational Research Association.

---

[1] I use the word paradox to mean a seemingly self-contradictory idea or concept.

[2] For in-depth discussions of this transition in education and assessment, I highly recommend Doll's (1993) book, *A Post-modern Perspective on Curriculum,* particularly Part III "An Educational Vision" and another excellent and readable article by Wolf, Bixby, Clemmitt, and Gardner (1991) "To Use their Minds Well: New Forms of Student Assessment."

# Chapter Twelve

# Understanding Music Media
Digital (Re)genesis or
Cultural Meltdown
in the 21$^{st}$ Century

*Peter Gouzouasis*

McLuhan and McLuhan (1988) proposed that communications media constantly reinvent themselves. From that perspective, digital technologies of the 1990s have enveloped analog technologies of the past century. The impact of the introduction of digitization has provided the seed for convergence across media platforms. Telephone, cable television, video conferencing, Internet, wireless technologies — all are melding to form what will become our primary information resource, and the home computer, or some "black plastic box" that will contain computer technology, is the technology platform for the playback and creation of New Media. RadioActive, InternetFM, Interactive TV, Web TV, Cable Web, New Media Network, ParaMedia — label it what you like. The way humans access all forms of information will change radically in the next 20 years, and music will be profoundly affected by the rapid evolution of digital media.

The lyrics of the Paul Simon song "A Simple Desultory Phillipic" told us "I've been Norman Mailered, Maxwell Tayored... I've been Rolling Stoned and Beatled 'til I'm blind...when the man says Dylan, he's talkin' about Dylan Thomas...the man ain't got no culture." One can imagine that if an updated cover of that tune were written today, one of the final verses would resonate with "I've been MP3ed and Firewired...I've been DVDed and MIDIed 'til I'm deaf." A tongue-in-cheek revision of a sarcastic lyric.

Whereas electronic media were the breeding ground of popular culture in the 20th century, digital media will proliferate pop culture in the 21st century as never seen before. With the speed with which New Media have developed, however, since the introduction of the desktop computer, one may easily predict meteoric advancements in the conjunction of communications technology with what is being addressed as "content" in popular media. Without acoustic media and visual media, however, "content" is empty. Moreover, without content, mass media are lifeless. Music, voiceovers, graphics, video, and film are the fundamental elements of, and provide conceptual frameworks for, human expression. We can agree that humans are not empty, lifeless beings (unless they are dead or drugged), so media would be meaningless without the fullness and richness of artistic content. And international, corporate broadcasting cartels (i.e., future Internet corporations) would not be able to sell commercial advertising time without content.

Given the nature of mass media, it seems most logical to represent historical knowledge of this topic in a rich, narrative form, where pertinent events may be woven together in a thematic style to create a story of what happened, what is happening now, and what may happen in the future to music and music education in the 21st century. The focus of this chapter is primarily rooted in the interpretation of historical precedents in technological innovation during a century when humans began it by sharing music making in the innocence of their front porches and firesides and ended it downloading MP3, Shockwave, LiquidAudio, and RealAudio files, knowing that those file formats would obsolesce in the wake of the next wave of New Media. Now teenage guitarists download tablature of any song written in note-for-note accuracy from an OLGA (On-line Guitar Archive) mirror site and unpack MP3 audio files of the same song — instant guitar lesson without the need for, or interference of, a stodgy, boring guitar teacher.

Strict historical research techniques could, in a sense, limit a writer to either a stale statement of facts or the creation of a chapter that would be a book itself of Reimerian or Gordonian proportions and conceptual density. Precedents for a more interpretive, rich, narrative style (Bruner, 1986, 1987, 1990) abound at the turn of the New Millennium, from recently minted dissertations to Internet-based research journals to books that comment on the (r)evolution that New Media will bring to all forms of knowledge representation. Bruner (1986) believes that narrative imitates life and that life imitates narrative, and draws comparisons between "life" as as a type of construction of the human mind and "narrative" as an analogous form of construction. Leggo (1995) suggests that writing is not self-expression but rather a form of self-construction. Narrative writing becomes a way of knowing and "be/com/ing" in the world, with lessons that inform us about the ongoing efforts to theorize the relationship between narrative and lived experience, and the relationship between narrative and living experience (p. 5). It is from those perspectives that narrative allows individuals to return to the past, live in the present, and project into the future — to live and revel in the remarkable speed of digital evolution. Stories composed of shared experiences may include interviews, story telling, field notes, journal records, letter writing, autobiographical, and biographical writing. As New Media emerge, WWW postings and announcements in written, audio, and video forms, traditional and electronic books, and newspaper and magazine articles form, inform and reform the narrative of our lives, and confound even the most aware musicians with the incredible speed at which music is changing, from both internal and external influences, in the year 2000.

## Hollow Logs and Synths
## Mr. Tambourine Man Meets Mr. Spaceman

Everything about how we use music in our daily lives (e.g., what, how, when, and where we listen to music) has been influenced by the advent of new sound recording and broadcast technologies over the past 100 years. All one needs to consider is the effect that the invention of long play sound recordings (LPs) had on all levels of the music profession, especially in music of Western cultures. For example, with LPs, entire symphonic compositions could be placed on one or two sides of a 10-inch or 12-inch vinyl record. Jazz improvisations grew from one-chorus expositions to 24-chorus marathon inventions based on standard changes of "Indiana" and "I Got Rhythm" (i.e., Charlie Parker's "Donna Lee" and "Anthropology," to name a few songs based on those popular tune chord progressions). The introduction of the long-play record had a direct effect on the live performance of music on the radio, to the point where recordings eventually eradicated resident radio station big bands and symphony orchestras. Some, but few, musicians survived the transition by moving from radio to either television or motion pictures as their main vehicle for music expression. One exception, Nelson Riddle (1921–1985), who worked with Tommy Dorsey, Frank Sinatra, Ella

Fitzgerald, Nat Cole, and Judy Garland and scored numerous films for screen and television, had a steady gig as a television band leader (e.g., *The Carol Burnett Show*). Ironically he is perhaps best known to younger generations for his recorded collborations with Linda Ronstadt. Doc Severinson served numerous years as leader of the *Tonight Show* band; and contemporary late-night talk show hosts have house bands to entertain live audiences, albeit mostly during commercials. That ritual is called "warming up the house." The LP evolution in and of itself forever changed the relationship between music and the music industry and profoundly affected the music profession and music itself. Difficult to admit, but by the middle of the 20$^{th}$ century music, with fewer viable, full-time jobs in the music profession, otherwise talented people were drawn into more lucrative professions and adapted to performing music for personal enjoyment and as a weekend avocation with modest salaries.

In many instances, the recording artist has replaced the performing artist. In many pop music instances, lip synching was the rule, not the exception in the 1990s. As early as the 1930s, without steady performance outlets, there was a trend for many musicians to find "legitimate" full-time jobs and perform music as an avocation. In 1929, Petrillo aptly described the emergence of new recording technology as "musician destroying musician" (in Leiter, 1953, p. 60) and believed that musicians were destroying their own profession by making recordings that would eventually replace them in numerous performance contexts. In what may be interpreted by some to be a revisionist perspective of this highly controversial figure in the music history of North America, James Petrillo — the brilliant, foresightful, feisty President who led the American Federation of Musicians (the AFM included all Canadian professional musicians) from 1940 to 1958 — seems to be the first musician to have recognized the broad power of electronic media in the music industry and the impact it would have on the entire profession of music and the evolution of music itself. A broad understanding of how the effects of technology on the development of music in the 20$^{th}$ century may actually be traced through the motion picture, radio, and recording industries. And although historical research may not be used to predict the future, past events may provide insights as to what we may encounter as new technologies continue to emerge in the 21$^{st}$ century.

## Music And The Movies — Nascent Points of Reference

In the innocence of the early 1900s, the initial effect of recording technology was the broadening of listening habits and an appreciation of a much more diversified music palette (Leiter, 1953). The introduction of recorded music actually enhanced the demand for live performance. Star performance status (e.g., virtuosos, child prodigies) had existed for centuries, but recording technology allowed for the dissemination of music without the need to travel to gain notoriety.

One of the first benefits of recorded sound was with the accompaniment of silent films and provision of intermission music by motion picture house orchestras (p. 55). It is difficult to imagine that in the United States alone, 22,000 musicians were employed in pit orchestras by 1926. However, the Vitaphone, which enabled movie operators to synchronize recorded sound with picture in their projector booths, was unveiled that same year. In 1927, Movietone technology, which melded film and sound into one medium, was introduced by Fox Film Corporation (p. 56). Because of union contracts with theaters, and the time it took for installation of sound technology in theaters the negative impact of the new technology on musicians was delayed for a few years. While there were 2,000 newly equipped theaters in the United States by 1929, that same year the theater industry still maintained jobs for 19,000 union musicians with a cumulative salary of nearly $1,000,000 per week. Impressive figures even by today's standards, yet by 1930 that figure fell to 14,000 theater musicians, reached a nadir with approximately 4,100 by 1934, and leveled off through the 1940s and into the 1950s (p. 57). Now musical theater audiences are frequently treated to stripped down pit orchestras featuring the sonorous sounds of synthesized strings pumped through digitally mixed sound systems. Yet, though some in academia may scoff at music forms that proliferated electronically, and now digitally, the proliferation of the popular music of the latter part of the past century may be interpreted as a great success of technological applications.

The AFM's actions to rebut the film industry, led by union chief Joseph Weber, took the form of print propaganda (e.g., cartoons, legitimate advertisements, editorials), and support from the print media took the form of urging the public to avoid listening to so-called "mechanically produced" music (Leiter, p. 59). In retrospect it was a heroic attempt of musicians who recognized the infiltration of our art form by mechanistic capitalists and an ironic battle of what at that time could be considered "mass medium against mass medium." The Music Defense League was an ingenious, non-monetary, coupon campaign run in a multitude of newspapers and magazines in the United States, whereby over three million persons clipped their coupons and sent them to the AFM to show support for live music performance (p. 60). When polled by a reporter of the *New York Daily News* (1930), five of six New Yorkers preferred live orchestras in theaters. While this strong show of support may have reflected one aspect of the music preferences of the populous, it was of little interest to the film industry which viewed live music as an extravagant cost that drove up the price of film production. It is difficult to imagine *Fantasia 2000* at the local OmniMax Theater performed with a live symphony orchestra in 2000, but that could be a reality if motion picture executives and media moguls decided live music was intrinsic to the artistic integrity of the film.

This historical overview of the emergence of "talking pictures" underlines the dramatic influence of the development of audio technology and its effect on the development of music itself, in this century. Whereas music began as part of the foreground at the start of this century — in concert halls, dance halls, theaters, and cabarets — we now seem to be left with the background drone of recorded, canned music in restaurants, stores, and elevators. And when music is in the foreground, it is frequently accompanied by the "chicken scratch" of disc jockeys at clubs and raves. It is difficult to imagine that the MUZAK Corporation began honing its craft in the 1930s, developing the "subliminal audio" model for corporations such as Digital Music Express, which offers 30 channels of commercial free, 24 hour, digital "music to shop by." The effects of electronic media still linger (and so do humans in supermarket aisles, audiating and humming along to "Golden Oldies" as we purchase our groceries) since how much live music there is on a Tuesday night in any metropolis is ultimately dependent on the promotional support of mass media such as radio, television, and the Internet.

## Click To Tune-In Next Century
## Live Music And Radio

In the early 1920s, in both Canada and the United States, when musicians first performed on radio, they did so to promote their playing and performed on radio for free. Interestingly, recordings of artists were played with the explicit intent of duping the radio audience into believing they were listening to a live performance. Thus in 1930 the United States Federal Communications Commission ruled that all recorded music be identified as such when broadcast (Leiter, p. 67). Another tactic that the AFM devised to stop the airplay of records was that all sound recordings have the disclaimer, "For Home Use Only" printed on the record face. That was almost as effective as the laughable "For Promotion Use Only" signature that is currently gold stamped on compact discs intended for airplay, but frequently pirated in used record stores and on radio stations across North America. In a famous test case between Fred Waring and WDAS radio station in Philadelphia, the Supreme Court of Pennsylvania ruled that "musicians have the right to prevent the unauthorized use of their recordings" (Waring vs. WDAS, 1937). However, three years later in the case of RCA versus Paul Whiteman, the U.S. Supreme Court ruled that the property of the musicians (i.e., band leader) ended at the point of purchase, thus opening up the floodgates of sound recordings on radio and further removing the musician from control of the music performance process (RCA vs. Whiteman, 1940 a, 1940b). That ruling would have profound effects on music across the North American continent.

Between 1931 and 1937 there were a number of attempts made by the AFM, from union local strikes to negotiated agreements to providing recording licenses to companies that exclusively used union members, to stem the technological threat to live music performance. In 1940, the U.S. Department of Justice ruled all previously negotiated agreements with the key stations of extant networks to be illegal. Soon thereafter, the inverse relationship between number of radio stations and number of musicians became pronounced. I have been a part of numerous live broadcasts of world class music performances and was the music director (I played a large role in choosing all the artists) of the 1986 Mellon Jazz Festival in Philadelphia,which honored the contributions of composer-saxophonist Jimmy Heath. The performance was digitally broadcast in cities all over the world via American Public Radio (APR). Every performer was a member of the American Federation of Musicians; the AFM played a supportive role in the recording of the music during the entire festival. So did record companies because the festival was marketed to them from the perspective of giving their artists global exposure.

Looking back on events in the history of the AFM may provide a perspective that the radio and record industry and new technologies used in those contexts and have had a dual influence on the evolution of music in North America. From a positive point of view, music was made accessible to broader audiences and made more popular; from a negative perspective, however, live performance broadcasts are not nearly as commonplace as they once were, and the role of professional performing musician, as a viable, sustainable occupation for talented individuals, may be considered an endangered livelihood no matter how much government intervention and regulation is foisted on Canadian listeners by the Canadian Radio-Television Commission (CRTC). By the late 1900s, live music as a common phenomenon was ultimately dependent on promotion and exposure in a variety of electronic and print media. In Canada, and at one time in the United States (e.g., Kool and Newport Jazz Festivals), monetary support from tobacco companies also has had a profound influence. On continental and international levels, the advance review of the artist's work, the promotion of a new recording, the promotion of a concert tour, the additional air play provided by supportive radio formats, the on-air interviews, the pre-concert interviews (many are recorded for the promotion of future concerts), and the live on-air post-concert appraisals are all fine tuned by mass media and affiliated industries to profoundly influence our concert going, our listening habits, our recording purchases, and our music tastes.

As the former music director of a 50kw jazz radio station (1983–1988) with a signal that covered the entire area of the fourth largest major market in the United States (WRTI, Philadelphia), my programming and promotional structures were heavily influenced by commercial radio practice. In fact by the mid-1980s, National Public Radio (NPR) in the United States, once very similar in sound and feel to CBC Radio in Canada, was being dictated by "suits" from the affectionately labeled "Minnesota Mafia" who eradicated the earthy sounds and sophomoric programming structures of public radio. Though some community radio stations in Canada (e.g., CITR, Vancouver) still maintain what can kindly be described by public radio professionals as "mosaic programming structures," the CBC has long succumbed to the CRTC's archaic, iron-fisted rules on Canadian content and programming policies.

So I was faced with playing the "new, improved radio game" or losing my position. As a musician whose main interests were the promotion of musicians and live music performance, that was not a choice, so I succumbed to playing within and around the rules of the game. Efforts to promote jazz artists were frequently successful if a new current album were placed in a hot/heavy air play category bin with nine other records and if that category received three air play slots per hour. That frequency of air plays would continue for four to six weeks, during which time I would report the "Hot" records to *Radio and Records* (an industry magazine that tracks air play across North America, which ironically, no longer tracks "pure" jazz radio but something known as "smooth jazz" or NAC/Smooth) as being in the heavy rotation of air play. Through music and general program directors, other radio stations would be very aware of our air play patterns and play frequencies, as promotions people at all the labels made sure people in "the business" knew that another major station was playing the record they were peddling, like hucksters selling raw fruit and vegetables. The only thing they lacked were the melodious voices of street vendors.

*Radio and Records Magazine* (http://www.rronline.com/) recently (2000) listed the following 11 music formats in their charts. Canadian artists, who are actively charting, and their hit songs are identified where possible: adult contemporary (AC) (Celine Dion, "That's The Way It Is" and Sarah McLachlin, "I Will Remember You"); Active Rock (Smashing Pumpkins, Megadeath, Metallica); Adult Alternative (Bruce Cockburn, "Last Night of The World"); CHR/POP (Ricky Martin, Jennifer Lopez); CHR/Rhythm (Mariah Carey, Will Smith); Country (Shania Twain); Hot AC (Celine Dion, "That's The Way It Is, Sarah McLachlin "Ice Cream," and Alanis Morissette "That I Would Be Good"); NAC/Smooth (Grover Washington, Jr., Spyrogyra, Bob James); Rock (Filter "Take A Picture"); Urban (Montell Jordan, Donell Jones); and Urban AC (Whitney Houston, Mint Condition). A quick perusal of the AC, Hot AC, CHR/Pop, and CHR/Rhythm charts will alert an astute reader to the fact that many artists and songs are so called "crossover" hits. That supports the notions that (1) the industry itself merely treats music as a commodity, and (2) most people in the industry know very little about music itself.

The record label promotions people who tried to describe the music on their current recordings frequently astounded me. When I would cite particular "non-jazz" music elements that were on their recordings as reasons for not giving their products air play, their only response was that other stations were playing their artists and that I should "do good business" with them and play their recordings. In other words, even after the infamous Payola scandals of the 1960s and '70s, business ethics permanently replaced music sensibilities. It is important to note that because a musician controlled the jazz airwaves, we frequently played music by Canadian artists who recorded for Justin Time, Zebra (an MCA affiliate that had Vancouver's "Skywalk" on their artist roster), Verve, Pablo, Concord, and other labels. Canadian content was an important element of the airplay rotation in Phildadelphia without the CRTC's intervention. Nationality was never an issue; quality music was, and still is, the issue, for a handful of independent thinkers in the music industry. Those factors are clear evidence that there are many music directors who lack(ed) the convictions and music knowledge to reject mediocre music, in any radio format and that with the exception of a few persons, the majority of program directors and music directors who work in the radio industry possess mostly superficial, "liner note enhanced," music knowledge. Nothing I have heard in the past 12 years in major markets across North America can make me retract that callous statement.

With those facts in mind, Canadian tax revenues would be better spent on aggressive, professionally managed promotions and commercial artist development personnel rather than out-of-tune government bureaucrats and amateur grant writers. *Billboard Magazine's* second longest selling album in history is Shania Twain's "Come On Over," which, as of January 2000 is # 2 and has been on the charts for 114 weeks. Shania Twain is a fabulous Canadian performer, recently named Best Female Performer and Female Country Artist by the American Music Awards (January 2000), and the CRTC has had nothing to do with creating her incredible success.

The music promotions "machine" works in mysterious ways that reach far beyond the imaginations of listeners, or "consumers." For a week before a concert, if it was an artist that both myself and the staff respected and enjoyed, we would play a new release and more recent releases of that artist's music once per hour in morning drive (5:00 a.m. to 10:00 a.m.) when there are the largest listening audiences for radio. If we really wanted to "hype" an artist, the morning person would play the targeted music and give away a pair of tickets to the artist's concert in the first quarter of the hour (:00 to :15), when people most listen to radio programming, a well-known fact in the industry. The main record shop in Philadelphia at that time would frequently complain that we should stop playing certain records when they sold out of those titles. That is because, while there is no research data available outside the music industry, there is a strong positive correlation between airplay and sales. The industry does not want "us" to know how feeble-minded the music listening public is for fear we would revolt and start making music in our homes again instead of passively listening to recordings.

There is much joy in helping promote the careers of musicians, and there is no greater way than to place an entire radio station at their disposal. Dizzy Gillespie, Art Blakey, George Adams, Ella Fitzgerald, Sarah Vaughn, Tal Farlow, Joe Pass, Grover Washington Jr., Emily Remler, Stan Getz, Gerry Mulligan, Mel Lewis, Mel Torme — and many others that I had the pleasure of interviewing on the air — all deserved the honor and flattery of media hype while they were among us. Unfortunately, the hype is usually reserved for popular artists in various rock and country music genres. Now that the jazz greats are all gone to that "big band in the sky," we can no longer enjoy their music in our concert halls and jazz clubs. We can all fondly recall their joy — an exuberance fueled by their deep love of and respect for music — and the audiences jam-packed into smoky bars. And now even the smoke is gone in bars across many North American cities. Even though aficionados are the "keepers of the flame" during lean promotional times, it is electronic media that transmit their message, albeit infrequently, beyond the small audiences of jazz bars, concert halls, and home stereo systems. And rich promotion is not happening for what most academicians and trained musicians would consider quality music, regardless of stylistic and cultural biases.

To continue a focus on North America's "other music," our first indigenous popular music form, because it takes a major promotional and artist development effort to mount financially successful concerts, only people who live in large metropolitan areas (i.e., a "major metro") have the luxury of hearing major performers on a regular basis. Moreover, even where jazz radio stations or specialty programs do exist on community run stations and late night CBC or NPR, local musicians have a difficult time competing with mass media because mass media in general are difficult to access by local musicians. The phenomenal success of Diana Krall is an anomaly.

Most local musicians, however talented they may be, lack access to professional recording resources and more important, exposure to the general public. Unless they have a recording contract with adequate distribution channels, most musicians do not have a professional calling card with which they may promote their music to the mainstream masses, even where promotional outlets may exist. True, some may be able to record a one-off CD in a basement digital recording studio, but selling your CD at a gig does not make platinum. The electronica group Trance Control, who earned the most money from MP3.com's "Payback for Playback" promotion, earned $4,556 in November 1999. That is the state of Internet sale of audio downloads and does not include sales of CD, concerts, or merchandise. Marketing and distribution strategies will probably change in the very near future, but for now the masses seem more interested in downloading every song The Beatles recorded in MP3 format and cramming them onto a single CD for $15 (US) than having the music of a new band. And with more people recording more music of vastly differing sonic and music quality, only the commercial promotion and monetary support that mass media can provide will separate the garage band around the corner from the next rock superact.

My work with high school jazz and rock guitar students and 100s of hours of exploration on a broad range of guitar WWW sites strongly confirms that perspective. The guitar began its journey to become the most popular instrument of the 20th century when it was first plugged into a theater's public address system. And the development of the guitar synthesizer in the late 1980s had the same effect on the status of the guitar as the development of the piano when it followed the clavichord and harpsichord.

## The Industry's Effects On Music: Why Do You Think They Call Them Hits?

To reiterate, mass media have the most prevalent impact on the music preferences of people living in Western-influenced societies. Our music cultures are directed by huge multinational corporations, and they are usually driven by record promotions hucksters and record charts in *Billboard*, which tracks sales, and *Radio and Records* or *The Gavin Report*, which track air play. Payola (i.e., monetary payoffs to music programming personnel) was (is) not the evil of radio industry — it and other subversive forms of so-called "payment" were (and in some cases still are) part of the reward system for staying and playing within accepted music industry structures. Moreover, in the past few years record labels have shrewdly circumvented federal Payola laws by buying sponsorship time blocks to promote new product in test markets. In light of that perspective, it is the music tastes and whims of musically illiterate executive producers and lawyers that dominate what we hear, how much we hear it, when we hear it, and where we hear it — not just in North America, but on much of our planet. And with the convergence of various technology platforms and the convergence of Internet and "content providers" (i.e., music companies such as Warner, Columbia, and Atlantic Records) our music choices and tastes will become even more defined by mass media.

Clearly, as a former music director and industry insider, I do not treat the business of music lightly. And obviously I am a harsh, sarcastic critic. On numerous occasions I frequently observed record sales soar in *Billboard* for new recordings of new artists that are reported in "heavy" rotation in *Radio and Records*. Some artists had traditional drawing appeal while others were newcomers to the music industry, but the results were always the same. The obvious, strong correlation between air play and sales was never so real to me as when those heavily favored jazz artists drew large crowds at the concerts that we promoted over the airwaves. Yet sadly, there are very few musicians and truly knowledgeable people in control of music play lists that affect the music tastes and sales patterns of major metropolitan areas, small towns, and rural farming areas. It is no mere subjective statement that the mass media and record company marketing personnel directly influence the music preferences of North American society. Canadian recording artists would fare much better in both national and international marketplaces if the CRTC were replaced by a professional promotional team that "worked" the commercial music industry for Canadian artist airplay. After all, to preserve Canadian music culture in the 21$^{st}$ century we will need to extend far beyond geographic boundaries. As they say in the business, "ya gotta work the channels," and the channels are constantly expanding with the evolution of New Media.

## Where Does Music Stand?

From a historical perspective, when "house bands" were typically heard on radio in the 1930s and '40s, the music director contracted the musicians and arrangers to perform, compose, and arrange music for their listening audiences. True, various products (e.g., soap, candy) were sold during those programs to sponsor the broadcasts, but both the listenership, and to some extent advertisers, were much more naive about the power of mass media. Sponsors were attracted to the music programming of a Cab Calloway, Glen Miller, Bob Crosby, Jimmy Dorsey, or an Elliot Lawrence — it was the quality of the music and the performers themselves that drew the listening audiences. Now, no matter how sophisticated their music tastes, most music directors must program according to narrowly defined style slots — Adult Contemporary, Country, Oldies — to attract a listenership that will sell commercial time slots. It is no secret that the Adult Contemporary (AC) format draws a large listenership among women, 18–35. That, in turn, leads to sales of particular products and services through specific types of commercials targeted toward that demographic population. One need only listen to the AC stations in their market to notice the products and services that are sold to the station's target audience. Music truly is an amazing business in that the relatively small segment of the profession that is interested in the promulgation of music for music's sake rarely, if ever, figures into the music industry's formula for "artistic" success. And if the commodification of music was not clear in the past, the objectification of music as "content" was magnified tenfold by the recent merger of America-On-Line (AOL, including AOL-Canada) and Time Warner, BCE and Teleglobe, and Rogers and Videotron.

Consider what it takes to become a popular recording musician and how many fabulous musicians are rarely or infrequently recorded. We can all name favorites that deserved more media attention. Moreover, consider the effect of the recording bans of the 1940s (Leiter, pp. 132–148) on the documentation, or lack thereof, of the evolution of North American popular music. One such example is found in the jazz form known as Be-Bop, where the embryonic stages have been historically focused on Dizzy Gillespie and Charlie Parker, and justifiably so, yet a number of other contributors to development of that style were grossly overlooked. Fats Navarro, Dexter Gordon, Wardell Gray, Allen Eager, Bud Powell, Tiny Grimes and Charlie Christian were some of the other obvious contributors in the embryonic stage, yet the significant gaps in the recorded history of the evolution of Be-Bop may directly be attributed to the infamous recording bans.

In retrospect, those musicians were brave and heroic. The last major attempt of musicians to make a strong stand in defense of live performed music, and in retrospect for the profession as a whole, was made in the 1940s. Few people in our profession recall the recording bans of the 1940s, let alone remember the reasons why they occurred. Essentially the issues involved were the commercial (e.g., radio broadcast) and non-commercial (i.e., home, personal) use of "mechanical" music. Interestingly, it may be argued (Leiter, 1953, pp. 137–138) that a shortage of shellac, primarily imported from India for the manufacture of records and the high cost of vinyl actually had more to do with the suppression of record production than the 27-month ban on all recordings that contained instrumental music. Nevertheless, the first strike ended in November 1944, when RCA and Columbia finally capitulated to paying royalties to the AFM, partly because (1) Decca Records and numerous minor record labels and transcription companies had reached an agreement with the union in the summer of 1943 and were recording all the new instrumental artists; (2) quotas on the import of shellac were increased, and a significantly higher number of records could be produced; and (3) recording artists, most notably Jascha Heifitz, were jumping labels and signing recording contracts with Decca (pp. 138–140).

That much of the turmoil between the AFM and the recording industry coincided with World War II made this issue highly political, even involving the United States Congress and President Roosevelt. Music was treated as a commodity for the morale of the troops and civilians during the Allied wartime effort, and politicians interested in preserving and promoting their personal music tastes and political interests were threatened by Petrillo's skills in manipulating the music industry for the sake of musicians and the live performance of broadcast music. Perhaps the most devastating political blow was the Lea Act, nicknamed the "Anti-Petrillo Act," of April 1946 which severely prohibited the powers of the AFM, established the radio industry as a record-playing medium, and prohibited:

> (1) payment of exactions for producing or using recordings or transcriptions; (2) imposition of restrictions on production, sales, or use of records or transcriptions; (3) payment of exactions for rebroadcast of programs. Any violations were subject to imprisonment up to one year, or to a fine of not more than $1,000, or to both. (pp. 158-159)

Leiter believed this law was precipitated by Joseph E. Maddy over the infamous Interlochen incident and arguably exemplifies the notion that the record and radio industries merely needed to pit musician against musician to solve their biggest business problem, musicians themselves.

The recording ban of 1948 was "reimposed because of the technological unemployment resulting from the use of records" (p. 166). It officially lasted 348 days, was less effective than earlier bans, and ended because (1) record companies had stockpiled enough recordings to release new material for a number of years, (2) public opinion was negative toward the AFM, (3) foreign record imports hampered the AFM's bargaining position (the manufacture of records had ceased in the United States and Canada, with support from

Great Britain, Mexico, Cuba, Chile, and South Africa), (4) bootleg recordings made their "debut" in North American society, (5) Petrillo had adopted a bargaining position with Congressional members, and (6) legal and governmental pressures from transcription companies and the United States Congress were growing ("Triumph of Honesty," 1944, p. 21).

This topic of study itself could well constitute an entire thesis that could form a revisionist story of the emergence of modern jazz. We do have many recordings from those seminal years of Be-Bop, yet through the analysis of bootleg recordings of live performances — many made with wire recording technology which was invented in 1890 and was widely used by amateur recordists in live concerts — one may find numerous instances of how the development of a music style was shaped by a broad number of people listening to each other perform. Jamming, learning riffs, singing along, and playing along with records — all are forms of human learning, of humans assimilating and accommodating music, and of humans developing a new music of their culture. And the history of the development of North American music over the past 100 years is testimonial to the power of electronic media. Western media homogenized culture on a global scale. Moreover, the infinite waves of New Media development and their implementation will have an even more profound impact on the retention and development of music in the 21$^{st}$ century.

## Video "Thinks" It Killed the Radio Star. What Will Eradicate Video and TV?

In 1999, **Music Music** aired a frightening, self-examining discussion of music videos called "Has Video Killed the Radio Star?" In this stark, confessional exposé, industry insiders referred to music videos as "electronic wallpaper" and "nothing but commercials" for the recording industry. The general consensus among executives who were interviewed was that the video audience is losing its "sight of reality." From their perspective, all viewers see is material nice clothes, nice cars, sex, money, and superheroes. Music is merely an afterthought, an accompaniment to digitized film. In fact, one insider referred to that phenomenon as the "superheroes syndrome" — I see money, I like money, I want money like those people." Jody Mitchell, the Director of A & R for EMI Music Canada, spoke of "bright colours" as the focus of videos. All this is more evidence that we live in a visual society, where even music, an aural art form, is debased and plastered to the background.

Video director Hype Williams believes that there is a "cult among directors" of music videos. Doug Atkins considers himself a visualist who takes sound and transforms it into a visual image. Paul Hunter uses his music videos as a vehicle for getting breaks in the film industry. One famous rap musician called producing a music video "getting crazy money...getting away with crime" as many times, the videos cost more than the records themselves to produce. As members of the group Barenaked Ladies said, "video directors can *make* a shit record." In other words, the music aspect of a recording may be horrendous, but if the video is good, the record will sell. Lou Robinson, Director of A & R for RCA Records spoke of how the Dave Matthews recording "What Would You Say" was released without video support, and video was used as an after market tool for exposure in a push to platinum sales status. These insights provide more evidence that heavy airplay rotation on a station such as Much Music can guarantee a hit record.

Mitchell Rowen of the CVC Report spoke about the fragmentation of production in music videos, in that although there has been a reduction in the overall production of music videos, there has been an increase in music videos from hip-hop acts and a decrease in music videos from rock acts. CVC's WWW site (http://www.music-video.net/programing.htm) currently offers excellent links for exploring both traditional mass media and New Media. As Rowen stated, "A great video can't necessarily help a great song, and a bad video can't hurt a great song as well. But a great video can make a bad song." He also warned of what labels will do with the rights to have music videos broadcast on the WWW. Some industry analysts believe it will "compromise" both the audio and the video, as if the audio still has seminal importance. NBTel, a leader in research and development of broadband technologies, place their focus on the streaming of music video that will be made possible by improvements in bandwidth. Those factors are yet additional, compelling evidence that in the very near future, the CRTC will have no control whatsoever over the listening and viewing habits of Canadians in any mass media. Perhaps then it will become apparent that it is more important to promote Canadian music culture commercially on a global scale, not restrict foreign content. We might hope some bureaucrat will understand the importance of a proactive Canadian music marketing strategy because it must be put into action, sooner than later. Foreign content can never be stopped in this supercharged information age.

## The Dawn of a New Era: Genesis or Genocide?

The development of North American popular music forms this past century began as an aural-oral process. Why did it become popular? One reason is that most of the people who listen to music in North America listen to radio, have been doing so since the invention of the amplitude modulation (AM) band, and still listen to it. And since the recent digitization of radio transmission equipment, AM is already being broadcast in the same stereo sound quality as its FM counterpart. Automobile manufacturers are the main impediment to the next transformation of broadcast technologies. Pioneer Electronics released the first digital AM/FM receivers in 1999, and Canadian cities are the first implement digital radio.

To reiterate, radio was created for the masses, and its advertised products are consumed by the masses. Popular music, which evolved on radio, first with live and eventually with recorded performances, became the folk music of the 20th century. What we think of as folk music is music of our past — sonic skeletons that line the yellowed pages of music texts collected by preservationists, rarely performed by anyone let alone the new generation of children in our schools. These words are written from the perspective of a person who has spent considerable time every day of the past year transcribing, arranging, and performing fiddle music from the British Isles and North America — in MIDI and AIFF formats. New, digital acoustic technologies may allow us to maintain and even revive, many forms of traditional Canadian music. New technologies, however, have also enabled the masses to produce even more music. The Byrds sang, "So ya wanna be a rock'n roll star?... Just get an electric guitar and learn how to play." If you want to become a New Media star, the updated version would advise a person to "just get a laptop computer, some video and sequencing software, and a synththesizer and take some time and learn how to make AIFS, MP3s, and Quicktime movies."

As pop in its general form is the music of the masses, consumption trends of popular music are the foremost indicators of music preferences. Some form of jazz, blues, and rock 'n roll has been the predominant music of North American society for the better part of this past century, and it has defined much of North America's culture — from music trends to social trends. Music heritage of 20th century generations was born out of the making of analog recordings, not the notation, of music. What will become "folk music" to 21$^{st}$ century North Americans was popular music to those of us who have lived and listened in the 20$^{th}$ century. When adolescents think of the term "classic" their focus is on rock and roll music of the 1950s to 1970s, not on music of the Renaissance or Baroque periods. From a radical, iconoclastic perspective, so called traditional "folk music" is music for music archaeologists, and those who base major teaching approaches on the elements and foundations of those songs are not necessarily teaching the music of our culture but music of past cultures. Though radically stated, unless our profession takes advantage of current technologies and takes a collective, proactive stance, we may be considered the generation that allowed the music we prefer to perform, listen to, and teach to die on the yellowed pages of textbooks and tattered sheet music.

As a music academic who loved counterpoint and harmony classes in undergraduate and graduate school, I loathe, but accept the idea that music notation is dead. Even Paul McCartney had the audacity to address a gathering of the 20$^{th}$ century's most important composers and gloat that he composed his entire opera and everything else he has created as a music illiterate (he claims to not read or write music in the traditional sense of the term). The notion of so-called "illiterate musicians" well predates The Beatles, and music fluency, not music literacy, will become the educational issue of the 21$^{st}$ century. Desktop computers (e.g., iMac) enable anyone with scant music and video production knowledge to become an expert producer of music. But in close examination, those best prepared to produce the content and context for this exciting new medium are broadly trained, open-minded, honest musicians. Although as contexts may change, content essentially remains the same, and music is context-sensitive on a number of levels (e.g., music sounds different on vinyl than compact disk; music is listened to differently on a car radio than it is on a turntable or personal cassette player). And as enhanced interactive, digital media may eventually replace some of the more recent digital forms of the creation and retrieval of music information, acoustic media will retain their importance and perhaps be considered on the same level as visual media. Certainly, all forms of acoustic media are fundamental to New Media.

## Media Mergers
## Conflicts and Contradictions of Convergence

Tom Rosensteil, director of the Project for Excellence in Journalism (Washington, DC) and Bill Kovach of the Nieman Foundation for Journalism (Harvard University) believe that "when media companies synergize their brands, they do not add to them. They dilute them" (*New York Times*, 2000, p. A27). They offer numerous examples in journalism contexts to support the perspective that economically motivated reorganizations "will be the end of independent press." I would argue that this influence moves far beyond independence of press and will directly affect the convergence all forms of information on continental and global scales.

Paradoxically, on the one hand New Media have created an information explosion never before experiences by humankind. From political newsletters (The Drudge Report WWW site receives one million hits every 24 hours) to independent filmmakers (www.alwaysif.com; www.Ifilm. com; www. Atomfilms.com), the Internet has been a democratic, freewheeling equalizer for anyone with a desktop computer, an ISP, a little old-fashioned know-how, good ideas, and time on their hands. Some believe that the open-endedness of the Internet enterprise explains why it grew so rapidly. On the other hand, the constant evolution of how digital information is manipulated may now signal the death knell for national individuality and cultural diversity. For example, the International Federation of Journalists believe that the merger threatens "democracy, plurality, and quality in media." Ironically, what we now consider the biggest takeover in corporate history (AOL and Time Warner) and the creation of the world's largest media and entertainment company may be considered mere "pocket change" later this century.

Ten years following the merger of what was then considered a megamerger of media giants, Time Inc. and Warner Communications, traditional bastions of media, have been enveloped by New Media (Hansell, 2000, p. A1). Context devoured content (read that as "Godzilla Eats Tweety Bird") to form a corporation with a stock market value roughly equal to the GDP of Mexico (p. C11). And when cable companies are soon forced to share cable lines with rival companies, as local telephone companies are being forced to do with so-called rivals, the types of wire (telephone, cable) or wireless (microwave, radiowave) technologies we use to share digital information will not be of primary concern. Yet even though new technologies for accessing digital information are being introduced on a weekly basis, contexts and contents seem to be coalescing without regard for what will ultimately become the "black box" we will have in our homes and offices within the next 20 years.

Time Warner and AT&T own the two largest cable systems in North America (e.g., the newly christened Rogers AT&T in Western Canada). AOL provides Internet service of over 50% of North American households. Seagram (USA Networks, Universal Music Group), Walt Disney (film studios, ABC, ESPN), Viacom-CBS (film studios, numerous broadcasting properties, MTV, Simon & Schuster), News Corporation (Fox, British Sky Broadcasting, HarperCollins), NBC and other old media will soon merge or form alliances (the Japanese term "karagee" is frequently used these days) with information technology providers such as Microsoft, AT&T, MCI Worldcom (Sprint) and new generation platforms such as Yahoo, Amazon.com, and eBay. The blur of hardware and platform convergence may ultimately lead to the blur of software convergence, which will probably lead to a homogenous muck of what we currently think of as cultural diversity. Like it or not, the future of music may lie in global homogenization, and any differences in music styles and tastes will be found in relics of past generations. Information is both power and economics, perhaps inextricably so, and the people who develop content may have an opportunity to shape global culture (i.e., music — their content can be freely distributed by broadband networks for interactive entertainment, education, information and e-commerce through desktop computers, televisions sets, MovieFones, and wireless hand held devices). In the Fall of 1999, AOL acquired Spinner.com, the Internet's largest music service, and Nullsoft, which makes the music player Winamp for $400,000,000 (U.S.). Both technologies will allow users to download a 20,000 item catalogue from EMusic.com for 99 cents per individual song. And even those devices and platforms will soon become obsolete. However, new content will always be needed, and music will always be a marketable commodity, even if established pop musicians in North America and Europe are featuring turntable scratching deejays (DJ Lethal, DJ Premier, DJ Homicide) who give hope to people who cannot play drums or guitar (Farley, 1999, pp. 60–61).

## Where Will Music Extend?

Our music culture is defined by our music environment, and the environment as we enter the next millennium is extremely "hot" and about to become substantially "warmer" (Gouzouasis, 1995a). Music styles and forms will continue to evolve, or devolve in the opinions of some, and the music of various cultures will continue to meld into various types of continental and world musics. To a great extent, new storage and recording technologies have already empowered the masses in the creation of music. We can send, store, and retrieve more information than ever before. In this century, the exchange of music ideas and music related information should be further enhanced. Elaborate slide shows with reel-to-reel tape soundtracks of the 1970s and early 1980s have given way to computer-based extravaganzas that include fluidly orchestrated, digitized audio, graphics, and video. The Sony Walkman was introduced to North Americans in September 1979; some claim it revolutionized music listening. Even cassettes (invented in the early 1960s) and compact disks (CDs, invented by Phillips in the early 1980s; 44kHz/16 bit technology) will soon give way to recently released MP3 players and Super Audio Compact Disks (SACDs are 96kHz/24 bit technology). From the perspective of a vinyl addict of the past century (I own over 2,500 LPs), I'll just burn CD copies of my old LPs and enjoy the music itself, not the technology.

Music and sound technologies play a large role in multimedia and that role will soon expand. It took over 50 years for radio and television to radically transform all aspects of music, yet in fewer than 20 years the desktop computer has had an even more dramatic impact on the way than music is created, used, enjoyed, and consumed. A relatively "new" technology called "enhanced CD" (DeLancie, 1995) enables recording artists to develop their own interactive multimedia modules, to create interfaces for their music on a typical, audio compact disk. An enhanced audio disk allows the computer user not only to listen to the music on a traditional compact disk player, but also learn more about music on a variety of levels through interviews, biographical information, and hopefully insightful music discussion and critique. The latest desktop computers (e.g., iMac) enable anyone with scant music and video production knowledge to become a producer of music instructional videos. The people who may be best prepared to produce the content and context for this exciting new medium are musicians. It is, however, more likely that this new level of technology will do more to proliferate additional channels of Much Music, MTV, and VH1 rather than quality children's music and Canadian folksongs and instrumental music.

The music profession still has a small window of opportunity to shape the direction of music development, music applications, and music content for New Media in the 21$^{st}$ century. However, though technologies seem to be in place, human resources lag far behind. The vast majority of all levels of music educators are unable to debug minor word processing problems, let alone create interesting AIFF and Quicktime files for general classroom or music classroom use. One way the music profession, especially those at colleges and universities involved in the education of musicians, has the potential to play a leading role in shaping the future of existing and emerging New Media is through training, certificates, undergraduate programs and graduate programs. Music, and the realm of all new acoustic technologies, needs our direct involvement as musicians, not as ethnomusicologists, Baroque performance experts, and theorists, if we would like to see music evolve in the 21$^{st}$ century. We may either take the lead in the New Media revolution or sit back idly and let the corporate conglomerates and musically illiterate techno-theorists continue to control our global music culture.

There are a number of ways that the music profession, specifically music education, may become proactive in applications of emerging technologies. First, the Internet has become a breeding ground for innovative ideas where inexpensive, yet globally-reaching projects can still easily be mounted. At the turn of the new millennium, this platform is still a relatively level, yet fertile, playing field. MP3, Liquid Audio, Real Audio and other new sound transmission technologies give us the capability to provide quality music instruction on a massive scale. Technologically enhanced music instruction should take the form of a Canadian national project, such as demonstrated by The Interactive Music Project (Gouzouasis, 1999; Gouzouasis & Green, 1998). This electron breaking site has shown the potential for music instruction delivery on the WWW for over five years. Second, a network of cross-continental sites with a unified design theme and specific task assignments needs to be started immediately and promoted on global levels.

Multiculturalism will take on very different meaning in a digitally enhanced music society, and we will need to redefine our notions of multicultualism on all levels in the 21$^{st}$ century. Corporate culture has become as important as geographically and ethnically defined culture. Time Warner sold 119 million recordings last year to capture almost one fifth of record sales in North America alone. That is a far cry from a company that was responsible for producing the first talking picture, *The Jazz Singer*, and numerous animation classics (*Looney Tunes* is now AOL content; that is "What's up, doc?"). Tim Berners-Lee (Luh, 2000) the man who invented the World Wide Web in 1989, recently wrote that "We should all learn to be information smart.... We should learn to distinguish between quality information and quality links." While that is a noble, idealistic standard, one may question how that will be done if it is nearly impossible to teach adolescents to distinguish between quality music and chicken scratch.

Electronic, analog sound recordings, and transmission technologies have permeated the planet's airwaves for over 75 years. It can easily be argued that the music styles of various cultural and ethnic groups have been merged and submerged numerous times over the past 3,000 years. In the past, changes were influenced by war, repression of peoples, and ethnic cleansing; now changes will occur on the digital battlefield in corporate skirmishes involving the music technocracy fighting for content rights. When the time comes to provide direction in the development of quality content, we need to have at least one voice promoting diversity and integrity in music. A unified, proactive music education group would seem to be just that group, but many of us have difficulties agreeing on appropriate curriculum content let alone WWW content.

At each technological epoch, relatively few musicians and educators took advantage of the opportunities that became available though technological innovations. Amateur musicians with home recording studios and shell web sites have shown what can be done with seemingly few resources (see Digital References for examples). Some of the most innovative WWW sites in the world are music-based and have strong, educational influences, yet our profession has not even acknowledged their existence (see the Digital References for suggestions). Yet academicians and professional musicians, those who would like to believe "know what is best" for the masses in terms of music taste and aesthetic experiences, seem oblivious to another opportunity that will rapidly pass as Western art music and national folk forms become music material for an elite minority — the keepers of our archaic past.

That the historical perspective outlined in this paper may serve as point of reference in renewing our awareness is clear. While Leiter (1953) did not consider FM radio and television to be a technological threat, he did consider kinescopes, the 1950s equivalent of videotaped broadcasts and crude technological precursor of music video, as potential to the "displacement of musicians in the future" (p. 183). The definition of "musician" was clearer to us in 1950 than it is now. Now anyone with a desktop recording studio can make themselves a "musician" in the Y2K sense of the term. Thus the crux of our paradox — music may be the only profession that has simultaneously been most positively and negatively affected by technological developments of the 20$^{th}$ century. Sadly, it seems that this trend will continue unless our profession makes a serious effort to put innovation ahead of preservation, and proactive involvement before whining, reactivity, and inactivity.

## References

Berners-Lee, T. & Fischetti, M. (1999). *Weaving the web*. San Franciso: Harper-Collins Publishers.

Bruner, J. (1986). *Actual minds: Possible worlds*. Cambridge MA: Harvard University Press.

Bruner, J. (1987).Life as narrative. *Social Research, 54* (1), 11–32.

Bruner, J. (1990). *Acts of meaning*. Cambridge, MA: Harvard University Press.

DeLancie, P. (1995). Music & multimedia '95: Enhanced CD a hot topic at convergence conference. *Mix, 19* (9), 56–63, 177–178.

Farley, C. J. (1999, October 18). Rock's new spin. *Time Magazine*, pp. 60–61.

Gouzouasis, P. (1994). Multimedia constructions of children. *Journal of Computing in Childhood Education, 5* (3/4), 273–284.

Gouzouasis, P. (1995). Music the medium: What's the message? *Canadian Music Educator, 36* (6), 15-20.

Gouzouasis, P., & Green, B. (1998, June). The Internet Music Project: Gender, music ability, motivation, and music achievement issues in distributive computer mediated interactive instruction of adolescents. Poster session presented at the meeting of the *Association for Advancement of Computers in Education*, Calgary, Alberta. Available: CD Rom.

Leiter, R. D. (1953). *The musicians and Petrillo*. New York: Bookman Associates.

Leggo, C. (1995). Storying the word/Storying the world. *English Quarterly, 28* (1), 5–11.

Lohr, S. (2000, January 11). Medium for Main Street. *The New York Times*, pp. A1, C10.

Luh, J. C. (2000). Tim Berners-Lee: An unsentimental look at the medium he helped propel. *Internet World:In Print*. [Online document]. Available: http://www.internetworldnews.com/article_bot.asp?inc=010100/1.01. Interview & Issue=1.01

McLuhan, M. (1964). *Understanding media:The extensions of man*. New York: McGraw-Hill.

McLuhan, M., & McLuhan, E. (1988). *Laws of media: The new science*. Toronto: University of Toronto Press.

Music in our city. (1931, December 7). *New York Daily News*, pp. 22–23.

Hansell, S. (2000, January 11). America OnLine agrees to buy Time Warner for $165 billion; media deal is richest merger. *The New York Times*, pp. A1, C11.

RCA Manufacturing Company Inc. v. Whiteman, 114 F. 2nd 86, CCA 22, July 25, 1940.

RCA Manufacturing Company Inc. v. Whiteman, 311 U.S. Supreme Court 712, December 16, 1940.

Rosenstiel, T. & Kovach, B. (2000, January 14). The bad business of media mergers. *The New York Times*, p. A27.

The triumph of honesty. (1944, November 20). *Time Magazine*, pp. 21–22.

Waring v. WDAS Broadcasting Station Inc., 194 Atl. 631, October 8, 1937.

## Digital References

*All jazz guitar.* Available: http://www.alljazzguitar.com/

*All music guide.* Available: http://www.allmusic.com/

*Billboard online.* Available: http://www.billboard.com/

*Danman's music lessons and song library.* Available: http://www.danmansmusic.com/

*Guitar college home study guitar courses.* Available: http://www.guitarcollege.com/

*Guitar player magazine.* Available: http://www.guitarplayer.com/

*Guitarre spielen.* Available: http://www.guitarplaying.com/

*Harmony central: The internet resource for musicians.* Available: www.harmony-central.com/

*Joe Diorio jazz guitar.* Available: http://www.joediorio.com/

*Listen.com. The music download directory.* Available: http://www.listen.com/

*Liquid music network.* Available: http://www.liquidaudio.com/

*MUSES computer laboratory.* Available: http://www.cust.educ.ubc.ca/wprojects/MUSES/

*Music scene international.* Available: http://www.musicscene.com/home.html

*On line guitar archives.* Available: http://www.olga.net/ & http://renegadeolga.net/

*Radio and Records Magazine.* Available: http://www.rronline.com/

*SONICNET: The online music network.* Available: http://www.sonicnet.com/front/index.jhtml

*Vision music.* Available: http://www.visionmusic.com/

# Chapter Thirteen

# In the Meantime
## Finding a Vision for Multicultural Music Education in Canada

*Charlene Morton*

*In this land of unparalleled cultural diversity, the time for rhetoric and happenstance is past.*

(Campbell, 1994, p. 75)

In her critical review of multicultural music education in the United States, Campbell (1994) speculates that the gaps that exist

> between the goals of education at large and music education in particular, between musical and cultural goals to be achieved through music instruction, between actual teaching practices and the policies set by the professional society, and between what [Music Educators National Conference] has accomplished and what leadership it has the potential to give regarding music's definitive role in the multicultural education movement...may be due to their partial vision, lack of concentration, and unsteady aim. (p. 72)

I expect that the verdict for multicultural music education in Canada would be much the same; that is, as Canadian music educators, we are failing to position the aims and objectives of teaching music within the aims and objectives of education, specifically, multicultural education. So, although we might have a "partial vision" in that most music educators embrace some notion of multiculturalism, many of us remain ambivalent or confused about the thorny issues of identity, difference, and equality, and, subsequently, have distanced ourselves from what Taylor (1994) describes as the politics of recognition:

this latter term designates something like a person's understanding of who they are, of their fundamental defining characteristics as a human being. The thesis is that our identity is partly shaped by recognition or its absence, often by the *mis*recognition of others, and so a person or group of people can suffer real damage, real distortion, if the people or society around them mirror back to them a confining or demeaning or contemptible picture of themselves. Nonrecognition or misrecognition can inflict harm, can be a form of oppression, imprisoning someone in a false, distorted, and reduced mode of being. (p. 25)

In my chapter, I assume that, as with any initiative related to multicultural education in Canada, I should begin from two key premises: first, preventing nonrecognition or misrecognition is a moral imperative for multicultural music education, and second, Canadian federal multiculturalism policy is the official framework for this imperative. I begin by reviewing our national policy on multiculturalism, examining its merits as well as its inherent tensions. Next, I explore similar tensions in a sampling of articles on multicultural music education. In the final section, I return to the challenge of finding a vision for multicultural music education that goes beyond the rhetoric of celebrating diversity toward addressing the politics of recognition. My overall purpose is to bring the moral objective of Canadian multiculturalism policy to the task of articulating a cogent and motivating vision for multicultural music education.

## Official Policy and Related Initiatives

The Canadian Multiculturalism Act was adopted by Parliament in July 1988, providing a statutory framework for existing policies which began with the adoption of the Canadian Citizenship Act (1946) and support for the United Nations' Universal Declaration of Human Rights (1948). Also known as Bill C-93, the Canadian Multiculturalism Act "imbues the principle of racial and cultural equality with the force of the law" (Leman, 1997, p. 16), spawning organizations such as the Canadian Race Relations Foundation and spending approximately 25% of allocated multiculturalism funds on "fighting discrimination" (Multiculturalism and Citizenship Canada, 1991, p. 13). The Canadian Multiculturalism Act also provides for partial funding of the Heritage Project and other public history initiatives such as the popular video and television series *Heritage Minutes* as well as less familiar projects such as the Heritage Summer Institute, a national eight-day summer school which began in 1997 for public school history teachers. In an address to the Winnipeg Canadian Club, Dr. Thomas S. Axworthy, Executive Director of the CRB Foundation (which initiated the Heritage Project) explains:

> Memory matters! It matters to us as individuals because it locates us in time and place and gives meaning to our lives. It matters to us as citizens because through an ordering of the past into discernible patterns, we can better understand how past choices have present day consequences. History also matters to us as Canadians, as the men and women who inhabit this particular and peculiar attic of North America. What we remember, what we stress as significant, what we omit from our past, and what we don't know or understand about the stories of our fellow inhabitants, is critical to our ability to endure as a collectivity. [undated pamphlet]

Those who are familiar with the popular one-minute segments of the *Heritage Minutes* can appreciate how well the Heritage Project has broadened our knowledge of everyday Canadian history and history makers. These 60-second narratives help Canadians "preserve, enhance and share their cultural heritage" (Canadian Multiculturalism Act, 1988, 3.1.a). Similarly, the preservation, enhancement, and sharing of musical heritage also locates us as individuals and as members of communities. Therefore, what we choose to teach in our music classrooms or for the concert stage is indicative of "what we stress as significant, what we omit from our past, and what we don't know or understand about the stories of our fellow inhabitants" (see Axworthy above).

Having made these observations, I add a critical comment: few of the *Heritage Minutes,* such as "Nitro," "(Jennie) Trout," and "Maurice Ruddick," reveal the historical evidence of racism and sexism in Canada. Because this video series is also packaged for use in school classrooms, educators should consider enriching this promising educational tool with a critical-thinking component exposing a tendency to reproduce a sanitized version of Canadian history. In doing so, we would support another important facet of the Canadian Multiculturalism Act which is to "assist ethno-cultural minority communities to conduct activities with a view to overcoming any discriminatory barrier and, in particular, discrimination based on race or national or ethnic origin" (5.1.g). Highlighting this federal mandate, the Department of Multiculturalism and Citizenship Canada has made it a major priority to eliminate racism.

The Department recognizes that other levels of government and key groups, such as the media, police, educators, social service providers, employers and labour groups, as well as individuals and communities, must be involved in fighting racism. A large part of the multicultural budget is devoted to working with these players to eliminate racial discrimination in Canada. [For example,] in 1991, Parliament passed legislation setting up the Canadian Race Relations Foundation with $24 million. (Multiculturalism and Citizenship Canada, 1991, p. 20)

Skeptics of state-sponsored multicultural education remind us, however, that this is not the first time that governments have used the language of inclusion, national unity, and equality while still maintaining capitalist economic policies and corporate power structures that counter or negate "romantic" plans for sociopolitical change.[1] One skeptic, William Watkins (1994), views multicultural education as another form of minority education driven by suspect political motives, explaining that "a brief review of colonial education, which existed well into the twentieth century, suggests that the education of minorities has always been driven by political motives [but n]ever has acceptable minority education challenged the economic structure" (p. 102). He goes on to explain that, because educators "embrace a strain of democracy totally separated from economics,...[one that] values free participation and association as ends in themselves," education will continue to be ineffective in eliminating racism, sexism, or classism (p. 113). Countering this strong criticism, Morrow and Torres (1994) explain that one cannot generalize about the links between economics and ineffective political reform. They point out, for example, that "racism goes back to its precapitalist roots and has been associated with many different types of social formations" in addition to slavery and colonial rule (p. 55).

In addition to the legislated commitment, there are federal initiatives implemented to enact the "the spirit of the law." Although multiculturalism policy in Canada is officially a federal concern, and public education is the official jurisdiction of provincial governments, the federal government can and does intervene in public school education using national policies, particularly in the area of citizenship education. Several factors, including demographics, influence the government's perception that it must better secure and preserve some notion of Canada as an entity. Sears (1997) explains that Canada's multiculturalism policy became a perfect vehicle to provide assistance and direct grants for the development and dissemination of educational materials, the provision of professional development for teachers, and the organization of professional and community conferences. Other means of influence were through the National Film Board, the Canadian Broadcasting Corporation, Canada Studies Foundation, Open House Canada Program, and numerous travel and exchange programs. In short, Sears reminds us that the federal government continues to maintain an interest in education as a vehicle for promoting national identity and unity, adding that there is good reason for referring to the Department of the Secretary of State as "Canada's unofficial federal Minister of Education" (p. 13).

Here, then, is a statutory framework that offers directives in advancing Canada's diverse cultural heritage, in promoting equitable participation and recognition of all Canadians, and in assisting in the elimination of discriminatory barriers to such participation. Furthermore, federal funding is funneled through many different institutional channels to ensure the implementation of multiculturalism policy, including initiatives in the school system. Bill C-93, however, is not a philosophical manuscript; so, although well written and justified in intent, it manifests inherent tensions in how it deals with the "diversity of diversity." By "diversity of diversity," I mean that Canada is not a one-dimensional kind of multicultural nation; rather, it is a multicultural nation that is home to three kinds of ethnically defined societies: indigenous peoples, immigration societies, and nationalities in competition (Moodley, 1999, p. 138). Although the Canadian Multiculturalism Act contains clauses that address the particulars of these three kinds of societies, it does not acknowledge the inherent dissonance in provisions such as those to "preserve and enhance the use of languages other than English and French, while strengthening the status and use of the official languages of Canada (1988, 3.1.i). In other words, how should we understand or reconcile a need to strengthen the status and use of the English and French languages, both officially sanctioned, in comparison to a need to rebuild dead or dying Native languages or a need to preserve and enhance immigrant languages thriving outside Canada?

Given these tensions in federal policy, it is not surprising to find similar tensions in the adoption of multiculturalism in school music programs. I am not suggesting that problems in multicultural music education are a result of our national policy. Rather, I am acknowledging that there are problems implementing multicultural policies at all levels, and I am proposing that they are related to a general ambiguity about how diversity (or, the "diversity of diversity") can be encouraged while maintaining a sense of nationhood. Nonetheless, I appreciate the potential for music educators to address these problems if we utilize official multiculturalism as a statutory framework as well as a moral platform on which to build a cogent vision for multicultural music education.

In the next section, I explore two themes related to the politics of recognition in the literature on multicultural music education in Canada: philosophical perspectives that address how we rationalize a multicultural mission and pedagogical issues that speak to how we accommodate multicultural education. To accomplish this task, I draw upon a small sampling of articles published in the *Canadian Music Educator* as well as a sampling of the literature on multiculturalism that examines identity, diversity, and nationhood.

## Singing Hallelujah, Singing the Blues
## Tensions in Multicultural Music Education

A transcript of a discussion group at the Arts Symposium, held at Simon Fraser University in March 1990, reveals a multitude of concerns that music educators grapple with in their search to better understand and implement multicultural music education (Walker, 1991b). Included in this summary are participants' questions about key concepts such as Canadian identity, Canadian culture, art, art versus culture, culture versus cultural studies, and, of course, multiculturalism and multiculturalism policy, as well as concerns about practical implications: how to teach, with which resources, or with whose experts. The participants asked whether they should use comparative studies of different cultures and whether they should emphasize the similarities or the differences. In selecting multicultural repertoire, they wondered if they should adopt a global or provincial perspective in making their choices. In calling upon "ethnic experts," they ventured into identity issues: what defines an ethnicity and what defines an expert. Finally, they raised their concerns about integrating the arts to recreate broader cultural understandings of music and the implications for music education *per se*.

Questions also voiced included concerns about racism, a problem assumed to be more commonplace in drama and theatre than in music. One participant wondered if multiculturalism was simply a "reaction to immigration" rather than a strategy to better appreciate and respect ethnic diversity (Walker, 1991b, pp. 27 & 29). Similarly, there was a concern about resistance among some ethnic groups, parents, and teachers against multicultural curricular choices from "our culture" rather than from "our own culture" and about the displacement of the canon and the preservation of the "dominant culture" (pp. 28, 33; see also Davey, 1991).

This transcript-summary captures common concerns that also permeate the literature on multicultural music education. In articulating similar concerns, however, many music educators have also offered points of clarification as well as pedagogical strategies. Much of the Canadian literature attends to the development of resource materials and classroom strategies (Hanley, 1993), a trend that has also been documented in a review of American research between 1973–1993 (Quesada & Volk, 1997). The literature reveals two recurring themes that have shaped our "partial vision" (Campbell, 1994) to date: (1) an appreciation of multiculturalism manifest in efforts to address the needs of increasingly diverse school populations and (2) an appreciation of multiculturalism manifest in an increasing awareness of diverse notions of music and musicianship.

Papers from a meeting of the Society of Ethnomusicology in Toronto which were then published in the Winter 1998 issue of the *Canadian Music Educator*, frequently address these two themes. Veblen (1998), as editor of this special issue, explains that the categories of race and ethnicity are ambivalent and fluid, creating much debate about the racialized foundation of multiculturalism policy. To illustrate the context-dependent nature of ethnicity, she draws our attention to census forms in Canada as well as the United States. Augmenting the debate and confusion about ethnicity and identity is the fact that population demographics continue to change quickly while the music teaching profession remains relatively middle-class, white, and female. Veblen concludes by assuming that teachers will follow through with their "professional responsibility to portray the world as accurately as possible…regardless of the racial mix of a specific class" (p. 4).

In the same issue, Elliott (1998) writes in terms of musical diversity rather than human diversity. Recalling his earlier thesis that, because "MUSIC is inherently multicultural…music education ought to be multicultural in essence" (1995, p. 204), he highlights the variability of music. His examination of musical choices does not, unfortunately, explore issues of identity, race, or nationhood. Driven by a mission to promote music-as-practice, he concedes that some musical practices "may be more appropriate than others *educationally*" and, therefore, "difficult choices must be made." His focus on musical growth is apparent in his recommendation that teachers select music from students' background because, "in this way, our students will mostly likely achieve a match between their novice level of musicianship and the first musical challenges they meet in their music education curricula," (p. 15). In short, Elliott's version of multicultural music education gives exclusive priority to increasing the awareness of diverse notions of music and musicianship.

Most music educators would admit to a predisposition toward nurturing musicianship in their students or, at least, encouraging a fuller appreciation for the many different kinds of musical experience. Miller (1991a) states that the learning outcomes for any approach to multicultural music education should be "the enhancement of a global view of music" (p. 11). In Part II of the same article, however, her focus shifts from purely musical considerations to include the human dimension of multicultural education. Her observations illustrate a sensitivity to the cultural conflict new Canadians experience in the music classroom. For example, she explains that the "physical fabric" of most Canadian music classrooms creates a monocultural environment defined by art-music instruments such as the piano (Miller, 1991b, p. 15). She also calls for better federal funding to support the full import of Canada's multiculturalism policy, including its antiracism projects (p. 17). In these ways, Miller seems more prepared than Elliott to attend to a multicultural perspective that takes up the politics of recognition.

To summarize, Veblen's and Elliott's treatment of the premise "given diversity, teach diversity" takes a vision of multiculturalism in two different directions. Veblen's bottom line is that we should better "portray the world." Wolf (1994) offers a further account of this position:

> [The] failure of recognition is extremely pervasive in our educational institutions, and it constitutes a level of insult and damage in need of immediate remedy.... The insult portrayed here is an insult fundamentally to individuals and not to cultures. It consists either in ignoring the presence of these individuals in our community or in neglecting or belittling the importance of their cultural identities. Failing to respect the existence or importance of their distinctive histories, arts, and traditions, we fail to respect them as equals, whose interests and values have equal standing in our community. (pp. 80-81)

Elliott's vision, on the other hand, sees diversity as an issue of epistemological significance; that is, he promotes multicultural music education as a means to further an understanding of musicianship no longer dependent on aesthetic ideals of art music. Many music educators have come forward in support of Elliott's challenge to aesthetic ideology (Bowman, 1993; Regelski, 1998; Rice, 1998). Although I add my name to those who support this epistemological debate, having explored similar concerns about what kinds of knowledge are deemed worthy (Morton, 1996), I caution that this debate provides only a partial vision for multicultural music education. I would prefer that, in addition to promoting diverse music repertoire and practice in order to augment students' understanding of music and musicianship as a means to displace elitist notions grounded in art music canonicity, we retain some semblance of the moral enterprise of multiculturalism policy.

Taylor (1994) explains that "enlarging and changing the curriculum is essential not so much in the name of a broader culture for everyone as in order to give due recognition to the hitherto excluded" (pp. 65-66), that is, to acknowledge the suffering from nonrecognition as well as misrepresentation. Music education literature does not, however, explore the negative impact of past omissions or stereotyping on members of minority groups. Simply put, there is no moral imperative to address the systemic lack of concern for past and present discrimination that afflicts ethnoracial minorities in their everyday lives, including the pain caused by stereotypes reproduced in school music and the absence of culturally accurate contexts for multicultural repertoire already in place (Tator, Henry, & Mattis 1998, p. 181). Furthermore, we have yet to acknowledge and address the negative impact of bias in music on the attitudes of dominant white populations toward ethnoracial groups.

Also included in this special issue edited by Veblen is a paper by Rice (1998), inviting us to examine ethical issues manifest in day-to-day conflicts that might arise in implementing multicultural repertoire. He believes teachers can avoid conflicts associated with trying to find the "best music" as well as the best way to represent or present that music if they better appreciate (five) different ways people come to know music: music as conversation, music as text, music as history, music as art, and music as commodity. I agree that misreading how someone understands "the nature of music" can create misunderstandings, but I would add that conflict also arises because each of these five ways of understanding music is an aspect of culture-making and, by extension, an identity issue. So, although Rice's hypothesis is a good reminder that "conflict between these metaphors generates some of the ethical dilemmas" (p. 8) in multicultural music education, it falls short of acknowledging the politics of recognition.

McCarthy (1998; see also McCarthy, 1999), on the other hand, articulates the interpersonal and intrapersonal complexity of identity issues in the classroom. She begins her paper by acknowledging that the multicultural movement in education has forced us to rethink our mission and visit — perhaps for the first time — the "issue of representation" (p. 17). She observes the significance of interpersonal issues of identity as she addresses the question of balancing multicultural traditions from local, state, and global communities. She presents a refreshing look at the challenges of working with not only *strange musical traditions* but also with *strangers*. Her explanation of why minority or immigrant students sometimes resist sharing their music in class is at odds with Rice's interpretation of this kind of classroom misunderstanding. Rice (1998) explains that this kind of ethical conflict is a result of people's varied understandings of *music*. McCarthy, on the other hand, takes up where Veblen left off in her analysis of the contingency of identity: McCarthy explains that teachers "need to be sensitive to bicultural tensions that frequently exist for immigrant students who are afraid of being perceived as 'other' if they share their songs or dances" (p. 19). For immigrants, the hyphenated reality of citizenship in a new country can unsettle their sense of identity, especially for young adolescents who, through the process of "growing up," willingly or involuntarily expose themselves to playful explorations of who they are.

Another valuable aspect of McCarthy's paper is her effort to pursue ideas explored at the 1994 Milwaukee conference where "music educators, ethnomusicologists, and folklorists addressed the value of partnerships between music in schools and their communities" (p. 17). Continuing the dialogue by revisiting and reworking old themes and problems can be an efficient way to generate solutions and find new direction. Similarly, the article by Willingham (1998) in the same issue summarizes papers and events at this Society of Ethnomusicology Conference, reiterating many of the concerns as well as contradictions presented seven years earlier at the 1991 Arts Symposium (Walker, 1991b). The article also identifies five obstacles to developing multicultural music education: lack of teacher education in non-Western idioms, lack of resources, narrow teacher expertise, discriminatory certification criteria, and lack of direction from provincial education authorities. Although the need to articulate a more comprehensive vision for multicultural music education is absent, the list offers an opportunity for educators to revisit identified problems in implementation.

The last paper in this special issue looks at the use of world musics, or, rather folk music, in instrumental method lesson books, noting the national origin of the repertoire. Authors Holmes and Volk (1998) explain that, although they have major concerns about using "'adjusted' songs for didactic purposes" and about "a lack of accurate information about the songs themselves and their place in their respective cultures," they believe that "world musics are an appropriate source for method book material" (pp. 30–31). Similar observations have appeared in numerous articles published over the years in the *Canadian Music Educator* to the effect that folk music should continue to have a role to play. Often couched in reassuring terms that it is, relatively speaking, business-as-usual, the pedagogical advice usually emphasizes the "similar generic features in music from different origins" in contrast to the rare contention that "it is not good to assume that each musical practice shares universal formal elements" (Willingham, 1998, p. 26). In other words, there are bound to be some comparative features.

Much of the literature supports the thesis that, although the repertoire is more varied, there are enough substantive similarities among musical styles, genres, and cultures to facilitate the integration of non-Western music into traditional music curricula (Ash, 1995; Day, 1987; Kuzmich, 1988, 1995; Montgomery, 1991). Similarly, in art education, a comparison of British Columbia's past and present art curricula reveals that today there is "much more emphasis on studying art from a variety of cultures.... Students are to look for cross-cultural similarities in the roles and functions of art" (Irwin Irwin, Chalmers, Grauer, Kindler, & MacGregor 1997, p. 243).

Montgomery (1991) quotes Nettl in explaining that, no matter how few characteristics might be similar, these similarities can be found and utilized. Echoing Campbell's (1999) assertion made during the keynote address at the October 1999 Kodály Society of Canada National Conference, Montgomery and others have consoled music educators with the advice that, in adopting multicultural repertoire, one need not "throw the baby out with the bath water." She explains that, although folksong repertoire "may need to be expanded," folk music will continue to be the mainstay of elementary music programs (Montgomery, 1991, p. 13).

Miller (1991a, 1991b) underlines Montgomery's observation that repertoire might need to be expanded. She explains that the mix of folk songs in authorized elementary school textbooks, even today, greatly favours European sources and that "finding authentic materials and teaching foreign languages is a problem," particularly those of Hong Kong, Vietnam, and El Salvador (Miller, 1991, pp. 11, 15, & 17). So, although music education in Canada since the 1960s has associated itself with the promotion of multicultural heritage through the use of folk music, including folk song arrangements for choir and band (Hanley, 1993, p. 27; Volk, 1998, pp. 140–144), a review of teachers' manuals and concert program notes reveals a superficial appreciation of different cultural perspectives and authentic non-Western musical experiences. Research by Haughton (1984), conducted at the administrative level of the Ontario Ministry of Education, confirms a hypothesis that "dominant interests in music and education" prevail (p. 38). Haughton concludes that "no other discipline makes the distinction between the culture of the school and the culture of the pupils so graphically apparent as music education" (p. 56).

Carpenter (1994) reminds us that it was Pierre Trudeau who stated that "a democracy is judged by the way the majority treats the minority" (p. 123). She recalls this statement to highlight that academic and amateur ethnic folkloristic endeavours undertaken by Anglo-Canadians could be characterized as paternalistic, sentimental, and exploitive (p. 134). Extrapolating from Carpenter's strong criticism, we might reconsider how music educators rationalize the use of folk materials in general, such as in the reconfiguration of folk songs for string and band programs as well as the arrangement of folk melodies to enhance choral repertoire. The question is of intent and contribution: Why do we bring folk materials into the classroom, and what contribution does music education bring to folk traditions?

Montgomery's rationale is that, because singing is the key practice in elementary school music classrooms and is a universal musical activity, elementary music education can readily accommodate new multicultural repertoire. She also points out that the elementary practice to teach "sound before symbol" readily accommodates the many aural traditions in non-Western music. These are appealing and feasible pedagogical possibilities; others, however, recommend that a search for similarities among different cultures should be balanced with pedagogical and philosophical investigations that examine the implications of contrasting and contradictory musical standards as well as contrasting and incompatible world views. Musical literacy as a learning outcome is a case in point. Kennedy (1998) explores this issue in her review of Blacking's work, comparing Venda and classical musical practices, but she does not speculate on setting aside literacy-based programs to make room for different musical or extra-musical outcomes such as those learned through musical narrative and kinesthetic experiences. Another example of a musical world view that is not readily absorbed by curricula based on the European folk song traditions is aboriginal music.

Taylor (1994) explains the broader context of approaching the study of different or unfamiliar cultures:

> Indeed, for a culture sufficiently different from our own, we may have only the foggiest idea *ex ante* of in what its valuable contribution might consist. Because, for a sufficiently different culture, the very understanding of what it is to be of worth will be strange and unfamiliar to us. To approach, say, a raga with the presumptions of value implicit in the well-tempered clavier would be forever to miss the point. What has to happen is what Gadamer has called a "fusion of horizons." We learn to move in a broader horizon, within which what we have formerly taken for granted as the background to valuation can be situated as one possibility along-side the different background of the formerly unfamiliar culture. The "fusion of horizons" operates through our developing new vocabularies of comparison, by means of which we can articulate these contrasts. So that if and when we ultimately find substantive support for our initial presumption [that all human cultures]...have something important to say to all human beings, it is on the basis of an understanding of what constitute worth that we couldn't possibly have had at the beginning. We have reached the judgment partly through transforming our standards. (pp. 66–67)

The transformation of musical standards and the introduction of new vocabulary to identify new musical and extramusical horizons is imperative if music education is to be perceived as a contributing discipline in multicultural education. Bartel (1993) explains that "cultural differences serve to amplify this need [for new vocabulary]" (p. 20). Expanding on his conclusion that, although research indicates that "teachers need to provide vocabulary to students that allows them to respond [verbally] in the cognitive and affective domains" (p. 20), I add that marginalized domains of musical experience, such as the kinesthetic and phenomenological, might now, in a multicultural program, assume equal status with traditional learning outcomes. Bowman (1993) reiterates the potential to expand and transform dominant perspectives, explaining that "musical value does not exhaust itself in the aesthetic" and, therefore, we need to "identify and describe [how] diverse musics do lay claim to excellence" (pp. 27 & 29).

Wilson and Bowman both expose inherent contradictions in the mission of multicultural music education. Wilson (1995) points out the incongruencies in the Ontario Ministry of Education document, *The Common Curriculum* (1995), explaining that:

> although there are nods to the reality of multiculturalism in Ontario schools, the outcome statements insufficiently acknowledge the barriers and lack of common assumptions among different ethnic and racial groups. In a sense, in the arts, there is not an existing *common curriculum*. (p. 22)

He believes, nonetheless, that there are "certain elemental arts learnings that are at the foundation of all the arts" that could be the basis for a new standard of creativity under the rubric of aesthetic education (p. 22). Bowman (1993) also notes that, because the profession is searching for the ultimate advocacy argument (and multiculturalism serves this purpose now), it fails to consider the philosophical and pedagogical contradictions of its claims. In contrast to Wilson's expectation to maintain the rubric of aesthetic education, however, Bowman, exposes the "tension between the pluralistic foundations of multiculturalism and the subtle but deep-seated monism of aesthetic ideology" (p. 24). Regelski (1998) supports Bowman's contentions, explaining that an aesthetic standard or "conception of taste" is exclusive and should not serve as a basis for school programs (p. 41). Thus, any recommendations to underline similarities among different musical cultures should be tempered with the understanding that, although there could be some comparative features, these features might not be significant or appropriate in articulating the cultural value of musical experience outside the context of art music.

In contrast to perspectives that advocate business-as-usual, Morin (1992) explores the challenges. She sees three familiar problems hindering the progress of multicultural music education: (1) "prejudicial cultural dispositions and behaviours," (2) little exposure to communities outside one's own, and (3) an insecurity about incorporating new ideas and materials. She seems to appreciate the broader context of multicultural music education, explaining that "cross-cultural understanding has become a pervasive objective in education" (p. 27). She adds that any initiation in multicultural education is a long-term project, concluding that progress will take "considerable effort and creative thinking," but that these changes, like "any kind of educational reform," can meet with success (p. 29). I think, however, that, given Morin's account of the barriers and her set of solutions, recalling the complex concerns expressed by teachers in past professional meetings, and recognizing the difficulty of coming to know the value of unfamiliar cultures, few could be convinced by Morin's claim that multicultural music education is like any other kind of educational reform.

Nonetheless, many teachers are excited about multicultural music education. In his editorial comments, Walker (1991a) recounts the enthusiasm of teachers at a summer school session in New Mexico who demonstrated an increasing interest in "what they should be teaching rather than lesson or unit planning" (p. 7). This new focus on content may be a result of insecurities resulting from an intuitive understanding that, unlike Morin's (1992) contention, this kind of educational reform is not like any other. For example, Walker recounts a telling question put forward by one of his New Mexico students: "What should be the place of band and choir programs in our public schools [in the context of multicultural programming]?" In my literature research, I did not find any discussion on this question by secondary music specialists. So, although I grant that the kinds of questions teachers are now asking are indicative of changing attitudes, the shift is generally restricted to elementary school programs, perhaps because it can better accommodate singable and danceable repertoire (Quesada & Volk, 1994). A case in point is the *Canadian Music Educator*, vol. 33, no. 1 (1991). It contains four articles dealing with issues related to multicultural education. The fifth and last article in this issue, however, explains how to better the technical development of brass students using chromatic scale drills (MacLaughlan, 1991). It is unfortunate that this article sits so exposed in this issue, but it does serve to illustrate my point.

The reproduction of music education as band or choral programs is indicative of Morin's (1992) observation that most music educators have little exposure to ethnic or musical communities outside their own and, consequently, harbour insecurities about incorporating new material and implementing new perspectives. Furthermore, because it is difficult, if not impossible, to extract music from its cultural context for study, music educators must seek out new musical venues and unfamiliar community settings. Ellis explains how her university students in Australia first had to be initiated into the Aboriginal belief system before learning their music (Walker, 1993, pp. 30–32). Therefore, in contrast to Morin's optimism, it is perhaps more realistic to echo Walker's (1993) and Zenker's (1994) shared opinion that the shift to non-Western practice and repertoire is complex and, therefore, deserves time for deeper reflection.

✳ ✳ ✳

## In the meantime

*Diversity has apparently become (for some) an end in itself.*
(Watkins, 1994, p. 102)

*Instead of lip-service to salsa and/or subaltern heroes and holidays, a critical [multicultural] education would privilege common learnings resting upon warrantedly assertable arguments for positive democracy, social justice, and respect for bona fide diversity rather than the United Colours of Benetton.*
(Brosio, 1999, p. 25)

Conceding that implementing multicultural music education is a long-term project, what should we do in the meantime? My recommendations have to do with taking more care in presenting *diversity* as a rationale for implementing multicultural music education. One problem is the familiar rationale that multicultural music education is imperative because of "increasingly diverse school populations." The emphasis on demographics distracts us from the moral and political intentions of Canadian multiculturalism policy. I am no more convinced that "increasingly diverse student populations" is the reason we should implement multicultural education than I would be convinced that women's increasing presence in the workforce is the reason we should implement employment equity laws. Human dignity "encompasses all the social and collective aspects of individuals and their rightful place in the natural and cultural environment" (UNESCO, 1998, p. 24). These human rights belong as much to the individual as to the cultural group, and, therefore, are not to be enacted only at those times when "strength in numbers" forces the hand of dominant cultures.

Another troubling aspect of this familiar "diversity" rationale is that it provides no support for multiculturalism initiatives in communities that have not witnessed the same demographic changes. We should not assume that diversity or difference is a fixed entity (May, 1999, p. 33) across Canada and through time. Neither should we present (relatively) homogeneous, rural Canadian communities with an understanding of multiculturalism defined by the demographics of large Canadian urban centres. Because human (and musical) diversity shifts from region to region and from decade to decade, I suggest that teachers would be better served by a vision that highlights the moral imperative of multiculturalism rather than rationales or partial visions based on some notion of proportional representation. In other words, a vision for multicultural music education should recognize the "diversity of diversity" and should further support the struggle for recognition, two goals that should remain unaltered by changing regional, national, or global demographics.

In their policy guidelines, the Canadian Society for Education through Art (CSEA) addresses the importance of multicultural education for homogeneous and heterogeneous communities alike:

> A multicultural curriculum is not just for students who live in the most racially diverse communities. There is an urgent need for all Canadians to both respect diversity and find some unity in that diversity. (Irwin et al., 1997, p. 244)

Unfortunately, decisions about multicultural education are often made in Canadian urban centres, compromising effective and appropriate multicultural initiatives in rural Canada. A case in point is the appointment of people to the CSEA committee that dealt with the issue of multiculturalism. Irwin and her colleagues (1997) describe the committee members as "pivotal stakeholders," that is, "art educators and students living in a large cosmopolitan city where multiculturalism is accepted as a fact of life" (p. 237). The assumption is that, by reason of proportional representation, "pivotal stakeholders" are those who live in the most heterogeneous Canadian communities. I would counter this assumption by reiterating that, if multiculturalism "is not just for students who live in the most racially diverse communities" (Irwin et al., 1997, p. 244), then Canadians who live in less heterogeneous communities need to be part of the dialogue.

Another problem stemming from an unfortunate interpretation of *diversity* is an emphasis placed on the diversity of musical cultures, as articulated in the thesis that, because "MUSIC is inherently multicultural,…music education ought to be multicultural in essence" (Elliott, 1995, p. 204). Again, there is merit in teaching diverse musical traditions as a means of enriching musicianship. This goal, however, should not distract us from the moral and political imperative of education and the Canadian multiculturalism policy. I like to think that science, mathematics, and music teachers would not be satisfied (or comfortable) if their students simply mastered their discipline, technique, or craft. Rather, I like to think that teachers would only be completely satisfied when their students could use their new knowledge and skills for the common good. For example, David Suzuki teaches science with a vision that demands that we use science responsibly with respect for all species. Some might think I am adopting a vision of music education that is too far removed from its artistic specificity. I would counter that we can learn a lot about forming a vision for (multicultural) music education by considering why other disciplines deserve core-curriculum status, beyond the rhetoric of producing able scientists and mathematicians.

Before I summarize my comments, I want to return to Watkins's (1994) serious concerns about a kind of state-sponsored multiculturalism subsumed by capitalist economic interests. His criticisms serve as a legitimate warning about corporate interests in education in general, and, in particular, about the link between the music industry and music education. I suggest, however, that we, as Canadian citizens, adopt "the spirit of the law" and replicate the legislated commitment to eliminate discrimination, a commitment that can also be interpreted to address "a plurality of historically specific *racisms*, not all of which employ explicitly the idea of 'race'" (Moodley, 1999, p. 150).

Native education consultant Schupman has recently been quoted as saying that "the potential role of a music educator has not yet been realized in terms of broadening the multicultural horizons of students" (in Volk, 1998, p. 113). His original statement, however, reads: "the potential role of a music educator has not yet been realized in terms of broadening the multicultural horizons of students and of promoting human understanding and tolerance for racial and cultural differences" (Schupman, 1991, p. 34). The omission is indicative of a lack of moral and political will to include antiracism education as part of multicultural music education in the United States. This omission is also apparent in the resolutions, all based on demographics and tabled at the 1990 MENC inservice where Schupman made these remarks (Anderson, 1991, pp. 89–91; see also Volk, 1998, p. 203). Equally disappointing is the International Society for Music Education's revised constitution which speaks in terms of musical diversity and "developing creative and competent musicians" (Volk, 1998, p. 119). There is no doubt that an increased awareness of human and musical diversity has triggered more appreciation of the relevance and importance of multicultural education. As I have explained, however, diversity as an end in itself should not be the reason for implementing either multicultural music education or the Canadian Multiculturalism Act, which, in its preamble, reiterates the provisions of the Citizen Act, the Canadian Human Rights Act, the International Convention of the Elimination of All Forms of Racial Discrimination, and the International Covenant on Civil and Political Rights.

To summarize, I propose that our vision for multicultural music education should not be justified simply with reference to ethno-minority or musical diversity. Rather, it should acknowledge the significance of recognition, as well as address the negative impact of misrecognition and nonrecognition in shaping intrapersonal and interpersonal aspects of identity and community. As we work though this long-term project of implementing multicultural music education, our vision will demonstrate that "democracy really matters" (Brosio, 1998, p. 33), that we see it as part of the moral enterprise called education (Magsino, 1999, p. 20) and our personal paths toward critical self-interpretation (May, 1999, p. 34), and, finally, that we see it as an extension of official national policy enacted through the statutory provisions contained in the Canadian Multiculturalism Act.

## References

Ash, S. (1995). Equality of opportunity in music education? *Canadian Music Educator, 37* (1), 23–25.

Bartel, L. R. (1993). Response to music: An exploration of cultural differences. *Canadian Music Educator, 34* (5), 17–20.

Bowman, W. (1993). The problem of aesthetics and multiculturalism in music education. *Canadian Music Educator, 34* (5), 23–30.

Brosio, R. A. (1999). Diverse school populations and the corresponding need for multiple-identity coalitions: With a touch of class. *Paideusis, 12* (1), 24–36.

Campbell, P. S. (1994). Musica exotica, multiculturalism, and school music. *Quarterly Journal of Music Teaching and Learning, 5* (2), 65–75.

Campbell, P. S. (1999, October). *Music, education, and culture: Interfaces at the millennium.* Address presented at the Music for the Millennium Conference, University of Western Ontario, London, Ontario, Canada.

Canadian Citizenship Act. SC 1946, c.31.

Canadian Multiculturalism Act. SC 1988, c.31.

Carpenter, C. (1994). The ethnicity factor in Anglo-Canadian folkloristics. In B. Diamond & R. Witmer (Eds.), *Canadian music: Issues of hegemony and identity* (pp. 123-138). Toronto: Canadian Scholar's Press.

Davey, E. (1991). Equalitarianism and anti-intellectualism in music *education. Canadian Music Educator, 32* (3), 11–15.

Day, A. L. (1985) Resolving the Canadian identity crisis: Multiculturalism and its implications for Canadian education. *Canadian Music Educator, 27* (1), 11–14.

Elliott, D. J. (1995). *Music matters: A new philosophy of music education.* New York: Oxford University Press.

Elliott, D. J. (1998). Musical diversity and music education: Principles and practices. *Canadian Music Educator 39* (2), 11–16.

Hanley, B. (1993). Attitudes to multicultural music education: A Q study. *Canadian Music Educator 34* (3), 27–36.

Haughton, H. (1984). Music as social and cultural reproduction: A sociological analysis of education processes in Ontario schools. *Canadian University Music Review, 5,* 38–59.

Holmes, R., & Volk, T. M. (1998). World musics in instrumental method lesson books. *Canadian Music Educator, 39* (2), 27–31.

Irwin, R. L., Chalmers, F. G., Grauer, K., Kindler, A.M., & MacGregor, R. N. (1997). Art education policy in Canada. In B. Hanley (Ed*.) Leadership, advocacy, and communication: A vision for arts education in Canada* (pp. 231–249). 154). Victoria, BC: Canadian Music Educators Association.

Kennedy, M. (1998). Another champion of world music education: The curriculum according to John Blacking. *Canadian Music Educator, 40* (1), 27–28.

Kuzmich, N. (1988). The issue of creativity in music education. *Canadian Music Educator, 29* (4), 35–42.

Kuzmich, N. (1995). Canada and China, beliefs and practices of music educators: A comparison. *Canadian Music Educator, 37* (1), 31–35.

Leman, M. (1997). *Current issue review,* 93–6E. Ottawa: Research Branch, Library of Parliament.

MacLaughlan, A. (1991). New pedagogy for the beginning band: Teaching the harmonic levels using the chromatic scale. *Canadian Music Educator, 33* (1), 39–48.

Magsino, R. F. (1999). Multiculturalism in Canadian society: A re-evaluation. *Paideusis 12* (1), 7–21.

May, S. (1999). Critical multiculturalism and cultural difference: Avoiding essentialism. In S. May (Ed.), *Critical multiculturalism: Rethinking multicultural and antiracist education* (pp. 11–41). London: Falmer.

McCarthy, M. (1998). Multiculturalism begins at home: Music in schools and their communities. *Canadian Music Educator, 39* (2 ), 17–20. [incomplete]

McCarthy, M. (1999). Multiculturalism begins at home: Music in schools and their communities. *Canadian Music Educator, 41* (1 ), 41–45.

Miller, E. (1991a). Some ideas on implementing multicultural music in the elementary classroom. *Canadian Music Educator, 33* (1), 9–13.

Miller, E. (1991b). The problems involved in implementing multicultural music in the elementary classroom. *Canadian Music Educator, 33* (1), 15–19.

Montgomery, A. (1991). Music in the elementary grades: A multicultural perspective. *Canadian Music Educator, 32* (5), 11–15.

Moodley, K. (1999). Antiracist education through political literacy: The case of Canada. In S. May (Ed.), *Critical multiculturalism: Rethinking multicultural and antiracist education* (pp. 138–152). London: Falmer.

Morin, F. L. (1992). Guidelines for introducing ethnic musics into the curriculum. *Canadian Music Educator, 34* (1), 27–29.

Morrow, R. A., & Torres, C. A. (1994). Education and the reproduction of class, gender, and race: Responding to the postmodern challenge. *Educational Theory, 44* (1), 43–61.

Morton, C. (1996). The "status problem": The feminization of school music and the burden of justification. Unpublished doctoral dissertation, Ontario Institute for Studies in Education at the University of Toronto, Toronto.

Multiculturalism and Citizenship Canada. (1991). Multiculturalism: What is it *really* about? Ottawa: Minister of Supply and Services Canada.

Ontario Ministry of Education and Training. (1995). *The common curriculum: Policies and outcomes, Grades 1–9, The arts.* Toronto: Author.

Quesada, M. A., & Volk, T. M. (1997). World musics and music education: A review of research, 1973–1993. *Bulletin of the Council for Research in Music Education, 131,* 44–66.

Regelski, T. A. (1998). Schooling for musical praxis. *Canadian Music Educator, 40* (1), 32–43.

Rice, T. (1998). Ethical issues for music educators in multicultural societies. *Canadian Music Educator, 39* (2 ), 5–8.

Schupman, E. (1991). Understanding American Indian music and selecting resources. In W. M. Anderson (Ed.), *Teaching music with a multicultural approach* (pp. 34–38). Reston, VA: Music Educators National Conference.

Sears, A. (1997). Instruments of policy: How the national state influences citizenship education in Canada. *Canadian Ethnic Studies, 29* (2), 1–21.

Tator, C., Henry, F., & Mattis, W. (1998). *Challenging racism in the arts: Case studies of controversy and conflict.* Toronto: University of Toronto.

Taylor, C. (1994). The politics of recognition. In A. Gutmann (Ed.), *Multiculturalism: Examining the politics of recognition* (pp. 25–73). Princeton, NJ: Princeton University Press.

UNESCO. (1998). *All human beings: A manual for human rights education.* Paris: Author.

Universal Declaration of Human Rights. (1984). *Yearbook of the United Nations, 1948–49,* p. 35, General Assembly res. 217A (III).

Veblen, K. (1998). Pluralistic classrooms and the challenges of multicultural music education. *Canadian Music Educator 39* (2), 3–4.

Volk, T. M. (1998). *Music, education, and multiculturalism: Foundations and principles.* New York: Oxford University Press.

Walker, R. (1991a). Editorial. *Canadian Music Educator, 33* (1), 5–7.

Walker, R. (1991b). Multiculturalism in the arts: Art and arts in context. *Canadian Music Educator, 33* (1), 21–34.

Walker, R. (1993). Culture and music education: What? How? Why? *Canadian Music Educator, 35* (1), 27–33.

Watkins, W. (1994). Multicultural education: Toward a historical and political inquiry. *Educational Theory, 44* (1), 99–117.

Willingham, L. (1998). The sitar meets the saxophone: An informal report on the Society for Ethnomusicology Music Education Forum. *Canadian Music Educator, 39* (2 ), 23–26.

Wilson, M. (1995). Wisdom or Folly? Provincial outcomes in arts education in Ontario. *Canadian Music Educator, 37* (1), 21–22.

Wolf, S. (1994). Comment. In A. Gutmann (Ed.), *Multiculturalism: Examining the politics of recognition* (pp. 75–85). Princeton, NJ: Princeton University Press.

Zenker, R. (1995). Cross-cultural issues for music education. *Canadian Music Educator, 37* (1), 7–10.

---

[1] A case in point is how close, during the week of January 17, 2000, Canadian taxpayers came to paying for the privilege of keeping professional hockey in Canada.

# Chapter Fourteen

# A 2020 Vision of Music Education

*Harold Fiske*

*"Cabinet Ready to Invoke Updated War Measures Act to Deal With Emergencies January 1."*
(*London Free Press*, December 7, 1999)

Throughout the dwindling months of the 20<sup>th</sup> century, the year 2000 was anticipated with intense excitement, fear, awe, and panic. Between the stockpiling of celebratory champagne and caviar on the one hand, and the hoarding of makeshift home-defence supplies including firewood, candles, canned food, and bottled water on the other, a range of long-engrained and dependent social-cultural rituals, religions, politics, technological artifacts, and beliefs exposed a range of human emotions, concerns, neuroses, and psychoses. The clock-count toward the most significant or meaningless temporal event in a thousand years, depending upon one's point of view, generated a mixture of outspoken denial, vehement apatheia, and renewed hope.

The event has been truly a "psychological" one. While time itself is real enough (linked to the speed of light: see Hawking, 1992), its measurement is a cultural convenience, solved in different ways by different eras. Compared with the calendars of non-Western cultures or non-Christian accounting, two millennia are hardly worth noting. For the rest of us, however, it provides a momentous quantity of artistic and political material. I recall as a child over a half century ago, on first realizing the concept of "one year's" worth of time, calculating my age at the turn of the century. It seemed to be a very long time "from now" (longer, it seems, than the period from "now" to "back then"). I recall, as well, futuristic projections of what civilization would be like in the year 2000: spaceship-shaped cars, trim buildings, robot-controlled gadgets in every household, and, of course, enduring peace and economic opportunity. Surprisingly, some of this actually happened; less surprisingly, much of it did not. Why, however, was the progression to the "year 2000" such a traumatic one?

All humans have an internal model of the past through which they keep track of the present and calculate the future. Part of this model develops through experience, and part through models of history imposed upon us through ancestral documentation, folklore, textbooks, and formal instruction. For example, Western-trained musicians have an internal model of Western musical history: certain composers lived at such and such a time; some of these devised certain composition techniques, the employment of which (retrospectively) accounts for particular music-theoretic developments (e.g., the symphony). Other composers living in the "present" either utilize composition techniques drawn from well-developed musical traditions or experiment with new approaches that either build upon and modify older ones or self-consciously move in some new direction (e.g., the dodecaphonic system). Depending upon individual musical experience, listeners slot pieces, one way or another, into their respective historical contexts. This context provides understanding. Indeed, "neo-era" pieces (those of Igor Stravinsky, for example) have meaning only if one is familiar with the composer, piece, or period on which they are based. A well-engrained historical model affects performance practice and interpretation, music theory descriptors, music-cultural traditions, and historical theory — explanations of the origin and development of musical style, genre, and fashion.

The point is this: entering a new century, especially one yoked with the start of a new millennium, moves absolutely everything we know about anything, including music, "back" one hundred/one thousand years. Musically speaking, nothing will ever be the same for us ever again. While such "paradigm shifts" have occurred previously, this is the first time we have actually experienced one first hand. Our understanding of music will change and, consequently, so must our teaching of it. And while this is (merely) a psychological effect, one based on an internalized culture-concept of time, it engenders a real effect that will eventually be manifested in our musical/educational behavior. While it is an effect that will be real only to us — future citizens of the musical community will only read about it or absorb it indirectly through their particular experiences — it will be an effect that is recorded historically, analyzed, constructed and deconstructed, and given both due and undue credit for subsequent musical events.

Contributors to a 1976 book, entitled *Music Education for Tomorrow's Society* (Motycka), tried to estimate the style and content of music education for the turn of the "next" (i.e., 21$^{st}$) century. The writers were well-known mentors of the day: Gerard Knieter, Robert Klotman, Abraham Schwadron, Donald Shetler, Jack Heller, Warren Campbell, Richard Colwell, Robert House, and F. Joseph Smith. Each (all men, note — it was the prefeminist era) attempted to show the future state of music education based upon then-current trends, philosophical ideals, problems in need of fixing, hunch, or whatever. Predictably, the results were mixed. Several described what was then the case.

Klotman, for example, said that "research has shown that it takes approximately 50 years for an innovative idea to permeate the entire...school system" (a pace that we might envy today given faster-than-life accelerants such as the Internet, CNN, and others). "All one needs to do to predict the role of the musician in education," said Klotman, "is to examine the direction music education should pursue in the next 50 years" (p. 12). Klotman rightly foretold that music educators would be multimedia specialists and that popular music would take on increasing importance as would world musics, but (so far) wrongly saw the drudgery of teaching being eliminated(!) and the eventual obsolescence of competitive music festivals. He also hoped that music teaching would become more individualized. Shetler also saw the future of technology-driven multimedia: "each detail of [three projected technology-centered teaching situations] is based on production hardware, transmission systems, and learning models already available [i.e., in 1976].... [I]t should be possible to document activities of this sort with little difficulty before 2001" (p. 38; Shetler was mostly correct; in fact, his scenarios are largely in place now and, in some respects, superseded by today's even more advanced and faster technology).

Schwadron espoused the music aesthetics movement as "a now recognized humanistic science embracing all musics in all world cultures" (p. 21) and suggested that "a world philosophy of music education centered on aesthetic considerations is currently in the state of refinement" (p. 23), ideas that more lately have come under serious attack. He also hoped, as we continue to hope, to see music education placed at the core of the curriculum.

Knieter went even further saying that "we do this [i.e., communicate musically] through the aesthetic mode, with the aesthetic nerve [sic], by way of some secret passageways [sic] in the right hemisphere of the brain where dreams are played" (p. 1). Although stretching his metaphors to excess, he also saw the arts holding a self-actualizing function, a concept as apt today as it was then.

Other authors played it safe, simply providing a historical overview (Colwell & Shetler), outlining a new perceptual theory that could affect curriculum development (Heller & Campbell), outlining problems with graduate education and pointing to some probable changes, which interestingly enough turned out to be dead on (House), or critiquing philosophical methodology of the day and offering suggestions for change (Smith). While we may sometimes be amused by the contrast between several of the projected views and what actually transpired, anyone attempting to forecast similar matters is forewarned: Motycka's authors sometimes missed the boat, and it is highly likely that we will too! But it is also the case that Motycka's authors were often on the right track.

One way to project the future is to look at what today's music research is discovering about how humans acquire musical ability. What is discussed with university music education majors today may very well be represented by tomorrow's school music curricula. For example, behavioral theory and psychometric measurement were key research issues during the 1950s and 1960s. They clearly had an effect on curriculum design and educational philosophy (for example in the use of behavioral objectives) in the 1970s and 1980s. (The behavioral objectives movement was largely abandoned in the 1970s due to the frustration in articulating and measuring covert behaviors. The concept returned, however, in the 1990s in the guise of "outcome-based education." The demise of the outcomes-based movement now seems imminent for similar reasons.) So my strategy is this: I will first offer a summary of a few of the seemingly more productive ideas currently under study, emphasizing those in particular that influence undergraduate music education foundation courses. Then, given that today's undergraduates will increasingly influence school music education programs over the next two or three decades, I will take the plunge and offer some predictions about changes that may occur. What follows is an overview of some of the more relevant work of the music education research community. Readers interested in pursuing these further might begin with the citations included or the more general *Handbook of Research in*

*Music Teaching and Learning* (Colwell, 1992; an updated second edition is due in 2001).

## What We Think We Know About Learning Music

### Perception and cognition

The perception of music is an aural illusion where the ear is "fooled" into hearing a carefully structured object (e.g., a sonata). There is, however, no actual "carefully constructed (sonata) object" between the bells of the instruments (or speakers of a sound system) and the ear. Instead, all that exists is a collection of air molecules forced into vibration and a consequent series of sound pressure waves, produced by the bowing, blowing, and pounding actions of musicians on various metal or wooden artifacts or vocal cords. Listeners rely on their collection of auditory brain mechanisms to detect cues from the acoustic signal (encoded as an electrical-chemical brain signal) sufficient enough for the construction of patterns. Constructed patterns are initially very short in duration (e.g., an instrumental attack), but subsequently are pieced into patterns that are a bit longer (e.g., a single tone), and those that are longer still, resulting in successive tones linked together as a pitch-durational pattern (e.g., a melody) and ultimately a series of pitch-durational patterns, thereby perpetuating and enhancing the auditory illusion (of, e.g., a sonata). Two points are clear from this: (1) music is a *constructed* (not copied) outcome of *genetic* brain activity, and (2) music is an event (since auditory brain activity is time-dependent), not an object (music-notational analyses to the contrary).[1]

But the realization and interpretation of music is more than a perceptual event. Heard tones would not make much sense if the perceiver could not place this sensory information into a workable context: The brain needs to relate incoming information to previous experiences and their consequences or outcomes and to current beliefs held about the immediate social and physical environment. The social and physical-environmental culture provides a context (see earlier discussion) for musical comprehension and meaning, a frame of reference within which cognitive processes occur.

The interaction between context and perception is a hypothesis-testing process: perceptual outcomes are compared with expectations triggered by the listener's experiences. Context "holds" model-representations of previously experienced musical works. Because context is flexible and easily modified by new information and experiences, repeated encounters with a work that result in revised perceptual realizations will in turn cause the context to change. This modified context includes, at the least, a revised structural concept of the musical work, one that generates modified expectations for subsequent hearings of the same piece. Modifications, large and small, made to a listener's cognitive context is *prima-facie* evidence for musical learning (Royal & Fiske, in press). *Musical learning is any change brought about by interactions between listener-assumed contextual content (established prior to the current musical event) and ongoing perception of the current musical event.*

In other words, while the initial act of auditory perception is the outcome of mechanical auditory neural networks (Handel, 1989), the more significant substance of the musical event is subject to a number of flexible, interacting variables: formally and informally learned beliefs and assumptions about the currently heard music both testing, and being tested by, the realized tonal-rhythmic patterns. Clearly, in order for such a process to be effective and successful, it requires full attention and (cognitive) participation on the part of the listener. And, since listening is as well a part of both learning to perform and compose, it is necessary that music education find strategies that draw students into full, active participation in their own musical learning.[2]

*Cognitive development*

But how do children acquire the ability to formulate and test musical hypotheses? This has been a popular research question for the past 100 years. Carl Seashore (1938) concluded musical ability was an outcome of genetically-determined degrees of auditory "elemental capacities," a theory now long refuted. In the 1970s others proposed a (Piaget-inspired) series of musical developmental stages tied to age (Pflederer, 1964, 1967; Hargreaves & Zimmerman, 1992). Although loosening strict age-stage dependencies of earlier theories (e.g., Swanwick, 1994), researchers in the 1980s and '90s continued to emphasize the potential importance of apparent cognitive and affective psychological and physical developmental processes for designing music curricula (Hargreaves, 1986), a potential rarely taken advantage of by music educators. These processes, a far more complex combination than originally anticipated, affect basic auditory discrimination, cognition (Serafine, 1988), emotional responding, creativity (Davidson & Scripp, 1992), musical personality

(Kemp, 1996; Roberts, 1993), and sociomusical development (Hargreaves & North, 1997).

More recently, techniques have emerged that have enabled researchers to examine early childhood, even prenatal, musical development (Deliège & Sloboda, 1996). The immediate goal is to offer a comprehensive description of developmental auditory abilities, the parallels between speech development and musical development, the relationships between time and rhythm development, musical-societal interaction, musical-artistic development, and the characteristics and distinctions between youthful musical expertise and nonexpertise.

One intriguing theory suggests that the prerequisite auditory abilities for music are related to the development of those for speech. Speech reception and production are controlled by a unique set of networks unique to the human brain (Handel, 1989). These mechanisms acquire specific native linguistic fluency solely by immersion in a local speech environment. Further, auditory perceptual learning about the local sonic environment begins prenatally and is normally accomplished (without formal instruction) by the time the child is four to six years old, that is, prior to entering grade one. While vocabulary and language-use continue to develop throughout one's lifetime, the prerequisite perceptual tuning of speech mechanisms — which essentially involves the discovery of regularities in the acoustic stimulus — appears to occur primarily during early childhood. It is likely that the perceptual tuning process is, at least initially, relatively undiscriminating. In other words, in order to acquire linguistic ability, the brain must learn to process sounds of any kind before learning to discriminate one kind of sound (e.g., speech) from other kinds (e.g., barking dogs or music). If that is the case, then it is also likely that, in the act of finding pitch, timbre, and durational invariance in the speech environment, regularities in the musical (and the remainder of the sonic) environment are being discovered as well. If so, then the *perceptual* basis for music cognition is also developed *prior to the age of six years old* (Heller & Campbell, 1981).

The latter conclusion has significant implications for music education but has rarely been invoked. Knowledge, the accumulation of technical and historical information about music, can be acquired at most any age depending, of course, upon what has been previously learned and the relevance of the new material to the learner. Very young children can easily learn the names of musical instruments; music reading and the meanings of interpretive notational symbols can be taught to children younger than ten years old; teenagers are able to learn rudimentary music theory and history. But acquiring information about music is not the same as involvement in music. If it is the case that the brain's neural networks are "tuned" to the locally experienced (native) musical system during the same period as they seem to be for language (i.e., prior to age six), then it is necessary that very young children hear and sing a considerable amount of music. While there is considerable music available through the media, the quality and technical character of most of it is probably insufficient for valid or significant musical participation. On the other hand, extensive listening, as required by Suzuki's approach to string instruction, appears to satisfy the implications of music developmental theory.

### Creativity

Musical thinking is more than receiving and interpreting music. It is also about discovering new musical possibilities. Music education is sometimes reluctant to make a claim for developing composition skills, assuming instead a more generic opportunity for "creativity." But what is "creativity?" Is it a unique, isolated ability, one that is unrelated to other abilities, which manifests itself by means of "lateral thinking" in problem solving? Or is it an ability that is highly and positively related to general intelligence? Are the paintings produced by elephants (where the brush is attached to the trunk) a sign of creativity? If not, how do we classify these "works" against abstract paintings by professional (human) artists? (Most viewers cannot pick out the elephant's painting from the human's.) Is "creativity" an empty, and therefore, meaningless construct? Answers proposed so far are contradictory.

But the term "creativity" does seem to allow for a wider range of sound experimentation than is implied by the more assumably preplanned and structured "composing" activity. It also excuses outcomes that do not "sound like" legitimate compositions, those that are more exploratory and improvisatory in nature. Others think of composition activities as those generally requiring highly advanced musical and aural skills, where students are often taught privately rather than in a group. Nevertheless, creativity/composing has been the subject of music education research studies and investigations.

The possibility of including composing in the music education curriculum in addition to the customary performance ensembles was seriously considered in the United States during the 1960s. The

Contemporary Music Project for Creativity in Music Education (which began as the Young Composers Project in 1959), supported by large grants from the Ford Foundation in 1963 and 1968, placed young composers in the public schools writing music for their ensembles and leading students in their own creative activities. In 1965 the federally funded Manhattanville Music Curriculum Project supported a composition approach to musical learning. Further support came from the Tanglewood Symposium of 1967 (Bessom, Tatarunis, & Forcucci, 1974). Most recently, the National Standards for the Arts (1994) includes a number of composition/creativity activities for all American grade levels among its lists of expectations for school music programs.

Interest in the composition approach was found as well in Great Britain during the 1970s and '80s, becoming a required part of the English and Welsh National Curriculum in the 1990s. John Paynter was a particularly strong advocate for music education composition activities (Paynter and Aston, 1970). In Canada, R. Murray Schafer (1976) was equally well known. However, interest today by Canadian music educators in carrying out composition in the classroom is spotty at best.

Creativity/composition has been the main interest of several important music education researchers. Margery Vaughn became well known in the 1970s for her tests of musical creativity. The test is modelled on the Torrance Tests of Creative Thinking (Vaughn, 1977); improvised responses to melodic and rhythmic patterns are evaluated on the basis of four criteria: fluency, rhythmic security, ideation, and synthesis. Others have examined the creativity process itself. Peter Webster (1987, 1992) has proposed a model of creativity after the style of earlier work conducted in both musical and nonmusical research areas: intelligence modelling, cognitive modelling, and environmental-interaction studies, as well as the music composition and improvisatory process and its product, and musical analysis and learning processes. The result is a comprehensive portrayal of the presumed creative thinking process, its enabling skills and conditions, the role of both divergent and convergent reasoning, and the creative product outcome. While the model is hypothesis-rich, few empirical studies have been conducted so far that have tested the validity of Webster's model (Cairns, 1997).

John Kratus (1989, 1991, 1999) measured the developmental sequence of stages and the time young children working in groups devote to carrying out an assigned composition activity. Tracking the time the children took in exploring, developing, rehearsing, and talking through their ideas provides a view of the creativity process or composition event. Gary McPherson (1995/96) similarly analyzed the development of improvisation and its relationship to the ability to sight-read music, playing by ear, and playing music from memory.

George Odam (1999) recently conducted a long-term project that involved 26 secondary schools in England and concerned teaching methods and resources that are most effective for teaching musical creativity. His team was successful in identifying some of the prerequisite skills required for composing, the skills and techniques needed to teach composing, the key issues in teaching and managing classroom creativity projects, and strategies for helping children to work in groups on their composition assignments. Finally, Odam also identified some fundamental questions that are of concern to teachers involved in classroom creativity activities. Although the project successfully developed a list of practical guidelines specifically geared to finding the means and materials for achieving satisfying creativity experiences in the music classroom, no single approach or strategy appears to be preferred to another. One principal link found between the various observed teaching styles was the considerable interest in computer technology and electronic keyboards. Technology seems to facilitate the teaching of musical creativity, particularly for students who lack instrumental skills or experience.

*Culture and musical understanding*

The source of musical talent and the role of culture in fostering musical ability has long been debated. Robert Walker (1986) argued that music is exclusively a cultural artifact, both in design and intent, and that accounting for the Musical Experience depends wholly upon comprehending the culture from which a particular example originates. Western musical theory is rooted in acoustical principles that were determined more than 2500 years ago. Melodic intervals, scales, and harmonies essentially originate with scientific descriptors of the natural vibration ratios found in the acoustic environment. Very roughly, the discovery of the natural order of sound production carried the assumption that the human ear was designed according to this same natural order. That is, if sound production followed a set of laws, then these laws should lead to predictions about perception (interval discrimination, for example). Further, since these laws appeared to extend beyond acoustic descriptors to natural motion generally (such as the rotation of the stars and planets), then it only seemed right that music was "intended" to follow these laws as well. Thus, Western music theory: in order for music to be comprehensible, musicians should accommodate the link between the natural order of vibrating strings and the ear's propensity to find maximum sense in this order. Thus, a universal and natural system of music; thus the importance of music — at least for the ancient Greeks — in culture, theology, and society: obviously humans were designed to make music and to find communicative meaning in music.[3]

A primary feature of any music system is the kind of sounds that are employed. One way of investigating cultural sound differences is to examine time-variant changes in the formants of these sounds. For example, links have been found between the production of non-Western musical sounds and "cultural codes," where the choice of vocal and instrumental timbre mimics natural environmental sounds rather than seeking Western operatic or symphonic quality (Walker, 1992, 1993/1994). Further, while training in Western music entails recognition and discrimination between pitched intervals,

> many non-western musical sounds do not elicit clear western pitch concepts. Taken as a whole, the sounds of non-western music range from a clear western pitch connotation to those where there is little evidence of such pitch. . . . It might be postulated, therefore, that the greater variance in frequency at formant peaks the less pitch information is available in the sound. (Walker, 1993/1994, pp. 78, 83)

Western musical instruments (generally) produce clear, analyzable pitch (by means of cochlear mechanisms that function quantitatively), while other cultures' instrumental pitch is (largely) not quantifiably evident with the obvious exception of recorders, flutes, and so forth. Providing that the timbral spread of spectrum-consistent partials versus spectrum-inconsistent partials is a significant consideration in pitch perception, do listeners from the latter cultures actually perceive pitch? If not, then pitch is less important than timbre for delivering communicative intent in the music of these cultures. It may be the case, for example, that listeners trained predominately in Western music tonality are perceptually compelled to impose pitch (even roughly so) upon non-Western instruments, even for those where spectrum analysis does not yield a common fundamental frequency integer (see above). Neural networks tuned to detect pitch may have difficulty not finding pitch in situations where none is actually intended. If so, then the meaning-intent for such music must remain unclear to Western listeners attuned to communication-intent delivered primarily through pitch. The same, of course, can be assumed in reverse: if the non-Western listener's ear is not attuned for pitch differences, then for them discrimination between different tones played on a piano, for instance, must be timbre-based or at least based on a dimension other than pitch.

The problem is exacerbated by the tendency for Western listeners to "hear" Western-pitched intervals for differently tuned non-Western scale systems or even for cases where no pitched interval is even intended (Walker, 1987; see also Siegel & Siegel, 1977). This phenomenon has sometimes led theorists to erroneously assume that tonal intervals and harmony, those which define Western music, are the sought after, yet unachieved, goals of non-Western cultures. But, "pitch is learned from the particular spectral configuration of a wave form and such a learned concept is not exactly transferable across different wave forms." Therefore, "all musical sounds are culture specific and…the particular musical sounds produced by each culture have special cultural significance which is not merely a by-product or an epiphenomenal accident"(Walker 1993/1994, p. 84).

Cultural dominance theory stems from the view that the human brain is extremely malleable and primarily subject to cultural intervention. At first glance, this view seems to conflict with our earlier description of music cognitive processes. Indeed, Walker and many others claim that a culturally-determined interpretation of the Musical Experience cannot be held simultaneously with genetically determined brain design theories. However, it can easily be shown that brains are genetically predisposed to search for and to construct patterns from arrays of incoming acoustic stimuli (Fiske, 1990). Regardless of cultural origin, a variety of cues or variables assist the listener in determining the beginnings, midpoints, and ends of musical units (Royal & Fiske, in press). While culture-dominance theories are largely supportable, they are at the same time compatible with genetically imposed, pattern-determination brain design. Indeed, in order for cultural variables to have an effect on human behavior, they depend upon the brain imposing patterns on the stimuli that characterize that culture. A combination of the two theories therefore provides a more accurate account of cross-cultural perception and cognition data than either theory taken alone.

## Cultural determinacy and music aesthetic theory

A doctrine of aesthetic education has shaped the philosophy of music education during the last third of the 20th century, largely due to the work of Bennett Reimer (1970, 1989). In effect, music education as aesthetic education suggests that the content of music is absolute and expressive; this content is intended by composers to be found and identified by the listener (Sloboda, 1991). If so, then philosophy has suggested that one of our primary functions is to train listeners such that music's aesthetic content may be realized and enjoyed. This outlook has been challenged recently by Elliott (1995) and Bowman (1998) among others.

One argument links the question of aesthetics with multicultural awareness.

> The issue is not that music is a human activity, but that humans operate within socio-cultural systems of which music is only a part. The autonomous musical sound does not exist.... No system universally relating properties of culturally embedded sounds with the biology of the human nervous system has been identified which might explain...[the] complex human response [to music]. (Walker, 1996, p. 3)

The "'aesthetic experience in music' should not be regarded as a generic mechanical universal; the [construct] should refer to *particular cultural artifacts*" (Walker, 1996, p. 5, italics mine). If we accept that sounds "as cultural expressions which only have significance in the special terms of their cultural embedding,...[then] 'music' is a term developed specifically in the West to signify modern western practices." In short, "if a culture has no word for music,...then logically it follows that it has no concept of music" (Walker, 1996, p. 6). In other words, the term "music" is culturally loaded, a Western term that carries the aesthetic construct with it as a unique cultural value system. "Music" and the aesthetic construct are yoked; the Western word "music" entails aesthetics, where aesthetics is the underlying interpretation for "music." But since the "music" concept is an invention of Western culture (owed again to the ancient Greeks) as a way (from the 18th century onward) for representing the aesthetic construct, the aesthetic response is also a Western invention, one that does not easily apply to non-Western "music," at least from the point of view of the non-Western natives. Since "music" is yoked to aesthetics, both the term and construct apply only to Western music; neither applies universally.

## Summary

The above research areas, both empirical and philosophical, are umbrellas over a larger number of music education foundation issues that are currently considered important. An even larger number of published and conference-presented papers have examined bits and pieces of these issues. There has been over the past five decades or so strong impetus from music educators in North America, England, Germany, Sweden, Norway, Australia and, more recently, a few Asian countries for pursuing these research directions. At the moment, the problems identified seem vitally important, even theoretically basic, for any well-reasoned plan for developing music education curricula in the future. There are no signs that research in our field will soon cease, only that it will continually change. The problem for future researchers is to discriminate between momentary distractions — those that reflect misunderstandings about the Musical Experience — and momentous ideas about music, both culture-centered and brain design-centered.

*On the basis of this research, what are the implications for music education curriculum development?*

Considerable progress has been made recently by music education researchers, philosophers, and music psychologists in explaining the Musical Experience. While no one claims that the mission is accomplished, at least a glimpse of a picture is beginning to emerge, albeit a very hazy one. While there remains considerable disagreement amongst scholars, certain points have emerged from philosophy and research that seem to be worth pursuing as a basis for music education curriculum reform and development in the immediate future.

Musical learning requires involvement on the part of the learner. In Western cultures, "involvement" means learning to sing or how to perform on an instrument, learning how to listen to music, learning how to create/compose music, or, preferably, all three. Other cultures define their own learning activities based upon the unique role music has in the "local" community. The view taken here is that each activity is necessary, but not sufficient, for musical involvement and musical learning. The "involvement" requirement reflects the fact that music is not an object, but rather a time-dependent event, and that this event is not learned by passive perceptual "copying" but rather by cognitive "construction" activity. Merely playing an instrument, composing, or identifying a tune is not sufficient for making a claim for musical involvement. Required additionally is evidence that the learner both comprehensively understands a piece — structurally, historically, and culturally — and has formed a personal identity and commitment to the piece, in whatever fashion that results in individual meaning for a particular listener, whatever his/her age or stage of musical experience, interest, and development.

Given the above, curriculum development should proceed on the basis of how music is learned rather than from an analysis of music itself. How-music-is-learned is a very different construct from historical or music theory analyses-of-what-music-is. The conclusions of one do not normally match the conclusions of the other. For example, instrumental method books routinely teach the concept of rhythm from a systematic, step-by-step breakdown of the whole-note unit into half notes, quarters, eighths, and sixteenth notes. While there are perhaps valid psychomotor issues behind this reasoning (e.g., sustained embouchure development, breathing skills, and so forth), and while a hierarchy of durational values can be a useful abstraction for depicting rhythmic notation in a reductive manner, a perceptual and cognitive understanding of rhythm is simply not acquired in isolation of active musical participation and involvement. "Rhythm," as a complex interaction of patterns of durations and silences, is effectively acquired in more natural ways by preschool children moving (dancing) to music, mimicking singers heard on radio and television, and improvising nursery songs on their own or with others.

Elliott (1995) reminds us that the purpose of musical learning, and the essence of musicianship, is *doing it*, making music as an active, skilled, knowledgeable practitioner and listener. "Music education" tends to be identified by some practitioners as a body of information and skills. Too often information about music and psychomotor skill development become ends in themselves rather than as a means to engage students' involvement in musical events. "Information about" fails to capture the dynamics of time-dependent musical thinking and decision making that musical involvement actually requires. Possession of information *about* music does not necessarily reflect involvement in music, with concomitant experience as young performers or as young "composers." Further, the value of information *about* music for listening purposes is highly dependent upon its success in drawing students into the perceived event. Continued research by music educators concerning teaching strategies and materials designed to attract students irresistibly to music-as-an-experience, rather than presenting music as an isolated object distinct and separate from themselves as living organisms, is warranted.

A comparison of "average" levels of performance, solo or ensemble, between today's music performance standards and those 30 or 40 years ago reveals a significant difference. Today's performers, either professionals or university music students, generally play better than their teachers did when they were students. If music education has been successful at anything, it is in the area of instrumental performance skill. Not surprisingly, practice has been the subject of a number of research studies. Jorgensen and Lehmann (1997) review a rather extensive sample of the multidimensional nature of this very complex human ability: the conditions, processes, and evaluation of musical practising across levels of expertise, experience, and performer intent. Research concerning practice illustrates how research outcomes not only describe or explain a phenomenon, but can be put to good use as well. For example, partly due to such research, today's university-level applied music instruction is far more clinical than it once was. Where at one time applied instructors relied exclusively on their own experience and performance intuition, today's teachers take advantage of scientific evidence concerning embouchure formation, the breathing apparatus, and tongue placement, and their application under different performance demands such as range and loudness levels. Continued attention by music educators to practice research should enable performance instruction to be increasingly effective at preuniversity levels as well.

Although it is generally agreed that a complete musical experience includes performance, listening, and creativity/composing, the latter two activities are frequently overlooked, especially at the secondary level. Listening ability is often taken for granted, and many teachers shy away from endorsing creativity projects either from a lack of security in their own composing abilities or because well-planned creativity classes are quite time consuming.

Children certainly are born knowing how to listen; they just do it and do not need to be shown how. What they do need to be shown, however, is how to apply their natural sensory listening ability to music. In order to develop and maintain effective music listening programs (for any grade level), music educators need to carefully plan and create a suitable listening environment (including having available good quality playback equipment), nurture an attentive and focused listening attitude (modeled by an attentive, focused teacher), develop the department's lending library of recordings, arrange for live concerts, and provide instruction that leads students to discovering tonal-rhythmic organic activity in music (of any genre), helping them realize the musical intent and significance of melodic interrelationships. Evidence suggests that music listening occurs through a systematic, cognitively based hierarchy of listening decisions (Fiske, 1990), where determining the solution to one task is dependent upon solutions to all previous tasks in the hierarchy during a listening event. Note that this activity occurs regardless of genre, style, or cultural origin of the music. Skilled listening, a prerequisite for any successful level of musicianship, is marked (presumably) by an ability to negotiate relatively difficult levels of the cognitive hierarchy. To do this requires extensive listening experience, opportunities to discuss the music heard, a range of musical styles and examples, and a teacher who understands the listening process and desires to nurture it on the part of her students.

Similar requirements determine a successful creativity or composition experience. Prior to the availability of MIDI technology, composing activities entailed good notation skills linked with good aural abilities. Although a good "ear" is still highly desirable, technology has removed the need for notating musical ideas in order to retain and recall them. Music technology provides "memory" in which tonal-rhythmic ideas are easily retained, modified, or developed — even "assisted" by the machine. At the beginning of the 21st century, computers can be used to create original sounds, mimic traditional instruments, arrange or rearrange sounds and sound patterns, and notate music. Computers can also perform music, provide a sensitive, improvised accompaniment to a live performance, and invent original material following stylistic guidelines. Computers provide music educators with a seemingly unlimited resource for nurturing their students' creative interests.

Continued research and development of listening materials and strategies, and of strategies that help students to respond creatively is clearly warranted.

During the last decade of the 20th century there has been considerable discussion and research about teaching all of the world's musics, not merely Western music in school music programs (Campbell, 1991, Bowman, 1998, Reimer, 1994). This focus has resulted in considerable disagreement, concern, and confusion over questions concerning lost time from normal music activities, and the acquisition of sufficient expertise to teach "foreign" musics in ways that maintain their authenticity. If the above discussion is correct, then it would appear to be impossible, in principle at least, to present adequately a musical system that departs very far from the perceptual requirements of our own music. On the other hand, in an era where access to information is both rapid and extensive, it appears culturally insular not to introduce music to students other than from the Western culture. This is particularly the case given the increasing influence of non-Western styles on contemporary composers, both popular and serious. Indeed, the interest in non-Western musics and the counter effects of Western music on other cultures — which may lead some day to the amalgamation of the world's musics, a very unfortunate outcome if it ever occurs — may make this question moot. Continued research by music educators concerning the efficacy of exposing students to the technical aspects of foreign musical systems is warranted.

## Predictions for Music Education in the 21$^{st}$ Century

This is the risky part of the chapter because few of any projections I have ever made in the past have had any bearing on what consequently actually occurred. But it is also the fun part, and regardless of past success I will launch a few guesses. Note that what follows is not necessarily what I hope will occur, only what I am anticipating will occur. I will base most these predictions on current promising research directions and activities already taking place in music education. If the directions set prove to continue and to produce outcomes that are consistent with what has occurred so far, then I expect the following will take place.

### *Changes that will occur at the pre-preschool and preschool levels*

If we have learned anything about the development of musicality it is that formal music education begins far too late (see, for example, Trehub, Schellenberg, & Hill, 1997). Systematic musical experience must begin at birth, or even earlier. Within the next two decades Canadian music educators will take the lead in finding practical ways for involving preschool aged children in systematically planned listening material and rhythmic movement, the goal being the "tuning" of auditory brain mechanisms during their natural (speech-related) search for "local" (musical) auditory regularity and invariance. Preschool music specialists, with a background in early childhood development, trained in suitable learning theory, materials, and strategies, will devise techniques for delivering effective musical experiences through outlets such as television, local pre-school music groups that also train parents to sing and play music appropriately with their children, and similar commercial instructional material through the Internet, CDs, and commercial outlets such as department stores. Attempts will at first be hit or miss. Ultimately, however, such programs will become recognized by the public as a major contribution from music education to the perceptual, social, emotional, physical coordination, and, of course, musical shaping and maturing of all children.

*Changes that will occur at the primary-elementary level*

In Canada, the Kodály approach has led much of the thinking concerning primary music education for the past 30 years. The approach is particularly effective when carried out correctly in that it amalgamates ear-training, listening, performance (singing), creativity (such as melodic improvisation), movement (through games), and rudimentary music theory concepts (melodic continuity, interval direction, and so forth). When carried out improperly, however, where the mechanics of the approach (e.g., hand signs) outweigh more desirable musical ends, the approach becomes abstract, irrelevant, and unmusical. Clearly, using the Kodály approach requires a broad musical perspective and a strong theory of musical learning. Otherwise, the approach falls flat. For Kodály there was nothing unusual about the approach other than the fact that he found a way to apply normal European conservatory pedagogical philosophy to young groups of students. Hand signs (adapted from Curwen's 19th century ear-training technique) and a repertoire based on (Hungarian) folk songs assisted the teacher in providing productive musical outcomes.

Canadian primary music will continue to employ a Kodály-like approach but will (continue to) modify it to suit local needs and interests, especially multiethnic ones. Repertoires will develop and expand to include popular and non-Western music, and interesting accompaniments, composed by students themselves through in-class computer resources, will become routine. An incorporated performance-listening-compositional curriculum strategy will also be promoted as a model for amalgamating musical experiences at upper grade music classes as well, including those at the high school level (with the obvious need to find suitable musical materials and teaching strategies). The result will be a more musical, holistic, experience than tends to be the case when the curriculum is based on more robotic, simple rote singing, note reading, or instrumental technique.

### Changes that will occur at the intermediate grades

The intermediate level will build on a Kodály-like amalgamated model from the primary level, a prime aspect of which will be creativity/composition by means of computer technology. Concentrated composition/creativity experiences will be featured, including public performance. Choral ensembles will continue to flourish. Instrumental instruction, particularly the guitar and instruments borrowed from the folk and popular music cultures, will become an increasingly important part of music programs, as will small ensemble experience. Instruction in music listening with the goal of personal repertoire development will also take place systematically. Some of this activity is already the case; what I think will happen, however, is the solidifying of current experimenting into a confident theory of music instruction.

### Changes that will occur at the high school level

While high school choruses will continue to thrive, orchestras will continue to struggle, and there will be strong signs that the high school band is in jeopardy as well. Music at the high school level has in the past 40 years become increasingly insular and isolated from the musical community, both popular and serious. Ironically, part of this is due to the success of large ensembles. Band ensemble technique especially has demonstrated very impressive achievements in North America.[4]

So why do I expect the band's eventual demise in Canada? Unfortunately, the outcome of the symphonic band and wind ensemble experience has its end engrained in its own achievement: BAND is often a more social or team-competitive experience than a *musical* one. Although there is nothing inherently wrong about this social orientation, increasing sensitivity for greater individual musical understanding will ultimately require more effective means than normally occur in band rehearsals. Individual accomplishment in large instrumental ensembles, while common enough, tends to be more technical than musical. Musical comprehension is frequently very limited, and knowledge about music, beyond note reading, if provided at all, is largely abstract and disconnected from comprehensive musical understanding.

Bands have also attracted much criticism about limitations imposed by repertoire. Composers of school wind music have moved away from orchestral and Baroque transcriptions toward "educational" music written expressly for contemporary wind ensembles. But today's literature is largely banal, clichéd, musically vacuous, and often too technically difficult for most high school ensembles, offering little relevant repertoire for students to develop and expand their musical literacy. "Band" is a unique experience, one that is difficult to carry on after graduation except in communities having adult instrumental organizations. Although bands will carry on in 2020, their continued existence will be threatened in Canada by expanded interest in computer-based composition and individual, rather than large group, musical activity. Instead, small ensembles emphasizing popular music and local multiethnic interests, and opportunities for performing student-composed works (for various combinations of instruments including computers), will shape future high school music programs. Also featured will be the continued development of listening skills and the development of students' own personal listening repertoire.

Unless: Bands have the potential for revitalization providing that an important condition is met. The large ensemble experience must be felt by its participants to be musically exciting, musically involving, and personally musically important — not merely a social event. The literature must hold recognizable musical value and substance; the director must be musically confident enough to able to demonstrate legitimate musicality and to show students how to activate this substance, making a performance more than just a technical exercise. No student should leave any rehearsal or performance without knowing implicitly that s/he has participated in a valuable musical event rather than a flat, pointless, and rudimentary pedantic drill. The model for this level of musical excellence begins, for most music educators, at the university level. For that reason university music departments must provide their instrumental students with band directors who represent the conditions above.

## Music teacher education and training

University music education majors will be strongly affected by recent and future changes in philosophy on the part of musicologists, music theorists, psychologists, and music educators. Their own ideas on curriculum reform will be influenced by ongoing discussion and debate concerning music as one of the "multiple intelligences" (Gardner, 1983), multicultural musics (Campbell, 1991; Reimer, 1994), critical and reflective thinking as decision strategies (Woodford, 1999; Stubley, 1993), gender issues (Lamb, 1994; Green, 1997), postmodernism and poststructuralism (Tilley, 1995), and a host of other concerns not yet imagined. The musical canon, assumed as an absolute list of masterpieces of the Western musical art form, will be drastically modified, even eliminated as a concept of musicological theory. (This activity in fact has already begun to happen.) Part of the reason for this redefinition includes a societal removal of any hints of elitism, the new century becoming a new ("marked") era of contemporary music, the continued discovery of interesting "lost" composers and music, the abundance and availability of recordings of appealing music, and philosophical concerns about what makes a masterpiece in the first place.

Important new research questions will emerge. In the quest for showing the importance of music as an essential human experience, one deserving "basic" status in school curricula and educational policy (some quests never change!), empirical research will resurge as a means for fulfilling the need for scientifically based advanced study of musical learning. Philosophical and ethnographic research techniques will mature; students will study philosophical analysis methodology along with statistical techniques.[5] Qualitative research approaches, a feature of the late 1980s and 1990s will begin to disappear, having shown their inherent methodological weaknesses. The number of descriptive studies, however, will grow, having subsumed the earlier goals of qualitative researchers.

As well, principles of music theory will be reconsidered (in light of advances in music perception and cognition), and new approaches to music analysis will be devised. Students will acquire a wider range of ideas about what music is, what a musical experience consists of, and how music is most efficaciously explained to others. Music education students will also be introduced to a wider range of questions, concerns, positions, and outlooks about the role of music in society, music as an art form versus a social-cultural artifact, and will graduate with a generally strong philosophical and psychological perspective of education and the musical community, beyond the usual basic music technique or pedagogical skills. Most of this is already the case in many university programs.

Currently, music education philosophers are calling for wide multicultural consideration in school music programs (Campbell, McCullough-Brabson, & Tucker, 1994). However, there are signs, I think, that the "multicultural question" will soon be reconsidered and that a shift will occur toward curricula that emphasizes the unique character of the Western musical experience as it has developed among multi-world musics, each exceptional and valid in itself. Note that this shift will not be a regressive one, but instead will require some understanding of other musical systems in order to highlight the distinctiveness of Western music. The outcome will be a stronger perspective concerning the evolution of Western music over the past 2000 years and thus a better understanding of it.

The average performance level of university music majors will continue to improve and astound as research in psychomotor behavior expands and as the technical quality and manufacturing of wind instruments, especially, continues to improve. Further, music education majors will increasingly experience "foreign" musics and musical instruments as performers, gaining skill and experience with a few of these from (at last!) newly hired university ethnomusicologists. Ear-training skills will continue to be problematical, although ear training will become a recognized research area, eventually offering new and viable instructional techniques and effective computer-driven materials. "Popular music" studies will proliferate; courses in the next-current phase of music technology will no longer be considered elective but instead required, as will courses in designing creativity/composition experiences for children. But, for essentially the same reasons that bands are threatened at the high school level, university bands too may soon disappear. Unless: If the "band experience" is musically valid, then universities must assure their respect by hiring conductors who have the prerequisite knowledge of repertoire, conducting technique, and the ability to develop and maintain superb musical ensembles. So far, this tends not to be the case in Canada, with one or two notable exceptions.

## Conclusions

The intent of music education is to *cause* a musical *effect*. In order to achieve this goal music educators need to have an implicit understanding of the nature of the musical experience, an understanding of how musical behaviors are acquired, and an ability to identify materials and strategies that ensure goals and objectives are met. The philosophy and psychology of music, often viewed as irrelevant to theories of musical instruction and day-to-day teaching concerns, attempt to discover explanations and descriptors of the musical learning process and ways of enhancing this process. But questions about the musical mind and the interaction of ongoing musical developments with cultural evolution are extremely complex problems. Further, research is slow and ponderous, and subject to miscues, considerable debate, and continued evaluation by the scholarly community. The situation is additionally complicated when myths about the effects of music are promulgated, often by the media which frequently misinterpret and overgeneralize research outcomes. Two handy examples are the left-brain, right-brain excitement during the 1970s and the Mozart/music-makes-you-smarter debacle of the 1990s. In both cases, the explanation of certain research studies was distorted, leading to conclusions that common sense and a few minutes consideration would reveal as erroneous ones. We seem to have overcome these particular episodes for the most part, but undoubtedly new concoctions will emerge.

Musical learning is the outcome of *musical* experiences; musical experiences make students *musically* more knowledgeable and intelligent. To accomplish the goal of effective musical learning requires music educators who are musically accomplished and knowledgeable about the learning process. The current generation of undergraduate and graduate music education students have available to them information and ideas about the musical learning process that earlier generations did not. Presuming that today's students make this information their own, using it for curriculum design and solving problems of musical instruction, the future of music education is very bright indeed.

**Acknowledgments.** I am grateful to Betty Anne Younker and Paul Woodford for their comments on earlier drafts of portions of this chapter.

## References

Bessom, M. E., Tatarunis, A. M., & Forcucci, S. L. (1974). *Teaching music in today's secondary schools.* New York: Holt, Rinehart, & Winston.

Bowman, W. (1998). *Philosophical perspectives on music.* New York: Oxford University Press.

Cairns, R. J. (1997). *A test of selected aspects of Peter Webster's conceptual model of creative thinking in music.* Unpublished master's thesis, University of Western Ontario, London, Canada.

Campbell, P. S. (1991). *Lessons for the world: A cross-cultural guide to music teaching and learning.* New York: Schirmer Books.

Campbell, P. S., McCullough-Brabson, V. & Tucker, J. C. (1994). *Roots and branches: A legacy of multicultural music for children.* Danbury, CT: World Music Press.

Colwell, R. (Ed.). (1992). *Handbook of research on music teaching and learning.* New York: Schirmer Books.

Consortium of National Arts Education Associations. (1994). *National standards for arts education: What every young American should know and be able to do in the arts.* Reston, VA: Music Educators National Conference.

Cook, P. R. (Ed.). (1999). *Music, cognition, and computerized sound.* Cambridge, MA: MIT Press.

Davidson, L., & Scripp, L. (1992). Surveying the coordinates of cognitive skills in music. In R. Colwell (Ed.), *Handbook of research on music teaching and learning* (pp. 392–413). New York: Schirmer Books.

Deliège, I., & Sloboda, J. (Eds.). (1996). *Musical beginnings: Origins and development of musical competence.* New York: Oxford University Press.

Elliott, D. (1995). *Music matters.* New York: Oxford University Press.

Fiske, H. E. (1990). *Music and mind.* Lewiston, NY: The Edwin Mellen Press.

Fiske, H. E. (1996). *Selected theories of music perception.* Lewiston, NY: The Edwin Mellen Press.

Gardner, H. (1983). *Frames of mind.* New York: Basic Books.

Green, J. P., & Vogan, N. (1991). *Music education in Canada: A historical account.* Toronto: University of Toronto Press.

Green, L. (1997). *Music, gender, education.* Cambridge, UK: Cambridge University Press.

Handel, S. (1989). *Listening.* Cambridge, MA: MIT Press.

Hargreaves, D. J. (1986). *The developmental psychology of music.* Cambridge, UK: Cambridge University Press.

Hargreaves, D. J., & North, A. C. (1997). *The social psychology of music.* New York: Oxford University Press.

Hargreaves, D. J., & Zimmerman, M. P. (1992). Developmental theories of music learning. In R. Colwell (Ed.), *Handbook of research on music teaching and learning* (pp. 377–391). New York: Schirmer Books.

Hawking, S. (1992). *A brief history of time.* New York: Bantam Books.

Heller, J., & Campbell, W. (1981). A theoretical model of music perception and talent. *Bulletin of the Council for Research in Music Education, 66/67,* 20–24.

Hodges, D. A. (Ed.). (1996). *Handbook of music psychology* (2nd ed.). San Antonio, TX: IMR Press.

Humphreys, J. T. (1989). An overview of American public school bands and orchestras before World War Two. *Bulletin of the Council for Research in Music Education, 101,* 50–60.

Jorgensen, H., & Lehmann, A. C. (1997). *Does practice make perfect? Current theory and research on instrumental practice.* Oslo: The Norwegian State Academy of Music.

Kemp, A. (1996). *The musical temperament: Psychology and personality of musicians.* New York: Oxford University Press.

Kratus, J. (1989). A time analysis of the compositional processes used by children ages 7 to 11. *Journal of Research in Music Education, 37* (1), 5–20.

Kratus, J. (1991). Characterization of the compositional strategies used by children to compose a melody. *Canadian Music Educator: Research Edition, 33,* [special ISME edition] *33,* 95–103.

Kratus, J. (1999, September). *Investigations in the compositional processes of children.* Paper presented at the 5th conference of the Research Alliance of Institutes of Music Education, London, Ontario.

Lamb, R. (1994). Feminism as critique in philosophy of music education. *Philosophy of Music Education Review, 2* (2), 59–74.

McPherson, G. (1995/1996). Five aspects of musical performance and their correlates. *Bulletin of the Council for Research in Music Education, 127,* 115–121.

Motycka, A. (1976). *Music education for tomorrow's society: Selected topics.* Jamestown, RI: GAMT Music Press.

Odam, G. (1999, September). *Issues in the teaching of composing in the classroom arising from "The Creative Dream" project, 1997-1999.* Paper presented at the 5th conference of the Research Alliance of Institutes of Music Education, London, Ontario.

Paynter, J., & Aston, P. (1970). *Sound and silence: Classroom projects in creative music.* Cambridge, UK: Cambridge University Press.

Pflederer, M. (1964). The responses of children to musical tasks embodying Piaget's principle of conservation. *Journal of Research in Music Education, 12,* 251–268.

Pflederer, M. (1967). Conservation laws applied to the development of musical intelligence. *Journal of Research in Music Education, 15,* 3, 215–233.

Reimer, B. (1970). *A philosophy of music education.* Englewood Cliffs, NJ: Prentice-Hall.

Reimer, B. (1989). *A philosophy of music education* (2nd ed.). Englewood Cliffs, NJ: Prentice-Hall.

Reimer, B. (1994). Can we understand music of foreign cultures? In H. Lees (Ed.), *Musical connections: Tradition and change* (International Society for Music Education,) (pp. 227–245). Auckland, New Zealand: The University of Auckland.

Roberts, B. (1993). *I, Musician.* St. John's, NF: Memorial University of Newfoundland.

Royal, M., & Fiske. H. (In press). Cognitive context and musical learning: How to have it both ways. *The Bulletin of the Council for Research in Music Education.*

Schafer, R. M. (1976). *Creative music education: A handbook for the modern music teacher.* New York: Schirmer Books.

Seashore, C. (1938). *Psychology of music.* New York: McGraw-Hill Book Company.

Serafine, M. L. (1988). *Music as cognition: The development of thought in sound.* New York: Columbia University Press.

Siegel, J., & Siegel, W. (1977) Categorical perception of tonal intervals: Musicians cannot tell sharp from flat. *Perception and Psychophysics, 21* (5), 399–407.

Sloboda, J. (1991). Music structure and emotional response: Some empirical findings. *Psychology of Music, 19* (2), 110–120.

Stubley, E. (1993). Musical performance, play and constructive knowledge: Expression of self and culture. *Philosophy of Music Education Review, 1* (2), 94–102.

Swanwick, K. (1994). *Musical knowledge: Intuition, analysis, and music education.* London, Routledge.

Tilley, T. W. (Ed.). (1995). *Postmodern theologies: The challenge of religious diversity.* Maryknoll, NY: Orbis Books.

Trehub, S., Schellenberg, E., & Hill, D. (1997). The origins of music perception and cognition: A developmental perspective. In I. Deliège & J. Sloboda, (Eds.), *Perception and cognition of music* (pp. 103–128). Hove, UK: Psychology Press.

Vaughn, M. (1977). Musical creativity: Its cultivation and measurement. *Bulletin of the Council for Research in Music Education, 50,* 72–77.

Walker, R. (1986). Music and multiculturalism. *The International Journal of Music Education, 8* (2), 43–52.

Walker, R. (1987). Music perception and the influence of western musical theory. *The Canadian Journal of Research in Music Education, 29,* (1), 47–57.

Walker, R. (1990). *Musical beliefs: Psychoacoustic, mythical, and educational perspectives.* New York: Teachers College Press.

Walker, R. (1992). Formants in singers: Stylistic and cultural perspectives. *Voice, 1,* 19–46.

Walker, R. (1993/1994). Identifying cultural uniqueness in musical *sounds. Bulletin of the Council for Research in Music Education Bulletin, 119,* 77–84.

Walker, R. (1996). Music education freed from colonialism: A new praxis. *International Journal of Music Education, 27,* 2–15.

Webster, P. R. (1987). Conceptual bases for creative thinking in music. In J. Peery, I. Peery & T. Draper (Eds.), *Music and child development* (pp. 158–174). New York: Springer-Verlag.

Webster, P. R. (1992). Research on creative thinking in music. In R. Colwell (Ed.), *Handbook of research on music teaching and learning* (pp. 266–280). New York: Schirmer Books.

Woodford, P. (1999). Living in a postmusical age: Revisiting the concept of abstract reasoning. *Philosophy of Music Education Review, 7* (1), 3–18.

---

[1] See Fiske (1996), Hodges (1996), and Cook (1999) for further discussion about basic auditory perception.

[2] See Chapter 7 of Fiske (1996) for a more detailed list and discussion of principles of music cognition and learning.

[3] See Walker, 1990, especially Chapter 3, for his strongly developed historical argument.

[4] See Green and Vogan (1991), Chapter 14, for a history of the band movement in Canada, and Humphreys (1989) for a history of bands in the United States.

[5] Philosophical analysis is currently a standard component in the training of philosophers, but not as yet (music) education philosophers.